RELIGION

Religion

What It Is, How It Works, and Why It Matters

Christian Smith

PRINCETON UNIVERSITY PRESS

PRINCETON AND OXFORD

Copyright © 2017 by Princeton University Press

Published by Princeton University Press,
41 William Street, Princeton, New Jersey 08540

In the United Kingdom: Princeton University Press,
6 Oxford Street, Woodstock, Oxfordshire OX20 1TR

press.princeton.edu

Library of Congress Cataloging-in-Publication Data

Names: Smith, Christian, 1960- author.
Title: Religion : what it is, how it works, and why it matters / Christian Smith.
Description: Princeton : Princeton University Press, 2017. | Includes bibliographical
references and index.
Identifiers: LCCN 2017005886 | ISBN 9780691175416 (hardcover : alk. paper)
Subjects: LCSH: Religion.
Classification: LCC BL48 .S5937 2017 | DDC 200—dc23 LC record available at https://lccn.loc
.gov/2017005886

British Library Cataloging-in-Publication Data is available

This book has been composed in Adobe Text Pro and Gotham

Printed on acid-free paper. ∞

Printed in the United States of America

10 9 8 7 6 5 4 3 2 1

CONTENTS

ILLUSTRATIONS

PREFACE

My intended readership for this book includes not only academic scholars of religion, but also capable undergraduate and graduate students and the educated reading public. In order to make my argument accessible to non-specialists, I introduce more technical terms in quotation marks, to indicate their specialized terminological nature. I also confine to footnotes theoretical references and arguments more relevant to scholars, which the less technically inclined are welcome to ignore. I apologize to specialists who already know the terms and may wish my arguments to be better integrated in the main text. I also express my regrets to non-scholarly readers who may find footnotes to be a distraction. I hope nonetheless that in the end everyone is able to learn what they wish without much difficulty.

To help reinforce my claim that the theory of religion developed here is widely applicable across space and time, and not only relevant to Western or Abrahamic religious traditions, I provide throughout the book references, illustrations, photos, and epigraphs for concepts and arguments that represent various religious traditions around the globe. I do not purport to be an expert on all religions. I apologize in advance to my colleagues in religious studies, history, and various area studies who not only know vastly more about specific religions than I do, but who tend to focus on religious particularities, differences, and fluidities my sociological generalizations run over roughshod. I hope enough of theoretical value is found here, despite that difference. Not every religious tradition is represented in the illustrations and references in a way that is proportionate to their population size or importance. Nonetheless, I trust that the moderate diversity of examples provided is indicative of the full breadth of the theory's genuine relevance, and that different readers of diverse religious backgrounds can readily think of more examples from their own experiences.

I owe a big debt of gratitude to Martin Riesebrodt, whose book *The Promise of Salvation* has shaped my thinking greatly—chapter 4 of his book contains some of the most helpful 20 pages of religion theory I have read.

Without Martin's work, this book would not exist, and I hope mine does his justice. I only regret that I never seized the opportunity to meet him in person before his untimely death in December 2014. Tom Tweed, Donna Freitas, Kevin Schilbrack, Doug Porpora, Justin Farrell, Mike Wood, Cole Carnesecca, Feyza Akova, Kraig Beyerlein, and Brandon Vaidyanathan provided extremely valuable critical feedback on early versions of my manuscript, helping to improve my argument, for which I am grateful, even though they may not be satisfied with my revisions. I also need to thank for their helpful contributions to this book Amy Adamczyk, Bob Brenneman, Jessica Collett, Shanna Corner, Dan Escher, Patrick Graff, Slava Jakelic, Ines Jindra, Mike Jindra, Sarah Johnson, Linda Kawentel, Sallie King, Paul Kollman, Mary Ellen Konieczny, McKenna LeClear, Bridgett Littleton, Brianna McCalsin, Nicolette Manglos-Weber, Ebrahim Moosa, Atalia Omer, Griffin Over, Jerry Powers, Micah Rensch, Tricia Ross, Chip Rotolo, Peter Ryan, Trish Snell Herzog, Jason Springs, Anna Sutherland, Brad Vermurlen, and participants in the Research and Analysis in the Sociology of Religion workshop put on by the Notre Dame Center for the Study of Religion and Society in the fall of 2015 and spring of 2016. Notre Dame is an exceptional place to study religion, and I am thankful for the students and colleagues I had there, and for others with whom I connected from Notre Dame. Many thanks to Sarah Edmands Martin for creating the tree illustration in figure 2.1; to Olivia Hall for help with the photo images; and to Anna Sutherland for copyediting help. Two anonymous readers for Princeton University Press also provided me with very smart and valuable constructive critiques that guided important revisions and clarifications, for which I am also most thankful.

RELIGION

Introduction

The God of old bids us all abide by His injunctions.
Then shall we get whatever we want, be it white or red.
—TRADITIONAL GHANAIAN AKAN PRAYER ON TALKING DRUMS[1]

See, I set before you today life and prosperity, death and destruction.
For I command you today to love the Lord your God, to walk in
obedience to him, and to keep his commands, decrees and laws; then you
will live and increase, and the Lord your God will bless you in the land
you are entering to possess.
But if your heart turns away and you are not obedient,
and if you are drawn away to bow down to other gods and
worship them,
I declare to you this day that you will certainly be destroyed.
—DEUTERONOMY 30:15-17

Anyone who wants to understand the world today has got to understand religion. The majority of people in the world affiliate with a religion, and many do so fervently. Religious practices have been a part of *homo sapiens* life since the beginning of our discernable history.[2] No human society has

---

1. Quoted in Jerome Rothenberg and Diane Rothenberg. 1983. *Symposium of the Whole.* Berkeley: University of California Press. P. 137.
2. Colin Renfrew and Iain Morley, eds. 2009. *Becoming Human.* Cambridge: Cambridge

existed that did not include some religion. A broad array of religions exists around the globe today, with a single religion dominating society in some places, while in others many traditions mix, morph, and clash. Efforts by some modern states to do away with religions have failed. Though thin and weak in some regions, religion is robust and growing in other parts of the world. On top of their relevance to individuals, contemporary religions produce major political, cultural, economic, and social consequences around the globe. Human life simply does not boil down to secular economics and politics. Understanding many major problems today is impossible without accounting for religion's influences. Neither can we appreciate much that is widely considered good in the world without taking religious factors into account. Academic scholars and elites often ignore religion. In doing so, they risk ignorance about a crucial part of human life that frequently affects the political, economic, family, military, and cultural phenomena they care about. When we understand religion and its role in societies, we can better understand our world.

This book explains in general theoretical terms what religion is, how it works, and why and how religion influences people and societies. Offered here is not a comparative study of various religions, but a social scientific theory of religion that helps make sense of all religions. Readers will learn not about the particular beliefs and practices of some specific religions, but about the nature of religious beliefs and practices per se that make religions what they are. By learning to approach and understand religion theoretically, readers will become equipped to grasp and explain any specific religion that may interest them.

Real-life events in recent decades have made clear that religion remains a crucial feature of human life. One cannot glance at the news without seeing religion's impact on local activities, national politics, and international war and peace. Yet social scientists who study religion seem somewhat constrained in their ability to explain religion well. Some are tired from frustrating theoretical debates; others focus on trivial rather than important topics; and yet others doubt whether religion as a subject matter even exists to be studied. My own field of sociology of religion seems like it could use the re-energizing of a better theoretical vision that stimulates new work. So although today we all need to understand religion well, the available theoretical resources may not be up to the task. In this situation, my purpose is

---

University Press; Robert Bellah. 2011. *Religion in Human Evolution*. Cambridge, MA: Harvard Belknap.

to advance an approach that explains religion clearly in order to enhance understanding and help generate fruitful new research.

The Argument in Brief

I develop this book's theory of religion by answering five basic questions, which provide the titles of its five chapters. First I explain what religion is. Then I describe what causal powers religion generates for influencing people, institutions, and cultures. Next I examine the key cognitive process involved in practicing religion, namely, explaining events by attribution to the influence of superhuman powers. I then explore why people are religious (or not), and in particular why humans seem to be the one animal species on earth that practices religion. Finally, I consider the question of religion's future fate in modern societies.

I begin in chapter 1 by defining what religion is. Religion, I will argue, is best defined as a complex of culturally prescribed practices that are based on premises about the existence and nature of superhuman powers. These powers may be personal or impersonal, but they are always superhuman in the dual sense that they can do things that humans cannot do and that they do not depend for their existence on human activities. Religious people engage in complexes of practices in order to gain access to and communicate or align themselves with these superhuman powers. The hope involved in the cultural prescribing of these practices is to realize human goods and to avoid bads, especially (but not only) to avert misfortunes and receive blessings and deliverance from crises. Key to this definition is the dual emphasis on *prescribed practices* and *superhuman powers*, which distinguish it from other approaches that focus instead on people's beliefs or meanings (rather than practices) and on the supernatural, sacred, transcendent, divine, or ultimate concern (rather than superhuman powers). This emphasis helps to avoid problems that plague other theories of religion.

This approach to religion distinguishes between a conceptual definition of what religion *is* and the myriad reasons why people *do* religion. The conceptual definition, we will see, references public traditions, institutions, and cultural prescriptions. The empirical reasons why people actually do religion, by contrast, often involve not just the desire to seek help from superhuman powers but also a variety of other subjective motivations, some of which actually may not be particularly religious, such as wanting to meet friends at prayer services. I will argue that we cannot define religion conceptually by the reasons people practice religion, any more than we can define politics by adding up people's reasons for voting for certain candidates in elections. We need to differentiate theoretically between what religion itself *is* and why people *do* it, even if the answers to these questions overlap. Doing so maintains theoretical clarity and opens up many interesting research questions.

When people practice religion for whatever reasons, I argue in chapter 2, they create a variety of new social features and powers that are able to influence people's lives and the world. These include things like new forms of identity, community, meaning, self-expression, aesthetics, ecstasy, social control, and legitimacy. I call these religion's "causal capacities," things religions *can do* (again, distinct from what religion *is*). These causal capacities, we will see, are secondary, dependent, and derivative aspects of religion's core nature. Nevertheless, they are crucial in forming the character of specific religious traditions. The goods they offer are also some of the reasons why many people practice religion. And such causal capacities explain how and why religions exert influence on people's actions and in cultures and social institutions—in ways that, I will argue, are far more extensive and diverse than many observers realize. Why does religion matter? For social scientists, part of the answer is that religion can make a difference, sometimes a big one, in how people's lives and the world operate.

Having described what religion is and what it can do, I explore in chapter 3 the particular human mental process upon which the practice of religion depends: the making of "causal attributions" to superhuman powers. This simply refers to religious people coming to believe that certain things happen (or don't) in life because of superhuman powers. They can include both obviously religious outcomes (like feeling God's forgiveness) and more worldly ones (like a bountiful harvest); they can range from the profound (a miraculous healing from a fatal disease) to the seemingly trivial (remembering the right answer on a quiz). What matters here is that people attribute some event or condition at least partially to the influence of superhuman powers. And since religious people do not always get what they want, we will also examine the various ways that people interpret the successes (or failures) of their religious practices. Along the way, we will consider questions about the nature of "religious experiences," miracles, and other kinds of superhuman interventions in human life. We will also explore some common cognitive biases that routinely influence human thinking, to better understand how and why people can easily attribute ordinary life outcomes to the influence of superhuman powers.

I then turn in chapter 4 to investigate why humans are even religious in the first place. Why are there any religions at all? And why are humans the only species on earth that practices religion? I will argue that the answer lies in humans' unique possession of a complicated combination of natural capacities and limitations. Natural, unique human *capacities* make it possible for humans to conceive of and believe in superhuman powers that are not immediately present, and to find ways to try to access their help. And humanity's natural *limitations* provide good motivations for seeking such help. The uncomfortable existential space created by the collision of amazing human powers and severe human incapacities provides the grounds in which religions germinate, grow, and flourish. Seeking the help of superhuman powers to live in that difficult space—and to realize humanly good and avoid bad things within it—is the central reason why people practice religion. Humans also often practice religion because they enjoy the secondary causal capacities that religion affords. I will additionally reference a large body of recent research in the cognitive science of religion to suggest that the regular operation of ordinary human perceptions, the human brain, and common human cognitive processes work together to make religion a natural and fairly effortless way for people to think about and live in the world. Religion actually comes quite naturally, it turns out, given human neurobiology, cognition, and psychology.

Finally, in chapter 5 I answer the question of religion's future first by suggesting that until human nature fundamentally changes, many humans will almost certainly want to continue to practice religion; that humans will continue to generate new religions; that religions will continue to be internally transformed over time; and that some religions will grow in size, strength, and significance, while others will decline. Predictions about the inevitable decline and possible disappearance of religion in modern society are incorrect. However, such "secularization theories" are not completely wrong or useless. Properly appropriated, they offer valuable insights into social causal mechanisms that decrease religious belief and practices. But to understand how these matters really work, I argue, we have to discard the simplistic assumption that secularization theory is either right or wrong. Instead, we need to re-conceptualize our analyses to recognize the variety of causal mechanisms that operate simultaneously, in sometimes contradictory and sometimes reinforcing ways, to produce different religious outcomes, depending on the specific historical conditions and social contexts of particular situations. In short, our understanding of religion's fate in modernity (or anytime, actually) needs to take into account greater complexity, contingency, and path-dependency than has been typical in the past.

That summarizes the main argument of the chapters that follow. The remainder of this introduction focuses on related philosophical and metatheoretical issues, to which scholars should attend. Non-scholarly readers who might get bogged down in philosophy, however, may want to skip ahead to read the last paragraph of this introduction (which makes a point important for everyone) and then proceed to chapter 1.

Theoretical Influences

My argument in this book is shaped by three key theoretical influences: first, a substantive, practice-centered view of religion; second, the philosophy of critical realism; and, third, the social theory of personalism. The first of these is a view of religion that is defined substantively, in terms of the meanings of a type of actions, and focuses on human practices before beliefs, following the previous work of Martin Riesebrodt and Melford Spiro.[3] This approach understands religions as culturally prescribed systems of practices seeking to access superhuman powers in order to realize human goods and for help in solving problems, both minor and profound. I believe this is the best way to understand religion, but it needs elaboration.[4] I agree with Stephen Bush that the triad of religious experience, meaning, and

---

3. Martin Riesebrodt. 2010. *The Promise of Salvation: A Theory of Religion*. Chicago: University of Chicago Press; Melford Spiro. 2003 [1966]. "Religion: Problems of Definition and Explanation." Pp. 187–222 in Spiro. *Culture and Human Nature*. New Brunswick, NJ: Transaction. My argument also closely parallels that of Kevin Schilbrack. 2014. *Philosophy and the Study of Religions*. Malden, MA: Wiley Blackwell. Pp. 115–148, which I unfortunately did not discover until this book was nearly completed.

4. I use the word "best" here intentionally, as an alternative to the triumphalist "the only true," on the one hand, and the relativistic "just another interesting and useful," on the other. All human knowledge is fallible and can be improved upon, yet some ideas are better than others. "Best" here combines both a commitment to the defensible preferability of an idea, with an openness to future revisions, improvement, or perhaps replacement, something like "the approach that the best currently available reasoning about evidence compels us to affirm over others." Some have suggested that I claim merely that my argument is internally logically coherent with the first principles of critical realism, not true or more accurate than other approaches. But a critical realist, operating with an "alethic" theory of truth (William Alston. 1996. *A Realist Conception of Truth*. Ithaca: Cornell University Press), cannot settle for a mere "coherentist" epistemology defended by the likes of W.V. Quine (1978. *The Web of Belief*. New York: McGraw-Hill). Theories need to be not merely internally coherent, but adequate to reality, as conceptual representations of what exists and how it works (see Christian Smith. 2010. *What Is a Person?* Chicago: University of Chicago Press. Pp. 209–212).

power needs to be retained and integrated in a new way, and that religious practices provide the right theoretical framework for doing so.[5] Riesebrodt and Spiro, for their parts, pointed us very far in the right direction. But I think their ideas need developing and expressing in ways more accessible to wider audiences.

The second theoretical influence is the philosophy of "critical realism." Behind all theoretical and empirical scholarship stands some philosophy of reality and human knowledge ("metaphysics" and "epistemology"), and in the deeper background there usually stands a philosophy of what is good and bad, right and wrong (ethics). Many social scientists do not pay attention to the philosophies that underlie their work, but that does not decrease their influence. It only means they are less visible and acknowledged. Certain general background philosophies have especially influenced the study of religion.[6] While all have some valuable insights to contribute, each I think is inadequate by itself (and in some ways highly misleading and unhelpful). A better alternative is critical realism.[7] Many existing works explain and advocate critical realism, and I need not repeat their arguments here. A few comments should suffice to help make sense of what follows.

Critical realism tells us to think of all science as learning about what exists and how and why it works. What exists is a matter of "ontology,"[8] and

5. Stephen Bush. 2014. *Visions of Religion*. New York: Oxford University Press.

6. These are positivist empiricism, hermeneutical interpretivism, postmodern deconstructionism, and pragmatism. Hermeneutical interpretivism is correct in most of its basic claims; however, it is often insufficient in not taking seriously enough the scholarly aim of understanding not only meanings but also *causal* influences in human life. One important account of this position—drawing out, problematically, in my view, some Wittgensteinian ideas to certain wrong conclusions—is Peter Winch. 1958. *The Idea of a Social Science and Its Relation to Philosophy*. London: Routledge. Also see Phil Hutchinson, Rupert Read, and Wes Sharrock. 2008. *There Is No Such Thing as a Social Science*. Surrey, UK: Ashgate. Positivist empiricism and postmodern deconstructionism are more problematic.

7. Critical realism is a meta-theory or philosophy of science, including social science, not a specific theory of religion or anything else. It is not a general explanation of how a particular part of human social life works, but rather a higher-order system of ideas and claims about reality, how it is ordered, and how it functions that creates a realistic framework within which good specific theories can be constructed. It is possible to develop different theories about any given topic within the critical realist framework. This book proposes not "the" critical realist theory of religion, since critical realism can generate and be compatible with more than one substantive theory in some areas. Still, not every theory on offer fits critical realism. Many theories critical realism criticizes as presupposing the wrong ideas about reality, causation, science, explanation, and so on. What I develop here is one theory shaped by critical realism, though not the only possible critical-realism-informed theory of religion.

8. Here I make a distinction between ontology and metaphysics, working with the former and ignoring the latter. Ontology, as I mean it, is simply about what has being in reality, the

how things work is about "relational causal influences." Critical realism focuses our attention on identifying the important objects, including social objects, that *exist* in reality, on "entities";[9] using empirical evidence and our best reasoning abilities to learn what (often non-observable) *causal powers* those objects possess and can exert under certain conditions ("causal mechanisms"); and developing, from that knowledge, explanations about how and why the complex world operates the way it does to produce conditions and outcomes of interest. In short, this book first seeks to theorize the "social ontology" of religion and to describe how and why religion operates causally in human life as it does. Many other approaches tend to be skittish about naming what religion essentially *is* and either avoid the idea of causal explanation altogether or misconstrue the nature of causality. But it is impossible to do good social science while bracketing ontology and sidelining causality.

The best way to summarize critical realism is to say that it combines ontological realism, epistemic perspectivalism, and judgmental rationality, and insists that *all three be held together* in thought and investigation. That means that much of reality exists and operates independently of our human

---

character of entities that have being, that are. The phrase "religious ontology" merely references what religion is, which is conceptually distinct from what religion can do (causal capacities) and what religion is like (features). Metaphysics, by comparison, is more ambitiously concerned with the fundamental nature of all being and the ultimate constitution of the totality of reality. That is not a concern of this book nor of most of critical realism used in social science. So readers should understand that when I speak of ontology, I am making no larger metaphysical claims.

9. By "entities" I mean parts of reality, whether material (bricks, airplanes) or immaterial (beliefs, light waves), and whether "raw facts" (gravity, rivers) or "institutional facts" (money, states). Some thinkers find talk about "entities" problematic, objecting to the idea that distinct objects exist that have particular essences. Understood properly, however, talk about entities is legitimate and necessary. An entity is just something that has existence, that has being, and so is and exists. The word "entity" derives from the Latin word *ens*, meaning "being." To believe that some entities exist in reality is a necessary presupposition for having a discussion about how we should properly talk about things. But to believe in entities does not require a commitment to some kind of neo-platonic realism, namely, the belief that every instance of an evident thing represents the embodiment of a more real universal form or ideal. Nor does believing in entities force us to accept misguided essentialist accounts of reality that claim that some of what are only humanly constructed, historically and culturally limited institutional facts are actually natural, fixed, or necessary. Those kinds of claims confuse the general fact that some entities exist with specific natures with particular claims about certain entities as possessing particular natures when in fact they do not. We ought not to accept anti-essentialism wholesale only because particular retail claims about the nature of some entities have been wrong, oppressive, and damaging.

awareness of it (ontological realism[10]), that our human knowledge about reality is always historically and socially situated and conceptually mediated[11] (epistemic perspectivalism), and that it is nonetheless possible for humans over time to improve their knowledge about reality, to adjudicate rival accounts, and so to make justified truth claims about what is real and how it works (judgmental rationality). All three of these beliefs must go together to promote the acquisition of human knowledge. Stated negatively, critical realism rejects "ontological anti-realism" (that reality is itself a mind-dependent, human construction), "epistemological foundationalism" (that a bedrock foundation exists for human knowledge that is certain and universally binding on rational persons), and "judgmental relativism" (that truth claims are all relative and impossible to adjudicate). Only by holding critical realism's three key beliefs together, and rejecting their denials, can we practice good social science.

On the matter of understanding causation, critical realism rejects the dominant positivist empiricist view that causation is about the association of observable events, often demonstrated as the statistical correlation of measured variables. Instead, it takes the more realistic "natural powers" view of causation, according to which all real entities possess by their

10. Critical realism provides conceptual distinctions essential for making sense of reality. One is between the real, the actual, and the empirical. The *real* is what exists: material, non-material, and social entities that have structures and capacities. The real exists whether we know or understand it, possessing objective being potentially apart from human awareness of it, even when parts of it are not expressed in actuality. The *actual* is what happens in the world, when entities that belong to the real activate their powers and capacities. The actual happens in time and space, whether any person experiences it or not ("If a tree falls in the forest . . ."). The *empirical* consists of what humans experience or observe, either directly or indirectly. So what we observe (the empirical) is not identical to all that happens (the actual): The actual comprises much more than the empirical. And neither the actual nor the empirical is identical to all that has existence (the real). What is real is much greater than what *happens*, and to think otherwise is to engage in what critical realists call the fallacy of "actualism." The empirical is a subset of the actual; and the actual is the outcome of operations of entities that are real. The three should not be conflated. Maintaining these distinctions enables us to understand that certain entities can and do exist even if they are empirically not observable. Only when they activate their causal powers in ways that produce events in time and space do they become actual, and thus potentially observable. The causal powers of other real entities may counteract or neutralize their causal powers, in which case their effects may not become actual, even though their real causal capacities are operating. That we do not see or cannot experience or measure something at some place and time in the actual does not mean it is not real and potentially or actually exercising causal powers. To think otherwise conflates the real with the empirical, which is a huge mistake.

11. Certain kinds of non-cognitive knowledge—such as knowing how to ride a bicycle—may not be conceptually mediated but directly embodied.

ontological nature certain capacities that, under specific conditions, can make or prevent changes from happening in the world.[12] Causal explanation thus consists in describing the causal capacities of the real entities in question, the arrangement of the conditions that in temporal processes triggered or neutralized those capacities, and the consequences of the "causal mechanisms" that as a result operated as they did.[13] In other words, explaining causally involves narrating who or what the *agents* were, what they *could* do, what they *did* do and *why* under particular circumstances, and what happened as a *result*.[14] This book focuses on what natural causal powers religion possesses, the various ways those capacities are expressed, and their characteristic outcomes.

Critical realism also differs from positivist empiricism by emphasizing the complexity, contingency, and "path-dependence" of most causal pro-

12. Ruth Groff and John Greco (eds.). 2013. *Powers and Capacities in Philosophy*. New York: Routledge; Ruth Groff (ed.). *Revitalizing Causality*. New York: Routledge; Douglas Porpora. 2008. "Recovering Causality." In A. Maccarini, E. Morandi, and R. Prandini (eds.). *Realismo Sociologico*. Genova-Milano: Marietti; Bert Danermark et al. 2002. *Explaining Society: Critical Realism in the Social Sciences*. New York: Routledge. Pp. 52–53, 56, 59, 74; Douglas Porpora. 1993. "Cultural Rules and Material Relations." *Sociological Theory*. 11: 212–229; Stephen Mumford and Rani Lill Anjum. 2011. *Getting Causes from Powers*. New York: Oxford University Press; Anjan Chakravartty. 2007. *A Metaphysics for Scientific Realism*. Cambridge: Cambridge University Press; Brian Ellis. 2001. *Scientific Essentialism*. Cambridge: Cambridge University Press; Brian Ellis. 2002. *The Philosophy of Nature: A Guide to the New Essentialism*. Montreal: McGill-Queen's University Press; Andrew Sayer. 1992. *Method in Social Science: A Realist Approach*. New York: Routledge; also see Robert Koons. 2000. *Realism Regained*. New York: Oxford University Press.

13. Porpora. "Recovering Causality"; "Cultural Rules"; Danermark et al. *Explaining Society*; Sayer, *Method in Social Science*; Koons 2000. *Realism Regained*.

14. Causal realism applies to human actions. Immanuel Kant famously argued that the possibility of human freedom requires a disconnection from the deterministic forces of natural causation, then viewed in Newtonian terms. Critical realism sees no need to protect persons from life in a causally real universe, because it views causation not as deterministic but rather about "tendencies." Some causes in the natural world may be deterministic, but others are not. Causation is about natural powers, capacities, limitations, and tendencies, not linear, closed-system, deterministic forces. These operate in complex and interactive ways in different "open-systems" environments to produce various, complicated, and often unpredictable outcomes; many operative causal forces end up producing no observable effects. Human persons, in particular, enjoy many unique powers and capacities that are characterized by openness, creativity, agency, freedom, and unexpectedness (Smith. *What Is a Person?*). Critical realism thus understands human activity not as transcending but embedded in and shaped by a causally operative though not deterministic world. Causal realism thus does not compromise human agency in action. Persons remain the purposeful agents of many of their own significant motivations and actions. By "human agency" I mean *the capacity to exercise personal powers and capabilities to cause events to happen in the world*. Causally oriented social sciences thus do not need to eliminate humanistically oriented assumptions, studies, and approaches to human life, because freedom and determination are not opposites; agency and structure need not compete directly against each other for influence.

cesses in human life.[15] Other background philosophies that influence much scholarship today instead push hard for simplicity ("parsimony") against complexity. Some also seem implicitly to be trying to discover something like scientific "laws of social life"—conceived as the regular association of observable events ("if A [probably] B"). Critical realism says that reality does not work that way, and there are few if any such non-trivial laws to be discovered. What is regular and "generalizable" in the human world are not associations between events, but rather the natural causal capacities of different entities, the conditions that tend to activate them, and the characteristic outcomes they tend to produce in particular contexts. Understanding those better, and not correlating variables, is what good science is really about. Finding a correlation between variables explains nothing. At best, it gives us an interesting fact that may *then* need causally explaining. Yet understanding causal processes well requires a readiness to take seriously the complexities, contingency, and path-dependency involved in real causal operations. More than obsessive parsimony, we need in our accounts "adequate complexity." This book's theory therefore does not take the form of "the more of variable X then the more (or less) of variable Y." Instead it speaks about natural causal capacities of real social (including religious) entities and their tendencies to operate in particular ways under certain conditions, while acknowledging the massive complexities involved.

Finally, critical realism influences this book in its commitment to "judgmental rationality." That is the belief that, with time, research effort, and good, reasoned arguments about the best available evidence, it is indeed possible to advance our human knowledge about reality and how it works. Science, broadly construed, can and does progress in its knowledge. Inquiring people at one time can better understand what is real and how it works better than similar people did at earlier times. That progress is not guaranteed, but it is possible and often actual. If this were not true, it would be pointless to research and to read and write scholarly publications, for none of it would be getting us anywhere. Even so, more than a few people today are skeptical about progress in scientific knowledge. Some think science does not discover but "socially constructs" truths about reality. Others fear the arrogance and conformism they think is implied by the idea of scientific progress. Still others worry about the lack of moral constraints on scientific

15. George Steinmetz. 1998. "Critical Realism and Historical Sociology." *Comparative Studies in Society and History.* 40: 170–186; Steinmetz. 2005. "Scientific Authority and the Transition to Post-Fordism." In George Steinmetz (ed.). *The Politics of Method in the Human Sciences.* Durham, NC: Duke University Press. Pp. 275–323.

advances. The first group is simply wrong, as I have argued elsewhere.[16] The second and third express legitimate concerns, yet none that negate the fact of possible scientific progress. We can believe in the advance of human knowledge about reality without being arrogant and oppressive or deeming science morally autonomous. But we cannot give up the hope of coming to better understand our world and human experience through systematic inquiry. And for that to happen, we cannot merely examine all the theories about a subject and let them stand. We should make reasoned judgments about which accounts seem to explain reality better than others.[17] That is what I seek to do in this book as it pertains to religion. To be sure, much of critical realism's influence I will not make explicit, but it definitely runs as the governing background meta-theory shaping this book's argument.

The third theoretical influence on this work is the social theory of personalism. I have written at length about personalist social theory elsewhere and will not repeat myself here.[18] Suffice it to say that personalism insists that all good theories of human social life build upon the essential facts of human personhood. The ground and emergent reality of all things humanly social are persons. So only a proper account of the nature, capacities, limitations, goods, and ends of human persons can sustain an adequate social theoretical account of human life. Personalism argues that humans have a particular nature that is defined by our biologically grounded yet emergently real personal being and its features, especially our powers, incapacities, tendencies, and natural goods. Human persons are not social constructions "all the way down," but natural entities with a real, identifiable condition and telic orientations, which are of course profoundly socially formed. Personalism observes that human persons have a natural proper end (*telos*) toward which to live—namely, *eudaimonia*, happy flourishing—that (by my account) is realized by the progressive attainment of six natural, basic goods. Religion potentially helps persons to realize those six goods and so move toward personal flourishing. This book's theory of religion, therefore, builds upon a personalist account of what human beings are, our natural capacities and incapacities, the natural goods of personhood, and the ends toward which our actions and interactions move. Its personalist

16. Smith. *What Is a Person?* Pp. 119–219.

17. See footnote 4.

18. Smith. *What Is a Person*; Christian Smith. 2015. *To Flourish or Destruct: A Personalist Theory of Human Goods, Motivations, Failure, and Evil.* Chicago: University of Chicago Press; also see Christian Smith. 2003. *Moral, Believing Animals: Human Personhood and Culture.* New York: Oxford University Press, which I would characterize as proto-personalist.

influences become especially clear when I discuss why humans are religious in chapter 5, but personalism is always running in the background, even if usually inconspicuously.

Final Clarifications

I said earlier that my definition of religion in this book closely follows that of Martin Riesebrodt, as developed in his 2010 book, *The Promise of Salvation*. How does my account differ from his? My definition of religion makes only minor adjustments to his, and so "my" definition might rightly also be said to be "Riesebrodt's definition." I do steer the framing and development of my theory away from his resolutely Weberian approach into a more clearly critical realist one. My definition combines what Riesebrodt separates analytically into the three separate steps of "defining," "understanding," and "explaining" religion.[19] I also adjust his definition by adding the phrase "align themselves with" to better account for religions lacking personal gods (about which more below). I may not subscribe to the details of his account of the phylogenetic and ontogenetic origins of religion.[20] And my book overall focuses much more on what Riesebrodt calls "religious-*ness*" than on religion itself. But I do not fundamentally disagree with any of Riesebrodt's thinking in his book, as I understand it; I rather wish to affirm, develop, and extend it.

That said, I do believe that Riesebrodt partly undermines his own project by two key terminological decisions worth mentioning. The first is his emphasis on the word "salvation," highlighted in the title of the book. This accent on salvation is odd, since Riesebrodt's theory seeks to be universal and his evidence and illustrations include Western and Eastern references, while the word "salvation" is closely associated with the Christian religion. Also, "salvation," for many, carries the connotation of eternal life in heaven, with life after death, not the more mundane affairs that Riesebrodt notes religions often concern. Having worked to develop a universal account of religion, why would Riesebrodt foreground a concept that seems partial and particular? I do not know. This cannot be blamed on the translation of his book from German to English, since the word in the original title, *heilsversprechen*, actually means "promise of salvation." To be fair, Riesebrodt's working definition of the concept of salvation is extremely broad. In his

19. Riesebrodt. *Promise of Salvation*. Pp. 71–91.
20. Ibid. Pp. 170–174.

analysis, the term refers to something general like "preservation or deliverance from harm, ruin, or loss," not the specifically Christian understanding of "rescue by God from sin and its consequences."[21] He also explicitly notes—although very late in the book and rather off-handedly—that "salvation" can be both "temporary" (temporal, relating to this world) and "eternal."[22] But however broadly one uses the term "salvation" in a theory of religion, in my view one cannot escape the particularly Christian meanings with which it is fraught. I therefore avoid the word salvation in this book and rely instead on the more general term "deliverance," which is also prominent in Riesebrodt, and should be less problematic, even if not perfect.

Similarly, Riesebrodt likes to describe religious practices as "liturgies." I understand his meaning and the useful connotations that term conveys. However, given the strong associations of the word "liturgy" with the worship styles of Catholic, Orthodox, and Anglican Christians, I think it best to avoid use of that term as well. Also, in this book I use the words "belief" and "beliefs" rather than "faith" to denote the ideas or premises about superhuman powers that help to make sense of religious practices. That is because the word faith too is freighted with associations with particular religious traditions—especially Christianity, and more particularly evangelical Protestantism—to serve as a useful term in discussing religion generally. At a time when the North Atlantic–centered world of social scientific study of religion needs to go global,[23] it seems advisable to use the more generic word belief instead of faith.[24]

My discussion of religion in this book focuses on what the vast majority of religions in the past and present have been and are like now, not on what

21. Ibid. On p. 89, he equates "the promise of salvation" with "the ability to avert misfortune, overcome crises, and provide salvation."

22. Ibid. P. 148.

23. David Smilde and Matthew May. 2015. "Causality, Normativity, and Diversity in 40 Years of U.S. Sociology of Religion." *Sociology of Religion*. 76, 4: 369–388.

24. By "beliefs" here I do not mean the professions of Western religious confessional systems. I mean, more generally, premises or propositions that people consciously or tacitly regard to be true—more precisely, mental attitudes of a certain kind directed toward premises or propositions that are taken to be true. Humans universally have and use beliefs of this kind in most of their activities, including the practicing of religion (see Smith. *To Flourish or Destruct*. Pp. 69–70; Lynne Baker. 1987. *Saving Belief*. Princeton: Princeton University Press). However, specific studies of religious traditions for which the concept of "faith" is indigenously "theologically" appropriate certainly ought to use that term in their analyses, since the character of science should always be driven by the nature of the subject being studied.

religion could or should be. My definition of religion also centers on "culturally prescribed religious practices," rather than people as religious practitioners and what they may or may not believe, including how much they
embrace or dissent from their religious traditions. This tilt toward practices
that are prescribed by cultural traditions—rather than religious people's
thoughts and feelings about their religions, including their critical, alienated, and dissenting positions—is, I believe, justified. I realize, however,
that it may seem to be biased toward the status quo, established orthodox-
ies, and authorities who have the power to determine "correct" practices
and, therefore, who is in and out, acceptable or not. So I want to be clear
that this book's theory need not privilege the religiously official and powerful. When understood and deployed well, it actually provides helpful tools
for those who wish to critique established authorities and traditions. The
theory situates observers to explore questions like these: Who "owns" religious cultures and traditions and why? How is religious authority maintained, perhaps even at the expense of religious ethics? Where are boundaries of religious unacceptability and therefore exclusion drawn, why there,
and how do they change over time? When and why might dissent from or
transgression of dominant religious practices actually become a religious
practice itself? How do religious communities negotiate dissonances between their official prescriptions and subjective dispositions of practitioners when the latter disagree with or do not fit easily into official standards?
In short, how do power, authority, continuity, voice, inclusion, exclusion,
alienation, critique, transgression, and dissent work in religions in the real
world?[25] Those are not the obvious or primary questions shaping this book's
theory, but the theory nonetheless can assist those with experiences, outlooks, and interests that raise such questions, as I hope will become clear as
the book's argument unfolds.

I do not in this book jump into debates that have been churning in religious studies and anthropology for years about whether "religion" is a
real entity or is something like the construction of modern, Western

---

25. For examples in my own field, see Korie L. Edwards. 2008. *The Elusive Dream*. New York:
Oxford University Press; Tricia Bruce. 2011. *Faithful Revolution*. New York: Oxford University
Press; Milagros Peña. 2007. *Latina Activists across Borders*. Durham, NC: Duke University Press;
Irene Sevcik, Michael Rothery, Nancy Nason-Clark, and Robert Pynn. 2015. *Overcoming Conflict-
ing Loyalties*. Edmonton: University of Alberta Press; Anson Shupe. 1998. *Wolves within the Fold*.
New Brunswick, NJ: Rutgers University Press; Kelly Chong. 2008. *Deliverance and Submission*.
Cambridge, MA: Harvard University Press.

colonizers.[26] My position follows Martin Riesebrodt's, explained deftly in his book, and I see no point in repeating it here.[27] Kevin Schilbrack's smart critical realist intervention in this debate I also embrace, as well as Tom Tweed's response to this issue.[28] As far as I am concerned, Riesebrodt, Schilbrack, and Tweed have gotten it right, by showing that the post-colonial critics may be largely correct, insofar as it goes, when it comes to religion as a *concept*, but that this does not negate the fact that humans have been *practicing* something real and identifiable that we call religion for countless millennia. We have learned much from the post-colonial critics, but their case has not dissolved the subject of religion.[29]

This book offers a social scientific account of religion (what anthropologists call an "etic" approach) that tries to take seriously the "insider" or "native" beliefs, categories, and meanings of religious traditions and people (what is called an "emic" approach) without being bound by them.[30] The

26. Michael Lambek. 2015. "What Is 'Religion' for Anthropology? And What Has Anthropology Brought to 'Religion'?" In Janice Boddy and Michael Lambek (eds.). *A Companion to the Anthropology of Religion*. Hoboken, NJ: Wiley Blackwell. Pp. 1–32; Russell McCutcheon. 1997. *Manufacturing Religion*. New York: Oxford University Press; Timothy Fitzgerald. 1999. *The Ideology of Religious Studies*. New York: Oxford University Press; Tomoko Masuzawa. 2012. *The Invention of World Religions*. Chicago: University of Chicago Press; Brent Nongbri. 2013. *Before Religion: A History of a Modern Concept*. New Haven, CT: Yale University Press; Jason Ananda Josephson. 2012. *The Invention of Religion in Japan*. Chicago: University of Chicago Press; Winnifred Sullivan. 2012. SSRC. "The World that *Smith* Made." http://blogs.ssrc.org/tif/2012/03/07/the-world-that-smith-made/.

27. Riesebrodt. *Promise of Salvation*. Pp. 1–70.

28. Kevin Schilbrack. 2010. "Religions: Are There Any?" *Journal of the American Academy of Religion*.78: 1112–1138; Schilbrack. 2012. "The Social Construction of 'Religion' and Its Limits." *Method and Theory in the Study of Religion*. 24: 97–117; Schilbrack. 2005. "Religion, Models of, and Reality." *Journal of the American Academy of Religion*. 73: 429–52; Schilbrack. 2013. "After We Deconstruct 'Religion,' Then What? A Case for Critical Realism." *Method and Theory in the Study of Religion*. 25, 1: 107–12; Thomas Tweed. 2008. *Crossing and Dwelling: A Theory of Religion*. Cambridge, MA: Harvard University Press.

29. I am also not directly engaging the dispute about whether religion scholars need be "caretakers" or "critics" of religion, as a recent debate has framed the matter (the correct answer is "neither"). See Russell McCutcheon. 2001. *Critics Not Caretakers*. Albany: State University of New York Press; Atalia Omer. 2011. "Can a Critic Be a Caretaker Too?" *Journal of the American Academy of Religion*. 79: 459–496.

30. Marvin Harris. 1976. "History and Significance of the Emic/Etic Distinction." *Annual Review of Anthropology*. 5: 329–350; Kenneth Pike (ed.). 1967. *Language in Relation to a Unified Theory of Structure of Human Behavior*. The Hague, Netherlands: Mouton de Gruyter; Russell McCutcheon. 1999. *Insider/Outsider Problem in the Study of Religion*. London: Cassell. If the first-order, emic perspective was sufficient to fully describe and explain social life—that is, if reality was so transparent to all of the actors involved in every condition and situation that their self-reports could articulate adequate explanations for those conditions and situations—then there

latter perspective (emic) concerns how reality is viewed and explained within the social group being studied; the former (etic) concerns how outsiders, like social scientists, define, categorize, understand, and explain the same social group using different, scholarly, "non-native" terminology and explanations. Taking an etic approach without discounting the emic sometimes involves switching between the two perspectives and navigating tricky tensions. One difficulty arises in adopting particular religious terms—such as "blessings" and "deliverance"—for use in general theory, without inadvertently dragging along the associated "baggage" from their original religious uses.[31] When scholars redefine through stipulation a "first-order" religious term for scholarly, "second-order" purposes, confusions can result. Yet scholars cannot invent entirely new, abstract conceptual vocabularies that are "untainted" by any first-order religious meanings by virtue of having no semantic connection to them. So we live in the tensions as best we can. Another problem is that religious people (the emic account) may disagree with social scientific interpretations of them (the etic account), setting up conflicts in views about what is "really" going on in religion and who has the correct perspective to see and know it. This book takes a primarily etic perspective, although it draws terms and provides examples from emic religious perspectives. Keeping in mind the emic/etic distinction will help this book's argument make more sense.

Finally, nothing in this book either directly endorses or invalidates the truth claims of any religious tradition. This book focuses on the human side

---

would be no need for any second-order social science or theory; the recording of first-order accounts would do. But the emic perspective is actually often limited and sometimes blurred if not mistaken, requiring an etic account adequately to understand and explain social life, even, sometimes, for the actors involved themselves. Doing this well is part of the responsibility and promise of the social sciences.

31. For example, my reservations about Riesebrodt's use of "salvation" and "liturgies." "Only an interpretive, that is, meaning-oriented theory of action, is capable of bridging the gap between religious internal perspectives and scientific external perspectives. Explanations that adopt external perspectives have to justify the outside point of view they adopt. In contrast, interpretive explanations arrive at their external perspectives by abstracting and systematizing internal perspectives. . . . They transform internal perspectives into an external perspective, which is different from the internal perspective but does not contradict them. . . . If we systematize the self-images that religions produce, we see that they contain a sufficient foundation for explaining religion in general. They illuminate the institutionalized meaning of religious practices and allow us to conclude that although this meaning is not identical with the meanings that practitioners attribute to their actions, it nonetheless corresponds to it. . . . Thus the sociological interpretation of meaning represents an abstraction and selective systematization of concrete cultural meanings, but not a break with them." Riesebrodt. *Promise of Salvation.* Pp. 71, 72, 89.

of religion, its nature and workings. The social sciences are constitutionally incompetent to make judgments about religion's metaphysical claims about superhuman powers.[32] Empirical social scientific research sometimes does

32. See Douglas Porpora. 2006. "Methodological Atheism, Methodological Agnosticism, and Religious Experience." *Journal for the Theory of Social Behaviour.* 36: 57–75. My general approach here is one of "compatibilism," a term that usually describes a position in the philosophical debate about human free will, which claims that determinism and free will are compatible. I am borrowing the word for the present discussion. Compatibilism here means that, in principle, genuinely different perspectives on religion—religious and social scientific—may very well be compatible or congruent with each other (though they are not necessarily). Alternative accounts need not be playing a zero-sum game, in which the more right one is, the more wrong the other must be. Instead, different types of accounts of religion might be taking different perspectives on the same subject, which are each valid, as far as they go, but also limited in what they can describe. With properly developed minds able to navigate the complexities of multiple, divergent perspectives on the same subject, we should be able to see how those perspectives provide insights that may be true to reality even if they are not identical with each other. And no matter which may be the thinker's own primary perspective, we should be able to learn from others. Religious practitioners may privilege the accounts of their own religious traditions, but they should also be able to learn from social scientists. And vice versa. Compatibilism does not guarantee or even argue that all perspectives and accounts are equally valid. Human knowledge is fallible and limited. Some claims may be wrong. Yet compatibilism is not really about judging the truth or falsehood of positions, but rather of their possible congruence. The compatibilist approach merely says that in principle, different, seemingly conflicting accounts may actually be true and able to stand together.

The viewpoints of the social sciences are constitutionally limited to making claims based on purportedly reliable empirical evidence and on retroductive and abductive theoretical inferences related to that evidence. Religious truth claims, by contrast, are usually based on different standards of evidence, such as purported divine revelation, historical tradition, mystical experiences, and personal enlightenment. The trouble is that what counts as authoritative evidence for any particular community of knowledge, practice, and discourse (scientific or religious) is particular to that community. Social scientists cannot be persuaded to claim anything as true based on the Jewish Bible or Qur'an, for instance. Likewise, many religious Jews and Muslims will not be convinced about the final truth of reality by analyses of empirical survey data and interviews. Compatibilism helps to mediate such differences. Social science and religion usually have two different purposes and types of authoritative evidence to which they appeal. They are rarely in direct competition. Each may be right or wrong in different ways. But rarely is one able to judge the validity of the other based on its own standards of evidence. Empirical social scientific evidence could never tell us if a transcendent God or Brahman exists as absolute reality, for example. Nor could scripture or mystical experience tell us much about the social processes by which people, say, undergo religious conversions or religious organizations suffer decline. The two simply have different interests, focuses of concern, and standards of judgment (see Christian Smith. 2016. "Why Scientists Playing Amateur Atheology Fail." *Christian Scholars Review.* 47). So they need not conflict.

The critical realism framing my argument in this book helps to explain why compatibilism makes sense, by observing that reality is differentiated, stratified, and complex, entailing complexities of "levels" of the real that each operate according to their own principles and mechanisms. Nearly everything in reality operates in "open systems" in which often overwhelmingly

hold implications for and can pose profitable questions and sometimes disturbing challenges to religious traditions. And social and natural science are capable of (in)validating some specific, empirically falsifiable claims made by religious actors, as when faith healers claim miraculously to cure diseases through prayer. But in general, the social sciences properly take an agnostic, or better yet, uninterested and disinterested, view of the veracity of the metaphysical and theological truth claims of religions, however important and interesting they may be in and of themselves.[33]

---

complex combinations of causal forces shape outcomes, including from "below" through emergence and "above" through downward causation. Furthermore, critical realism rejects philosophical materialism and empiricism, affirming instead that some very important aspects of reality are immaterial (e.g., motivations, values, light waves, etc.) and that much of what matters in reality cannot be accessed by direct empirical observation (e.g., causes, emotions, beliefs, etc.). That is true, critical realism observes, whether or not any religious claims are correct. But if that is true, then at least some religious claims come to be less alien to the reality that science studies. Critical realism and its meta-theoretical frame of thinking are thus compatible with atheism but also with many religious truth claims—in ways that positivist empiricism, for instance, is not. Because reality is highly differentiated and complex, it requires distinct sciences to focus on different aspects of reality, "cutting nature at its joints," to quote Aristotle, according to how those aspects seem to work in constitution (ontology) and operation (causality) at particular levels. That can range from subatomic particle physics to political science to cosmology. Critical realism also recognizes that the human quest to know as much as we can about reality is good and valuable. So whenever humans believe they have discovered some feature of reality that is not yet adequately understood, critical realism says to think hard about which tools and methods will best describe and explain that piece of reality, given its particular nature. The method is always determined by the subject of study, not vice versa. There is no singular "Scientific Method," but many methods that all seek to be most true and adequate to their subjects of study. In short, the human quest for greater knowledge about reality should be characterized by a wide-open, ever-learning pluralism of interests and methods.

33. To be clear, however, I am not here advocating a version of Steven Jay Gould's "non-overlapping magisteria" (aka NOMA), which says that science and religion represent entirely different kinds of inquiry, with science being in charge of *facts* and religion in charge of *values*, such that no conflict should ever arise between them (Gould. 2002. *Rocks of Ages*. New York: Ballantine Books). Gould's thinking was headed in the right direction, but did not get it quite right. Religion is not only interested in "values," but also facts (Francis Collins. 2007. *The Language of God*. New York: Simon & Schuster. Pp. 95, 165). Values ultimately are also always based on facts, as critical realism sees it, even if they are different kinds of entities than facts (Smith. *What Is a Person?* Pp. 386–399). Similarly, science is not just about facts; it presupposes and has implications for a host of values, such as truth, creativity, simplicity, persuasion, etc. (Imagine a science that is truly "value neutral" about the moral commitment to truth!) A better position would be to acknowledge that science and religion both have to do with facts *and* values, and to distinguish between the two in other ways. In compatibilism, the difference is *not* that science and religion "own" or are responsible for dissimilar *types of things* (facts versus values), but rather that they have *qualitatively distinct interests, questions, and standards of knowledge* with regard to sometimes the *same* objects of study (religion, in our case).

1

What Is Religion?

Come, Agni, praised with song, to feast and sacrificial offering:
Sit as Hotar on the holy grass! . . .
O Agni, him who, like a chariot, wins us wealth.
Do thou, O Agni, with great might guard us from all malignity,
Yea, from the hate of mortal man!
O Agni, come; far other songs of praise will I sing forth to thee. . . .
O Agni, bring us radiant light to be our mighty aid,
for Thou art our visible deity!

—HINDU SCRIPTURE, SAMA VEDA (1:1:1:1,5–7,10)

Our God, our help in ages past, our hope for years to come,
Our shelter from the stormy blast, and our eternal home.

—CHRISTIAN HYMN, ISAAC WATTS (1719)

The first step to understanding religion is identifying what religion *is*. What are we even talking about?[1] Scholars have long argued over many rival definitions of religion. Some have given up trying to define it.[2] Others have

---

1. Although my account eschews Durkheim's explanation of religion as grounded in the sacred and collectively constituted—proceeding instead along Weberian lines reframed by critical realism—my procedural insistence on defining religion up front is Durkheimian, not Weberian.

2. Andrew Greeley, for example, wrote, "I make no assumptions in the beginning of this exercise about a proper definition of religion. There exists a bitter and useless controversy in the

decided that religion does not even exist "out there" to be studied and understood, but is only a modern, Western invention imposed on the world for political and religious purposes.[3] I think, on the contrary, that religion is a real, distinctive, and enduring part of human life, and that we can describe its nature in specific terms.[4]

To properly identify what religion *is*, however, we need to do three things. First, we must turn our attention away from various debated *concepts* of religion and focus instead on the *reality* of religion as it is found in actual human lives and societies. Our initial point of reference needs to be not the many different ways one can think about religion, but the concrete realities of religions in the world that we are trying to think about.[5] Second, we need to put on hold our interest in the *ideas and beliefs* of religious people, and concentrate on their religious *practices*, that is, on repeated, religiously meaningful behaviors. The common bias toward an "intellectualist" view of religion needs to be corrected with a primary focus instead on people's reiterated actions.[6] Third, we must do more than ponder the

---

sociology of religion about what religion is, and whether one needs an explicit 'transcendental,' 'superempirical' referent for a belief system to be religious." Greeley. 1982. *Religion.* New York: Free Press.

3. See note 26 in the introduction.

4. I generally follow Riesebrodt in emphasizing three features of a good definition: "Religious practices should be differentiated as clearly and unambiguously as possible from other kinds of practices. First, this differentiation should be made in such a way that our everyday understanding of religion is not stood on its head; instead, the phenomena that are commonly considered religious should fall under the definition given. Second, the definition should not already contain the explanation of the phenomena.... Third, the definition should be compatible with religion's self-understandings as expressed in their practices." Riesebrodt. *Promise of Salvation.* P. 74.

5. Critical realists distinguish the "transitive" and "intransitive" aspects of science—the transitive being our ideas about real things and the intransitive the real things about which we have ideas. Confusing the two leads to enormous troubles. Here we begin with the intransitive fact of religion being practiced in the real world, regardless of the contingent history of our scholarly conceptualizations of religion. Skeptics might say that we cannot observe "religion" in the real world until we have first settled on a definition of religion. The epistemology presupposed by that view, however, related to a post-Kantian outlook exemplified in strong social constructionism, is one-sided and erroneous. In the development of human knowledge, working through an ongoing hermeneutical spiral, transitive concepts are just as determined by intransitive facts of reality as our understandings of those facts are partly mediated by our concepts about them. Humans can and do observe and make sense of real things happening in the world without pre-defined categories in hand that tell them what those things are. Otherwise, our human knowledge would amount to nothing but our starting-point concepts, and it is hard to explain where they would come from. See Terry Godlove's effective use of philosopher Donald Davidson to address this question. 2002. "Saving Belief." In Nancy K. Frankenberry (ed.). *Radical Interpretation in Religion.* Cambridge: Cambridge University Press. Pp. 10–24.

6. See Manuel Vasquez. 2010. *More Than Belief.* New York: Oxford University Press; Daniel

various arguments for and against different views of religion. We also need to make *rational judgments* about which approaches seem better and so deserve our assent. We need to choose between the best alternatives and move the discussion forward.[7]

What, then, is religion? *Religion is a complex of culturally prescribed practices, based on premises about the existence and nature of superhuman powers, whether personal or impersonal, which seek to help practitioners gain access to and communicate or align themselves with these powers, in hopes of realizing human goods and avoiding things bad.* The most common of these hopes is to avert misfortunes and receive blessings and deliverance from crises of many kinds; but other, more "spiritual" other-worldly, and sometimes sublime goods and bads are also often part of religious concerns. This definition of religion includes all the concepts that need to be included and avoids all the "accidentals" that ought to be excluded. It is specific and precise where it needs to be, yet also general and inclusive where needed. Let us unpack its meaning, phrase by phrase.

Superhuman powers is the pivotal idea in this definition. "Superhuman" here means that these powers are (believed to be) able to influence or control significant parts of reality that are usually beyond direct human intervention.[8] That is why humans need their help. Normally these superhuman powers are also not directly observable by human senses. Their sphere of influence may concern personal experiences, human social life, the natural environment, and life after death. Superhuman powers can make happen things that human powers cannot, at least in some situations—that is what makes them *super*human. This emphasis on power, on capacities to make things happen or prevent them from happening, is central to the reasons humans have for producing religion.[9]

A second defining feature of "superhuman powers" is that—according to the religious communities that take their existence and nature as prem-

---

Winchester. 2008. "Embodying the Faith: Religious Practice and the Making of a Moral Habitus." *Social Forces.* 86: 1753–1780.

7. Per critical realism's commitment to "judgmental rationality," described in the introduction.

8. Riesebrodt. *Promise of Salvation.* P. 75.

9. The centrality of powers also connects directly to critical realism's and personalism's emphases on the natural powers and capacities (and incapacities and finitudes) of real entities and persons that do (and in the case of religion are at least believed to) exist as part of reality. In all cases here, the (in)ability of entities to *cause* certain things to happen is central to human life and the interests of scientific understandings of it.

ises—they are *not* human creations.[10] Part of the very superhuman-ness of these religious powers is that they are (believed to be) not dependent upon human invention, activity, or production to exist. People may need to feed, please, or replenish the superhuman powers, but they do not create them.[11] This feature is crucial for distinguishing the superhuman powers that define religion from other types of superhuman powers that emerge from human activity but that are not religious. Examples of the latter—which I will call *humanly emergent* superhuman powers—include the Internet, global capitalist markets ("the invisible hand"), and state institutions. These (and nearly every complex human social institution) are "able to influence or control significant parts of reality in ways that are usually beyond direct human intervention"; they possess superhuman powers to exert forces of downward causation on human persons. Humans also engage in various practices to try to access and realize goods from these powers.[12] But the key difference is that they are the products of human design and activity, and so are not powerful in the way that *religious* superhuman powers are.[13]

This definition purposefully avoids the ideas supernatural, transcendent, ultimate, God, gods, spirits, higher beings, holy, numinous, ultimate

10. This was not a point of concern for Riesebrodt, to my knowledge, though important to add here.

11. It would be inaccurate, however, to say religious superhuman powers are always "self-subsistent" or "have their own ground of being," because some of them (ghosts, angels, saints in heaven, gods described in Hesiod's *Theogony*) do not have independent existences but are dependent for their being upon other superhuman powers. The most precise way to define religiously superhuman follows Schilbrack: the powers in question must be both not empirical and also not the product of any empirical thing, that is, they must be "superempirical" (and not merely "nonempirical") (2014. *Philosophy and the Study of Religions*. Malden, MA: Wiley Blackwell. Pp. 134–135, 139–140).

12. I intentionally use the word "goods" instead of "benefits" in this book to signal its grounding in neo-Aristotelian personalism rather than utilitarian rational choice theory; to suggest the vastly broader range of life (and possibly afterlife or "next-life") goods than utilitarianism, which ultimately references pleasures and pains, can; and in particular to recognize the many potential perceived goods of subjective religious experiences. Obviously I do not mean only material or consumer goods.

13. This distinction has potential implications for re-conceiving parts of secularization not as the straightforward decline or loss of religion (Taylor's "subtraction" theory, in Charles Taylor. 2007. *A Secular Age*. Cambridge, MA: Belknap) but instead as the displacement of practices oriented toward religious superhuman powers through a shift by many modern people toward practices devoted (to the point of sometimes being willing to kill and die) to humanly emergent superhuman powers, such as The Nation, The Economy, Science, Capitalism, Communism, and Mass Education. However, this is an admittedly speculative interpretation that is beyond the scope of this book's argument (but see, for example, William Cavanaugh. 2011. *Migrations of the Holy*. Grand Rapids, MI: Eerdmans).

concern, and the sacred, for good reason.[14] Debates about defining religion have taught us that none of these terms are adequate. For example, the idea of "the supernatural" presupposes a distinction between the natural and supernatural; yet some religions do not believe in anything supernatural but instead understand everything in existence as belonging to nature, with even superhuman powers belonging to the natural order of things. A similar problem compromises the idea that religion concerns the "transcendent," since many human religions have conceived their superhuman powers, the spirits of trees and streams, for instance, as immanent to this reality, not transcending it. Likewise, the idea that religion is about "ultimate" realities or concerns does not work, since many religions are concerned in part— and some are almost wholly concerned—with this-worldly, even mundane issues, like fertile crops and healing sickness, not ultimate things like eternity or "the meaning of life." God, gods, spirits, and beings are a problem because, again, not all religions believe in a God, gods, spirits, or higher beings. The notion of "the sacred" also fails to demarcate religious things for three reasons: Many things that some people treat as sacred (the nation, golf, shopping, etc.) cannot reasonably be considered religious, not all aspects of all religions are viewed as sacred, and the conceptual opposite of *sacred* is not secular or non-religious but *profane*. Human cultures always involve sacred things, but those things are not always religious.[15] Among all the possible concepts available to define religion, only one captures the crucial feature of all religions, and that is the idea of superhuman powers.

14. Scholars, even after reading Riesebrodt, sometimes still confuse "superhuman" and "supernatural" (and "theistic")—for example, Ammerman's critique of "Riesebrodt's picture of asking *supernatural* forces for assistance" and his focus on "practices . . . oriented . . . to the *supernatural*," in contrast to "Extra-*theistic*" spiritualities (2014. *Sacred Stories, Spiritual Tribes.* New York: Oxford University Press. Pp. 290, 292, italics added).

15. Defining religion in terms of the sacred also leaves us not only with an unclear, nonintuitive, substantively vacuous account of what "religion" is, but also with the allegedly inescapable condition of "Religious Man," necessarily expressed in all people, no matter how secular or irreligious they may be. By such a definition, everyone inevitably turns out to be "religious," one way or another, although religion turns out not to mean much. It then becomes difficult to make sense of real religious decline, of secularization, in cases when that does happen (see chapter 5). Indeed, this last point may help to explain the appeal of "the sacred" for defining religion; it offers one strategy for rescuing religion from the acids of modernity. "This expansion of the concept of religion seems to serve the repression of subjective processes of disenchantment rather than the pursuit of analytical goals. Some people find it easier to broaden the concept of religion to the point of meaninglessness than to admit to themselves and others that they [and many others in society] no longer believe in superhuman powers and their accessibility" (Riesebrodt. *Promise of Salvation.* P. 78).

The phrase "whether personal or impersonal" means that the superhuman powers in any given religion may or may not be believed to possess things like consciousness, thoughts, desires, intentions, and feelings. Some superhuman powers may be God, gods, spirits, sprites, ghosts, or demons with properties analogous to those of human persons, such as mind, will, and emotions. But others may be non-conscious forces, energies, or dynamisms, such as a common view of Hinduism's Brahman, which some humans believe they can tap or align themselves with through religious practices.[16] What kind of causal capacities do impersonal powers possess? Karma, for instance, exercises the inexorable force of causing all actions to be followed by their fitting consequences. The Tao, in some views, is a natural principle, essence, flow, or energy that, when properly known and followed, results in harmony, liberation, and happiness. Dharma operates similarly for many. Which kinds of superhuman powers

16. My approach depends on the idea that some impersonal powers can "act" in the sense of exerting causal forces on human life. Is this idea consistent with the *dharmic* religious traditions associated with many interpretations of Hinduism, Buddhism, Sikhism, and Jainism? I believe so, although fully explaining why would require a long chapter, and the matter is complicated by significant internal heterogeneity within many of these traditions, which lack centralized orthodox doctrines. For present purposes, we can briefly note that, according to a common understanding, *Brahman* in Hinduism, for example, is the Ultimate Reality of the cosmos, the highest Universal Principle, the unchanging and uncaused cause of all changes, often thought of as the material, efficient, formal, and final cause of all that exists. Brahman, though impersonal, thus acts in and upon life and the world causally. Because of ignorance and desire, many in this tradition believe, human existence is also subject to the powers of *samsara*, the repeated cycles of reincarnation. *Karma*, too, is an impersonal force or principle of cause and effect that determines future states of existence according to past and present actions, and so is fundamentally about active causality and the governing of good and bad human outcomes, which religious practices intend to influence. By aligning oneself with these truths and powers of reality and living according to *dharma*, a virtuous, proper, and moral life, the religious practitioner can move toward the liberation of *moksha* or nirvana. Although these superhuman powers are impersonal, their traditions still fit this definition of religion well. One might next ask then why gravity, an impersonal superhuman power arguably not absolutely unlike Brahman in some respects, does not count as religious. The answer is that (a) people do not view gravity as a power that can be communicated or aligned with through the exercise of culturally prescribed practices; (b) people readily view gravity (whether they theoretically understand it or not) as a natural *condition of the possibility of* misfortunes (spills, falls, drowning) and not a superhuman power capable of preventing them; and (c) no human community or tradition has developed prescribed complexes of practices to help people align with the power of gravity so as to obtain blessings and receive deliverance from crises. Gravity is thus an impersonal superhuman power, yes, but not the object of a religion. Usually, in fact, when humans do make natural superhuman powers religiously significant— for example, the sun or mountains—those powers are *personified*, as being or representing gods or spirits.

religious practitioners seek to access, whether personal or impersonal, depends on what their practices assume about them.

Religion consists in part of *a complex of culturally prescribed practices.* "Practices" are culturally meaningful behaviors that are intentionally repeated over time, such as making yearly offerings to the spirits of one's ancestors or praying every night before going to sleep. All four of those elements—meaning, behavior, intentionality, and repetition—must be present in the activity (though not necessarily in the mind of the practitioner, as I suggest below) to count as a genuine practice.[17] One person's mindless behavioral habit, such as repeatedly scratching his chin, is not a true practice by this account, since it is not culturally prescribed, is hardly intentional, and has no broader cultural meaning.

Religions are formed from networks of practices grouped together into complexes. A single practice does not make a religion. One does not simply burn some incense or read the passage of a text and thereby have a religion. Religions are composed of conglomerations of interrelated practices, sometimes so many that it takes a lifetime to learn to perform them well. Each of the practices has its own meaning, and each usually adds extra meaning to the others in the larger complex of practices to which they belong. Take a simple example: Folding one's hands for prayer and speaking the words of a prayer are distinct religious practices, neither of which absolutely requires the other. But when they are combined, each enriches the meaning of the other: The folded hands enact a reverence that is appropriate to the prayer and the prayer provides an expressive purpose with content for the folded hands. The combined meaning is more than the sum of its parts. Complexes of religious practices, which are part of even the simplest of religions, thus generate synergies and experiences that individual practices alone do not.

Practices, by this account, also need to be specified and commended by some culture or tradition.[18] Religious practices are never random, idiosyncratic, or arbitrary. If they were, then they could not be meaningful. They would simply be the strange doings of odd people. Religious practices are always culturally prescribed. The stipulations may cover *which* practices to perform; *how* to perform them correctly; and *when, where,* and *in what situations* to perform them. Often only certain people—shamans, mediums,

---

17. Making practices central to religion makes it "a *humanistic* definition of religion, in the sense that it does not exclude human agency or conscious aims" (Schilbrack. *Philosophy and the Study of Religions.* P. 122, italics added).

18. See the important clarification on the question of persons, not social units, as actors in the section Terminological and Other Clarifications later in this chapter.

priests, ordained clergy, laypersons—are allowed to engage in particular practices. In addition, some religious practices are prescribed to be undertaken by individuals, some by groups, and some by entire nations or societies.[19] Some religious practices are meant to be enacted once in a lifetime, while others are expected to be sustained over a period of time or even an entire life. Still other practices are supposed to add up to one whole, comprehensive way of life. Institutionalized cultural orders or systems thus always tell practitioners when and how to repeat the meaningful actions correctly, and who may repeat them. If a practice is not conducted properly by the right person, then it is often considered invalid and ineffective. This is why religions are almost invariably social activities—communities of memory engaged in carrying on particular traditions (figure 1.1).[20] In fact, in the absence of inherited historical traditions, most new religious movements simply *invent* them as needed.[21] Communal memory and the authority of historical tradition give religions some of their formative power, but because it is difficult to transmit practices faithfully across generations, they also make religious continuity challenging to sustain over time.

A long tradition in the sociology of religion, reflected in the theory of the French sociologist Emile Durkheim, among others, has insisted on a sharp distinction between religion and magic. In this view, religion is by definition a social fact, socially constituted and practiced, and therefore requiring collective practices to exist. Magic, by contrast, is thought to be a different species of human activity, partly because it is often an asocial practice performed by individual clients for instrumental, personal reasons, rather than taking place socially as a matter of group solidarity. Making this

19. Some studies of religion talk about religious "rituals" more than "practices." How, in this theory, are these two concepts related? While they are similar in nature, "practices" serves as a more general and inclusive term than "rituals." Practices I define broadly as culturally meaningful behaviors that are intentionally repeated over time. Rituals, by comparison, usually signify prescribed rites, ceremonies, or proceedings conducted in stipulated forms and sequences that are distinguished by their relative solemnity, formalism, traditionalism, invariance, rule-governance, sacral symbolism, and performance quality (Catherine Bell. 1997. *Ritual*. New York: Oxford University Press. Pp. 138–169). Not all rituals feature all of these characteristics, but that is the ideal type. Practices, while reflecting some of these qualities, can be more diverse, informal, and irregular. All rituals are practices, but not all practices are rituals. And so not all activities in which religious practitioners engage to access superhuman powers are or need to be rituals.

20. Daniele Hervieu-Leger. 2000. *Religion as a Chain of Memory*. New Brunswick, NJ: Rutgers University Press.

21. James Lewis and Olav Hammer (eds.). 2011. *The Invention of Sacred Tradition*. Cambridge: Cambridge University Press; Nicholas Roberts. 2015. *Political Islam and the Invention of Tradition*. Washington, DC: New Academic.

FIGURE 1.1. An adult Christian believer is baptized by church leaders via total immersion in a river near the village of Nyombe, Malawi, Africa. Baptism by water is a central religious practice in most Christian traditions. (Copyright: Joseph Project—Malawi / Alamy Stock Photo)

distinction between religion and magic was necessary for Durkheim and his followers because they believed that religion is the collective representation of that which a community considers to be sacred about itself.[22] But this distinction does not matter for us. The collective performance of practices is not an essential feature of religion, by my account; nor is Durkheim's emphasis on the sacred. Magic can and usually does involve "complexes of culturally prescribed practices" oriented toward superhuman powers, as this book's definition specifies. So, following Riesebrodt,[23] I see no need to divorce religion and magic conceptually. When magic is practiced in ways that fit the definition of religion advanced here, then it belongs to religion.

One could never enumerate a comprehensive list of religious practices. However, it is possible to compile a list of various practices from religious traditions past and present, both common and unusual. Such a list is compiled in no particular order in table 1.1. Later I try to sort these specific practices into some major types.

Linking the practices just discussed and the superhuman powers discussed earlier is the phrase *based on premises about*. Practices are culturally

22. Durkheim and Karen Fields (transl.). 1995. *The Elementary Forms of the Religious Life*. New York: Free Press.

23. Riesebrodt. *Promise of Salvation*. P. 78.

TABLE 1.1. The Variety of Religious Practices

Animal sacrifice	Observing holy days	Hanging images on walls
Scripture reading	Processions	Self-flagellation
Communal fellowship	Conducting crusades	Consecrating objects
Observing sacred laws	Requesting prayer support	Coming forward down an aisle
Human sacrifice	Practicing pacifism	Using prayer beads
Sharing sacred meals	Visiting shrines	Memorizing scripture
Hospitality	Praying to ancestors	Divination
Wearing amulets or talismans	Venerating sacred objects	Observing dietary restrictions
Plant harvest sacrifice	Constructing monuments	Conducting funerals
Reciting mantras	Kneeling	Making sacred art
Sacred dancing	Keeping silence	Walking labyrinths
Observing rites of passage	Receiving visions or appari-	Preserving bodies of the dead
Spoken prayers	tions	Reciting oral histories
Giving alms	Giving public testimony	Venerating animals
Lighting candles	Laying on hands	Using hallucinogens
Observing sacred calendrical	Closing one's eyes	Retelling sacred narratives
times	Folding hands	Offering food to priests
Spirit possession	Raising arms	Ritual sexual acts
Fasting from food	Trusting a divinity	Feeding spirits
Burning incense	Waving plant branches	Observing dietary restrictions
Making offerings	Obeying divine commands	Covering body parts
Meditation	Holy kisses	Revering names of deities
Sexual abstinence	Political blessings	Ritual breathing exercises
Blessings of fields	Housing divine statues	Abstaining from unclean words
Consulting oracles	Contemplating icons	Ritual physical exercises
Pilgrimages	Spiritual journaling	Avoiding taking any life
Ritual water on skin	Phallus worship	Renunciation of clothing
Blessings of houses	Spiritual direction	Reenacting cosmic mythologies
Conducting exorcisms	Ordination for office	Pastoral discipline
Singing worship songs	Spinning prayer wheels	Water purification rites
Studying sacred texts	Reciting the Rosary	Casting of spells
Blessings of marriages	Penance	Refusal of professional medicine
Celebrating festivals	Attending religious services	Pronouncing of curses
Water baptism	Confession of sin	Positioning talismans
Proselytizing	Believing the gospel	Coloring bodies
Genuflecting	Ashes on forehead	Burning dedicated objects
Wearing prescribed clothing	Endowing religious houses	Keeping vigils
Prostration	Praying to patron saints	Pouring libations
Religious conversion	Buying indulgences	Eucharistic adoration
Taking oaths	Teaching religion	Family visits with ancestors
Celebrating worship liturgies	Performing sacred dramas	present

prescribed and performed because of presuppositions about the existence and nature of superhuman powers that those practices are meant to access. If the superhuman powers were not believed to be able to influence matters of interest, their help would not be sought. The point here is simply that the imperative to perform practices references beliefs that some superhuman powers exist and have capacities for causal influence that humans can access through certain practices.[24]

We see, then, that, while the definition of religion developed by Riesebrodt and being advanced here is clearly centered on practice, it does not overlook the importance of religious beliefs. Religious practices are based on religious premises, and premises are beliefs of a certain kind. There is no religion without some beliefs. The beliefs need not be central to religion, or to its academic study, but they cannot be excluded, either. The role of beliefs in religion is also entailed in the very notion of practices itself. Practices are culturally meaningful behaviors intentionally repeated over time. For behaviors to be culturally meaningful, some beliefs must be operative. Meaning is more than beliefs, but it always depends upon some beliefs. Belief-less meanings do not exist (even if the emotional sensations that often accompany meanings do). And so, to initiate some religious practice, some people at some time must hold some beliefs. But even beyond that, the motivation to carry out practices presupposes a purpose for them. The presupposition of religious practices specifically is some premises about the existence of some superhuman powers that those practices aim to access. Thus, some beliefs are essential to religion's constitution, even if, again, they are not central to its performance and study.

Religious practices are also not prescribed aimlessly but have a definite central purpose: They *seek to help practitioners gain access to and communicate or align themselves with* the postulated superhuman powers.[25] This purpose should be broadly construed to include steps like making contact with,

---

24. The premises here refer only to beliefs about the superhuman powers, their existence and natures, not about larger worldviews or complete cultural systems.

25. My definition from here onward (the "which seeks to" and "in hopes of" parts) includes what Riesebrodt considers the distinct matter of "explaining" religion. He would say that my definition violates his second criterion of a good definition: it "should not already contain the explanation of the phenomena" (74), in order for explanations to be falsifiable. The transcendental realism in critical realism (see Roy Bhaskar. 1997. *A Realist Theory of Science*. London: Verso), however, justifies this move in a way that the transcendental idealism of Riesebrodt's post-Kantian Weberianism does not. My definition says that religion's purpose—accessing superhuman powers—itself *partly constitutes religion*, and is not merely one possible account of why religions exist and act, so it belongs in the conceptualization of religion's ontology. My definition

sustaining a relationship with, attuning oneself to, learning the will of, worshipping, attempting to manipulate, winning the attention of, honoring, pleasing, appeasing, feeding, bargaining with, and more. Which purpose is being pursued will vary by the religious tradition, the prescribed practices, and the nature of the presupposed powers. For this theory it is important to grasp that religious practices are not simply initiations of offers to make exchanges. Practices come in many forms and embody and express various modes of communication, interactions, and relations with superhuman powers. Exchange is only one of those possible modes, and in some religious traditions it is not emphasized. Religious practices in some traditions can just as well seek to foster connections to superhuman powers characterized by love and gratuitous gift-giving or pure spiritual well-being.

I intentionally include both "communicate with" and "align themselves with" in order to accommodate both religions with personal superhuman powers *and* those with impersonal superhuman powers. It is hard to imagine communicating with a force or power that is impersonal. Some religious traditions do not postulate personal gods or spirits, but instead affirm superhuman powers, forces, or dynamics, such as Brahman or karma. It is better to describe the practices of these religions as seeking to attune or align practitioners to or with these impersonal superhuman powers than to say they intend to "communicate" with them. For this reason, I added the phrase "align themselves with" to my definition.

These observations about premises and beliefs raise crucial questions about exactly *who* needs to believe for the practices to be religious. Do religious practitioners at any point in time or always need to believe the premises for their performances to count as religious? Must they always understand and agree with the content of the beliefs on which their practices are premised? What if they do not understand, or they dissent from, the religious tradition and practices? Can some people believe on behalf of others? The account I am advancing suggests the following answer.

Religious practitioners do not need to be aware of the cultural meanings of their repeated actions for them to count as real practices.[26] At times, practices can be performed mindlessly or while distracted. In some cases,

---

remains open to criticism and invalidation, of course, just as much as Riesebrodt's "explaining" religion remains falsifiable.

26. Schilbrack. *Philosophy and the Study of Religions*. P. 121; Michaelis Michael and John Paul Heady. 2012. "A Guru-Disciple Tradition: Can Religious Conversion Be Non-Cognitive?" In Morgan Luck (ed.). *Philosophical Explorations of New and Alternative Religious Movements*. Surrey: Ashgate. Pp. 77–95.

certain practitioners, such as young children, may have no idea about the meanings of their repeated actions. Specific religious practitioners also need not authentically believe in the premises and cultural meanings behind the practices they perform, in the sense of personally affirming the ideas as true.[27] Some people participate in the religious celebrations of Easter and Passover, for instance, who do not personally hold to the historical and theological claims that make those observances religiously meaningful. What matters is not that every practitioner is aware of and truly believes in the culturally meaningful premises of every practice, but rather that *the practice itself* is institutionalized in a complex of repeated actions that are culturally meaningful in religious terms, that is, oriented toward gaining access to superhuman powers. That distinction is important.

The *meanings* of religious practices as conceptualized here, in other words, derive not from the cognitive assent of the people engaged in them at any given time but from a variety of institutional sources, including historical traditions, sacred texts, and explanations by religious specialists. Religious practices are social realities irreducible to the beliefs of the people who enact them. Beyond the subjective experiences of practitioners, they involve various more or less objective "externalized" forms, such as prayer books, ritual dances, candles, the retelling of stories, and the slaughtering of animals—which Riesebrodt calls "supra-individual, objective levels of religion."[28] To count as a genuine religious practice, the repeated actions in some way need to be connected to an account of their cultural meaning.[29] Somebody somewhere needs to be able to explain at least some of the

27. Many people end up holding religious beliefs that are inconsistent with the teachings they are supposed to accept according to the prescriptions of their religious traditions, such that, to a significant degree, "theology doesn't determine people's actual thoughts and behaviors." D. Jason Sloan. 2004. *Theologically Incorrect.* New York: Oxford University Press. P. 4; Justin Barrett. 1999. "Theological Correctness." *Method and Theory in the Study of Religion.* 11: 325–339.

28. Riesebrodt. *Promise of Salvation.* P. 88.

29. So when discreet religious practices are removed from the larger complex of practices of which they were originally a part, and performed in institutions whose cultures involve no premises about superhuman powers, then they may cease being religious practices, despite their religious origins. Examples of this phenomenon include undertaking the originally Hindu, Buddhist, or Jain disciplines of yoga in exercise classes at secular health clubs for purely health reasons, and singing sacred choral music in an ensemble of a secular community music association. Riesebrodt argues that people simply performing religious behaviors does not mean that they are actually doing religion: "People can act religiously without practicing a religion. Someone who practices Zen meditation on Mondays, turns tables on Tuesdays, lays out Tarot cards on Thursdays, and goes to Mass on Sundays is performing religious acts, but the systematic connection among them is lacking. If this connection is produced only subjectively [within one person], if it is not shared

religious significance of the actions. But there are many ways for that to happen; it does not require all or even any of the practitioners at any given time to understand and affirm the truth of their premises for those actions to be religious. Also, practitioners can engage their religions even while disagreeing with, transgressing, or maintaining a distance from the established beliefs and practices. They may do so in hopes of seeking the truth, bearing witness to fellow practitioners, spurring reform of their religion, or fostering greater inclusion.

In any actual performance of a religious practice, different participants may undertake the same actions for different purposes—from repenting from wrongdoing, to conforming to group norms, to looking for an escape from boredom. However, as we seek to understand religion *theoretically*, our key point of reference, to repeat, must be the *culturally prescribed purposes and meanings* of the practices, not primarily the subjective interests or motives of the people performing them. Religious practices are to be performed, according to this book's definition, to help practitioners gain access to and communicate or align themselves with superhuman powers. That specifies the purposes or objectives of the practices. But here these objectives must be understood as *those of the cultures and traditions that prescribe the religious practices*, not the subjective intentions of the particular practitioners. The necessary theoretical starting place for understanding religion is *what a religious culture or tradition says those practices mean and intends its practices to achieve*.[30] The subjective intentions and attitudes of religious practitioners are of course very important, and they matter hugely in the study of religious*ness*. But for the purpose of defining religion theoretically, the subjective intentions of practitioners are not the key reference point.[31] Whether and when gaps may exist between the "official" intentions of the practices and the subjective purposes of the

---

with and confirmed by others, then these practices lack the social character of a religion" (Riesebrodt. *Promise of Salvation*. P. 76). But the line when such a practice becomes definitely not religious can be unclear.

30. Riesebrodt's discussion on this point is helpful, though he uses the term "liturgies" here more than practices (*Promise of Salvation*. Pp. 84–89).

31. "It is ill conceived to construe the object of the study of religion to be the inner experience of religious practitioners. Scholars of religion are not presented with experiences that stand in need of interpretation but rather with texts, narratives, performances, and so forth" (Robert Sharf. 1998. "Experience." In Mark Taylor (ed.). *Critical Terms in Religious Studies*. Chicago: University of Chicago Press. Pp. 94–116). Some of Sharf's arguments I think are confused and would be helped by a dose of critical realism, but his historicist and epistemological problematizing of religious experience merits consideration.

practitioners in any instance is an *empirical* question, one often worth investigating—but one that is not essential for clarifying our *conceptual definition* of religion.

For example, suppose we observe a religious congregation reciting from a prayer book a prayer for protection from evil. What matters for our purpose of defining religion is that the authors of the prayers, the tradition that adheres to that prayer book, and the culture that prescribes the recitation of those prayers—in short, the religious institution—mean those prayers to be offered to a superhuman power in hopes of receiving their protection from evil. That is the essential element for defining this activity as being part of religion. Whether the members of the congregation who are reciting the prayer actually believe in or fear evil is an analytically separate issue. Some may and some may not. But that does not matter for the purpose of *defining* religion. What matters is that the culture, the tradition, the institution prescribing the prayers delineate and intend them to be seeking to access a superhuman power in order to ward off evil. Particular religious people do often practice religion in hopes of gaining the aid of superhuman powers, more than many realize or admit. But their motivations are also subjective and potentially highly variable, sometimes even partly unconscious. Attempting to define religion theoretically by referencing practitioners' subjectivities is a misguided enterprise.[32] By contrast, the intended meanings of religious cultures, traditions, and institutions are more or less objective, public, and focused, and so provide firmer grounds for conceptualizing a definition of religion.[33] Empirically—that is, what we can observe about people's actual practicing of religions—what religious institutions prescribe and why people practice religions are nearly always coupled, but we often observe only a "loose coupling," not a tight fit. Our theoretical account of religion needs to account for that loose coupling. Again, an interest in understanding the subjective motives of religious people is entirely valid and often necessary. But that shifts our attention away from defining *religion* analytically—what we are trying to do in this chapter—and toward studying

---

32. Riesebrodt. *Promise of Salvation.* Pp. 82–84.

33. By analogy, "we understand a play or an opera not by interviewing actors, singers, musicians, or spectators but by grasping the meaning of the action . . . as expressed above all in the texts spoken or sung, in the sets and the staging, in the actors' gestures and mimicry. It is also determined primarily by the author, composer, and director, not by scholars or critics. In other words, the 'subjectively intended meaning' of religious action should not be interpreted subjectivistically. Rather, it is constituted in each case in the context of an institutionalized social and cultural meaning" (Riesebrodt. *Promise of Salvation.* P. 83).

religiousness empirically, a key distinction (discussed just below) that we need to grasp and maintain.

Presupposed by this need to communicate or align oneself with super-human powers through prescribed religious practices is the belief that the powers they are directed toward are not automatically or continually accessible or perhaps attentive to the religious practitioners; or perhaps that humans are easily out of alignment with those powers. In some cases, this is because the superhuman powers are believed to exist in a completely different realm of being, on another plane of existence, and reaching them requires breaking through a barrier or bridging a gap. In other cases, they are thought to require some mode of communication other than ordinary human speech. Sometimes the superhuman powers in question are believed to be so superior in mind, capabilities, or moral perfection that the limitations or corruptions of ordinary human life make them inaccessible in any way other than the prescribed mediating rituals. Then again, the superhuman powers may be considered so slippery, untrustworthy, or malign that particular practices are necessary to corner, pacify, or subdue them for human purposes. Some superhuman powers are thought capable of depletion, hunger, anger, or greed, and so need to be fed, appeased, or rewarded before or while being approached. Finally, in some religions, the superhuman powers (often viewed as impersonal in these cases, such as karma) are believed to operate with such an unyielding consistency of consequences or justice that the religious practices are necessary not to sway the superhuman powers but to bring human consciousness and behavior into sync with the workings of the invariable cosmic order or natural law that the superhuman power defines.

At the same time, nothing in this theory assumes that the superhuman powers that religious practices access are necessarily hostile, difficult, or resistant. They need not be greedy or self-seeking. In some religious traditions, the believed-in superhuman powers are gracious, loving, merciful, forgiving, benevolent, and always ready to hear and respond to the entreaties of their people. Some superhuman powers are more than ready, willing, and able to provide blessings and deliverance. The real difficulty in such cases, according to these traditions' accounts, is not the disposition of the superhuman powers, but humanity's aversion to properly acknowledging and honoring them. Even so, no matter how benevolent and accessible a superhuman power may be believed to be, religious people still perform some practices prescribed by their religious cultures to approach and interact with that power properly. Never are those relations conceived to be automatic, continual, or guaranteed. Religious practitioners in their "natural habitats" may not always recognize that this is what they are doing, but that is nonetheless (from an etic perspective) what is going on.

Why do religious cultures prescribe practices for people to access and communicate or align themselves with superhuman powers? And why do many (though not all) people often perform those practices? It is *in hopes of realizing human goods and avoiding bads, especially avoiding misfortune and receiving blessings and deliverance from crises.* (Elsewhere[34] I explain more thoroughly, and in the section "Why Are Humans Religious?" in chapter 4 of this text I summarize, my personalist account of motivating basic and non-basic human goods and bads; readers unfamiliar with personalist theory, however, can instead begin by thinking in terms of "what *people in particular cultures consider* to be good and bad for humans.") At root, humans approach superhuman powers for help in conditions and situations they cannot control and with problems that they cannot solve. Generally, when people are able to resolve their difficulties in a reasonable amount of time using ordinary, human means, they do so and leave the superhuman powers alone. But very often it happens in life that people cannot address or cope with problems with their own limited resources. Humans also often wish to have extra help, redundancies of assurance, and backup plans for matters that they can only partly control. Religion exists and in part attracts adherents because it promises people the help of superhuman powers to respond to problems, both small and enormous, immediate and perhaps eternal, that they believe they cannot solve themselves. *That is not all religion does, nor is it the only reason people are religious*, as we will see below. But realizing goods and avoiding bads, especially averting misfortune, obtaining blessings, and receiving deliverance from crises through superhuman means, are religion's core purpose, its ultimate raison d'être.[35] When that central purpose withers, whether for reasons internal or external to religion, then, I suggest, over time religion tends to wither, too.

The list of concerns for which people seek to access the help of superhuman powers is as long as all possible human frailties, vulnerabilities, hopes, anxieties, and inadequacies. Riesebrodt notes that "blessings and misfortune can be found in three domains: nature, the human body, and social relations."[36] Dimensions of salvation and misfortune are, he observes,

---

34. Smith. *To Flourish or Destruct.*

35. Even, ironically, when the stated purpose of a religious practice aims at purposelessness or inactivity.

36. Riesebrodt. *The Promise of Salvation.* P. 90. "With regard to nature, the focus is on such

the natural environment of humans, the human body, and interpersonal relations. Thus, for instance, disease and hunger, suffering and pain, need and repression, persecution and expulsion, flood and drought, war and annihilation are generally seen as misfortune, whereas health and abundance, successful hunts, fertility and large harvests, peace and social harmony are seen as blessings. In addition, there are transcendent expectations of salvation that transpose earthly blessings and misfortunes to another level. Here, for the saved, there are no disasters, no crises, no misfortune. They enjoy an eternal state of bliss. In contrast, for the damned or the souls that find no peace, a temporary or eternal state of suffering, pain, and torment is expected.

The latter, of course, only applies to religions that posit conscious existence with possible judgment and reward after death. But blessings can be very immediate, subjective, and positive too, such as enjoying a relationship with God and experiencing God's mercy, forgiveness, and love.

I must repeat a point made above. Religious cultures prescribe practices by which practitioners might realize human goods and avoid bads, such as avoiding misfortune and receiving blessings and deliverance from crises. That does not imply, however, that the means or processes by which that might happen are always instrumental exchanges between humans and superhuman powers. Religious practices come in many varieties and can produce possible effects (as explained by the religious traditions that prescribe them) through diverse means. Only one of those means involves mutually beneficial, tit-for-tat, quid pro quo exchange. Other religious practices offer the promise of goods through cultivated relations with personal superhuman powers that are understood to be irreducibly benevolent, gracious, tender, unmerited, uncalculated, and gratuitous. And in religions involving non-personal superhuman powers, exchange is simply impossible—one cannot broker an exchange with an impersonal force, principle, or power, like the Tao or karma. Through the right practices one either aligns oneself with them or not. Thus, the "in hopes of" part of this book's definition of religion should not be assumed to only involve transactional exchanges.

---

forces as thunderstorms, earthquakes, floods, droughts, volcanic eruptions, invasion of locusts, disappearing game herds, or epidemics. With regard to the human body, the themes of reproduction and mortality—fertility and birth, disease and death—are dominant. Social crises that become the object of religious practices are often closely connected with questions of social superiority or inferiority and with changes in social status. Such crises may concern domination, conflict and sanction, initiation, marriage, and death" (p. 90).

Critics of religion have at times alleged that religion is only about assuaging the fear of death by promising life after death. Some scholars have emphasized overcoming death as religion's essence.[37] Such views are inadequate. No limited set of concerns exists that religion specializes in addressing. Religions can and do engage *every* human concern, anxiety, hope, weakness, and calamity possible. No gain or burden, no dream or catastrophe, either possible or actual, present or future is beyond religion's capacity to address.[38] Consider, for instance, the practice of prayer (shifting now from the focus on religion to religiousness). People sometimes pray for automobile parking spaces to open up for them on busy days. Sometimes they pray to win the lottery. People pray for the miraculous physical healing of diseases. They pray for their children who are struggling with bullying in school. People pray for rain so their crops prosper, for wisdom or patience, for the end of addictions. They pray for political justice in their nations, to be received into eternal life, to avoid the damnation of hellfire. They pray to remember the correct answers on exams or to not be caught for stealing or lying. And some pray about haircuts and what to wear.[39]

Of course, some religions encourage a focus on certain kinds of misfortunes and blessings while ignoring others. Certain religions attend primarily to getting practitioners into heaven, while others do not even believe in life after death. Some religious practices are concerned with averting the curses of malevolent spirits or the "evil eye" enemies have imposed on them, while others seek to enhance mental and emotional happiness and well-being. Some appeal to superhuman powers for victory in war, others to bring much-needed peace and reconciliation. Many people just hope that God will grant them some support and serenity. Exactly which concerns

37. For example, "religion ... is the result of two incurable diseases from which humankind suffers: life, from which we die; and hope, which hints that there may be more meaning to life than a termination in death. Humankind ... is the only being of which we are aware that is conscious of its own mortality and is capable of hoping that death is not the final fact in human life. Thus, religion becomes possible when a being is conscious of the inevitability of its own death and becomes inevitable when the being has experiences that suggest that death does not have the final word." Andrew Greeley. 1995. *Religion as Poetry*. New Brunswick, NJ: Transaction. P. 26.

38. Recognizing this important "everyday" feature of religions, a recent wave of scholarship has shifted attention away from the official and dramatic and toward the ordinary aspects of religion. See Thomas Tweed. 2015. "After the Quotidian Turn." *Journal of Religion*. 95: 361–385; Nancy Ammerman. 2007. *Everyday Religion*. New York: Oxford University Press; Meredith McGuire. 2008. *Lived Religion*. New York: Oxford University Press; Courtney Bender. 2003. *Heaven's Kitchen*. Chicago: University of Chicago Press.

39. T. M. Luhrmann. 2012. *When God Talks Back*. New York: Vintage. Pp. 76–77, 94; Katharine Wiegel. 2004. *Investing in Miracles*. Honolulu: University of Hawaii Press.

tend to occupy the practitioners of different religions depends largely on the interaction of religions' inherited beliefs about reality in general and their superhuman powers specifically with the kind of problems people typically face in any given historical and social setting. Practices are most likely commensurate with the blessings and troubles that most concern people in particular social circumstances, and with those that their religions, by virtue of their premises, are best suited to address. Few Catholics living on the Upper West Side of Manhattan pray fervently for demonic exorcisms, just as few Pentecostals in sub-Saharan Africa pray for inner peace on days that the stock market is jittery.

Even so, humans everywhere seem to rely on religion to address certain concerns more frequently than others. And most religions are responses to these common concerns. These tend to be matters that confront all people at some time and that humans have severely limited capacities to avoid or resolve. Prime among these concerns are damaging accidents to body and spirit, misfortunes in the sphere of earning a living, bodily sickness, and death. No humans can avoid the last two events and few humans are fortunate enough to avoid the first two their entire lives. Even those with especially charmed lives may still be troubled by anxiety about the possibility of calamities that never befall them. Fortune brings worries of its own.[40] Apprehensive expectations and sustained hopes can motivate religious practices just as well as the suffering of actual problems. On the matter of death, having one's soul turned away from the halls of venerable ancestors upon one's passing because of an improper burial, or spending an eternity in hell because of sins one never repented of, or being reborn an "untouchable" or an animal in the next life because of bad karma are clearly disasters from which one would seek deliverance, assuming one believes the premises underlying those possibilities. Even in religions that do not posit an afterlife, practitioners may share the widely felt human concern to avoid death at an early age and eventually to die in peace rather than in suffering and disgrace.

In theory, religion is concerned with both goods and bads, blessing and misfortune, positives and negatives. But different religions vary in their emphasis on the positive versus the negative. Some are primarily about health, wealth, and happiness. Others are consulted primarily when trouble strikes. How and why religions differ in these ways and their results for human lives

---

40. Graeme Wood. 2011. "The Secret Fears of the Super Rich." *The Atlantic*. April. http://www.theatlantic.com/magazine/archive/2011/04/secret-fears-of-the-super-rich/308419/.

are matters for empirical investigation. Furthermore, the motivations to gain something good versus to avoid something bad operate with different intensities and dynamics. A large body of research shows that, across most domains of life, negative prospects, experiences, images, and memories generally have more powerful effects on human motivation and cognition than positive ones.[41] Psychologists call this a "negativity bias." Economists observe a related tendency that they call "loss aversion," which is people's propensity to prefer avoiding losses over acquiring gains—with most studies showing that losses are twice as psychologically powerful as gains.[42] This variation may be influenced by whether the positive and negative results are viewed as short-term or long-run prospects. Similarly, motivations to engage in different kinds of religious practices with different goals will likely vary by social class, types of people, and religious traditions (figure 1.2). However, we have good reason to expect that religious practitioners are generally more motivated to engage in practices seeking to avoid, relieve, and cope with misfortune and crisis than they are to attain blessings and other positive outcomes. But these are open empirical questions requiring research. So, too, does the question of differences between intrinsic and extrinsic religious motivations—that is, performing religious practices in order to achieve some external good or simply because the practices themselves have become intrinsically rewarding (for both of which this book's theory can account).[43]

41. Roy Baumeister, Ellen Bratslavsky, Catrin Finkenauer, and Kathleen Vohs. 2001. "Bad Is Stronger than Good." *Review of General Psychology.* 5: 323–370; Paul Rozin and Edward Royzman. 2001. "Negativity Bias, Negativity Dominance, and Contagion." *Personality and Social Psychology Review.* 5: 296–320; Kelly Goldsmith and Ravi Dhar. 2013. "Negativity Bias and Task Motivation." *Journal of Experimental Psychology.* 19: 358–366; Tiffany Ito and John Cacioppo. 2005. "Variations on a Human Universal." *Cognition and Emotion.* 19: 1–26.

42. Daniel Kahneman and Amos Tversky. 1992. "Advances in Prospect Theory." *Journal of Risk and Uncertainty.* 5: 297–323; Ido Erev, Eyal Ert, and Eldad Yechiam. 2008. "Loss Aversion, Diminishing Sensitivity, and the Effect of Experience on Repeated Decisions." *Journal of Behavioral Decision Making.* 21: 575–597.

43. Some readers may be tempted to think of mine as a broadly "functional" definition of religion, that is, one that determines what religion is by what religion distinctively does, by the social or psychological functions it serves (in contrast with substantive definitions that focus not on what religion uniquely does but on its unique substantive content). True enough, this chapter's definition does zero in on the central activity of religion: realizing human goods and avoiding bads, especially offering superhuman help with blessings, misfortunes, and crises. To that extent, it does involve a functional *dimension*—though one that is centered on the goods of *persons*, not "society" or mere psychology. But that does not make mine an essentially functional definition. Purely functional definitions of religion are doomed to vagueness and failure. My account of what religion does is more concerned with motives for producing and practicing religion than the

FIGURE 1.2. Celebrating the Hindu festival of Diwali, the "Festival of Lights," families bring food offerings to the gods in their Hindu center. The food is displayed before the gods prior to ceremonies and prayers, candles are lit, and the passing of flames from one candle to another is believed to bring good luck. (Copyright: Awesome Cardiff)

To clarify one last central point about this definition of religion: Religion is not most fundamentally a cognitive or existential *meaning system*. Rather, it is essentially a set of *practices* aimed at accomplishing things that humans consider to be good and avoiding bads. Some cultural meaning system is necessary to tell religious people what religious practices to perform, how to perform them, and why they are to be performed. But "making meaning" is not the heart of religion, not by this account. The heart is undertaking practices to realize goods and avoid bads, especially obtaining blessings and avoiding and coping with misfortunes and crises. That shifts this theory away from the dominant theme of theories of religion during much of the last century—that is, religion as a cultural meaning system[44]—

---

social functions religion serves (see Riesebrodt. *Promise of Salvation.* Pp. 72–74); and more central to my definition of religion than the "function" of solving people's problems is its focus on superhuman powers and the human practices that seek to access them. In Schilbrack's terms, mine is a "dithetic" definition of religion (*Philosophy and the Study of Religions.* Pp. 115–121).

44. Clifford Geertz. 1973. "Religion as a Cultural System." In *The Interpretation of Cultures.* New York: Basic Books. Pp. 87–125; Max Weber. 1978. *Economy and Society.* Berkeley: University of California Press. Pp. 399–634; Talcott Parsons. 1928–1929. " 'Capitalism' in Recent German Literature." *Journal of Political Economy.* 36–37: 31–51; Talcott Parsons. 1979. "Religious and Economic Symbolism in the Western World." *Sociological Inquiry.* 49: 1–48.

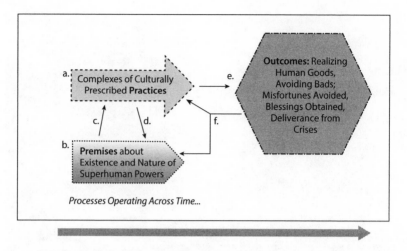

FIGURE 1.3. Schematic representation of religion's ontology

and toward a focus on practices performed, activities engaged, and their desired results.[45]

Having pulled apart, elaborated on, and illustrated a particular definition of religion, we can now put it back together, as represented schematically in figure 1.3. The large arrow shapes are meant to denote active processes performed in time, while the dashed lines are mean to suggest the semi-permeability and openness to change across time of each of the elements in question. The letters attached to arrows (a, b, c, etc.) indicate the distinct analytical aspects of the model, beginning with the priority of practices.

Types of Religious Practices

Religions prescribe many kinds of practices. Martin Riesebrodt identifies three distinct major types:[46]

1. *Interventionist practices*: These could involve "establishing contact in the sense of manipulation . . . for example, by wearing amulets or performing 'magical' acts"; "temporary interaction or even fusion with superhuman powers, as experienced in mystical trance and ascetic ecstasy"; or "activating superhuman potential that slumbers

45. Bush. *Visions of Religion.*
46. Riesebrodt. *Promise of Salvation.* Pp. 75–76; also see pp. 85–87.

within a person, includ[ing] practices of self-empowerment through contemplation and 'enlightenment' experienced thereby." This type includes *symbolic actions* facilitating "interaction [with superhuman powers through figurative activities] such as prayers, chants, gestures, formulas, sacrifices, vows, or divination.

2. *Behavior-regulating practices*: These "pertain to the religious reshaping of everyday life with respect to superhuman powers" and "usually concern the avoidance of sanctions or the accumulation of merits. . . . Such regulations regarding behavior are, however, valid as a religious practice only when they occur in accord with the will, the principles, or the sanctions of superhuman powers."[47]

3. *Discursive practices*: These refer to "interpersonal communication regarding the nature, status, or accessibility of superhuman powers, their manipulability, and their will, as well as techniques of self-empowerment. Discursive practices hand down and revise religious knowledge concerning interventionist practices and stand in a dialectical relationship with that knowledge. They are the foundation of religious interpretive cultures. Theology also falls under this rubric and should not be seen as limited to an academic discipline and intellectuals."

The lines between these categories are not always sharp, but these analytical distinctions help us to sort out divergent types of religious practices. According to Riesebrodt, social science should, for logical and methodological reasons, privilege interventionist practices over behavior-regulating and discursive practices in its theorizing.[48]

Riesebrodt also distinguishes different kinds of "general practices," which are "interventionist practices in which virtually all members of a religious community can or should participate." These include (1) *calendrical practices*, the observing of religious calendars that mark time, typically,

47. "They deal with such matters as how people should treat one another; what, when, and with whom they may eat; at what times and places they should carry out, or avoid, certain actions; how they should bury their dead. . . . In an intensified form, behavior-regulating practices can also assume the meaning of interventionist practices, for example, when they are interpreted as communication with superhuman powers or as a strategy of self-empowerment. Ethical behavior or the intensive study of sacred texts can be interpreted as a form of religious service and thus take on the quality of an interventionist practice" (p. 76).

48. Riesebrodt. *Promise of Salvation.* Pp. 85–87—which relates to the point just made about meaning-making, more closely associated with discursive practices, not being religion's center.

around three themes: "vegetative" (seasonal food growth), "astrological-cosmic," and "salvation-historical"; (2) *life-cycle practices*, which are "performed on occasions such as birth, entry into the religious community, the affirmation of the latter by young adults (initiation, complete membership), marriage, dying, and death"; and (3) *variable practices* that "react to unforeseen events," such as "risky enterprises, diseases, natural catastrophes, lovesickness, murder and sudden death, political crises, and poor harvests."[49] Common themes in many religious practices are worship and veneration, the marking of rites of passage, the making of sacrifices and exchanges, fasting and feasting, marking time through commemorations, celebrating festivals, and rituals of political and social legitimation. Pilgrimages and other forms of "crossings" are important in religious practices, too, along with "dwelling" in particular places.[50] Riesebrodt also notes that certain religious practices are to be performed by "laypersons," that is, ordinary religious people, whereas others are undertaken by religious "virtuosi," who as "advanced" religious practitioners radicalize ordinary general practices. "Whereas most laypersons are content to be protected from misfortune," he observes, "virtuosos seek salvation, whatever the cost. If the price of achieving eternal salvation is putting up with temporal suffering, virtuosos accept it."[51] Sometimes virtuosi may also be recognized or official religious leaders—clergy, seers, shamans, and the like—but very often they are independent souls, usually mystics and ascetics.

The Mutual Influencing of Practices and Premises

The idea that religious practices are "based upon" premises about superhuman powers should not be mistaken for the idea that premises come first and practices follow, or that beliefs are more fundamental than practices. Considering the prehistory of religion, it is impossible to say which came first, the premise or the practice. Considered analytically, the relationship must be seen as mutually interactive. Religious premises explain and justify particular complexes of practices, and the performance of practices often shapes religious premises. The practices and premises depicted in figure 1.3 are thus positioned in the same vertical space (rather than one preceding another) with each influencing the other (arrows c and d) (and both also

49. Ibid. Pp. 95, 91, 92, 99, 108, 111.
50. Tweed. *Crossing and Dwelling*; Jonathan Z. Smith. 1992. *To Take Place*. Chicago: University of Chicago Press.
51. Riesebrodt. *Promise of Salvation*. P. 122.

being influenced by the outcomes of practices [f]). Insisting on this mutual influence of practices and premises prevents this account from being a fundamentally cognitivist theory, one in which religion is viewed as something that grows out of people's heads. Of course, practicing religion requires cognitive activity. But by this account, embodied practices oriented toward superhuman powers define the core of religion.[52]

This practice-centered approach to religion is not an alien imposition; it is consistent with the view from inside religions. Consider, for example, how religious communities induct young members (children and perhaps converts) into their religions. No one first ensures that children have learned the cognitive content of the religious tradition, and only then allow or ask them to put that content into practice. No, newcomers begin by participating in religious practices, and only later—and sometimes never—are they taught the ideas and meanings that underlie the practices. That does not mean that those religious practices on their own cannot make sense to newcomers, however, because practices are *meaningful* repeated actions and so inherently embody and express their own significance. There are more ways of knowing in religion (and sports and music and many other activities), in other words, than simply grasping ideas.[53]

Consider, too, the assumptions about human dispositions and transformation embedded in many religious understandings of practices, even when they are not explicitly articulated. It is not that people first think or comprehend something religious and subsequently undertake a practice. Rather, the idea of many practices is to work the other way around: People need to start engaging in the prescribed practices and, it is hoped, as a result they should over time find themselves transformed in spirit and mind. Practices, in other words, are *formative*, not simply expressive. The sheer *doing* of them helps to bring into being that which they also embody. For example, the rabbi at the synagogue does not teach that the members of his congregation should try to feel generous toward the poor and, if they do, then give money. They should just do the right thing by giving, whatever they are feeling, and then ideally they will perhaps come to feel

---

52. I devote less direct attention in this book to bodies themselves than I could. Much good work on the matter exists, which I hope interested readers bring to mind, and more work could be developed in the future.

53. This emphasis on practice is consistent, too, with all we know about processes of religious conversion, which tend to begin with changes in significant social network ties; continue with changes in practices, identity, affiliation; and lastly (usually) involve revisions of religious beliefs (Stark and Finke. 2000. *Acts of Faith*. Berkeley: University of California Press. Pp. 114–138).

generous later as a result. American evangelicalism does not say to first get oneself to feel "spiritual" and then pray to God if that happens—no, one just needs to start praying and *that* will help one *get* more spiritual. Much of ancient Latin Christianity taught the rule, *Lex orandi, lex credendi* ("The law of praying is the law of believing" or "As we pray so we believe"), which meant that praying well leads to believing well, that liturgy forms theology, worship shapes faith. Different religions will express this dynamic in diverse ways, yet the underlying principle that religious practices are formative and not merely expressive undergirds many practices of most religions, from saying Islamic prayers five times a day (*Salat*) to Hindu meditation and beyond.

The point here, again, is twofold. First, cognitively centered, confessionally driven, intellectualist religions are rare—and most that appear to be are, upon closer inspection, less so than they seem. Religions, as with most of human social life, center on embodied practices. Second, the premises and practices that help to define religion are mutually influencing. The experience of performing practices can shape religious premises just as much as premises explain and justify practices.

Terminological and Other Clarifications

Having defined religion in this way, we can now distinguish four closely related but importantly different concepts. The first is the plural of religion, "religions." The word "religion" (singular), as used above, operates as a theoretical concept, referring abstractly to the class of all religions as particular kinds of practices humans perform. The word "religion*s*" (plural), by contrast, refers to specific, concrete instances of those complexes of practices performed in time and space. For example, Shia Islam, Jainism, and Wicca are actual religion*s*; as such, they are also *instances of* the abstract theoretical concept "religion" defined above. When we use the analytical term "religion," we must not think that it refers to some specific, "least common denominator" super-religion or trans-religious entity, which can be partitioned into "denominations." No such thing exists. All that exists in actuality are particular religion*s*. As defined above, religion exists only as an analytical, theoretical concept. So, when we wish to employ this theoretical concept, we should speak of "religion," but when we wish to refer to specific, concrete instances of religion, we should say "religion*s*" or "*a* religion."[54]

---

54. See Riesebrodt. *Promise of Salvation.* Pp. xii, 1.

The second concept to distinguish from "religion" is "religious*ness*."[55] The latter should be used to describe the religious features or involvement of particular religious practitioners[56]—and perhaps small units of practitioners, such as families, when their practices can rightly be described in the singular. "Religiousness is the subjective appropriation and interpretation of religion. . . . Religiousness is best understood as the result of a dialectic of institutionalized practices and subjective appropriation and interpretation," Riesebrodt writes.[57] How often someone (or a couple or family) venerates spirits, lights candles in the temple, fasts from eating at appointed times, or offers animal sacrifices are matters of their *religiousness* as persons (or small groups) practicing religion. And that refers to a different level of analysis than "religion," as defined above, which is concerned centrally with complexes of culturally prescribed practices, not the engagement of particular people with those practices. So when we wish to speak about "*how* religious" a distinct person (or couple or family) is, to what extent they have appropriated religion, we mean their "religious*ness*." By contrast, again, when we say "religion," we refer back to the complex of prescribed practices itself. This distinction between complexes of prescribed practices, on the one hand, and people's levels of involvement in those practices, on the other, is crucial to keep clear in our minds to avoid confusion. As I noted earlier, much of what follows in this book, especially after this chapter, concerns human religiousness, not religion as a conceptual category.

The third related but distinct concept is "religious tradition." This phrase adds to the concept of religion the idea of temporal continuity, that is, the similarity of religious practices as they are repeated over time, usually over generations and maybe millennia. As an abstract theoretical construct, "religion" as defined above can be considered analytically, apart from any concrete instantiation. But actual religion*s* as real complexes of practices situated in time and space always face the question of how much (or whether) they do and should try to remain the same over time. Some religions are highly invested in their own changeless nature; others have few problems developing over time. The idea of a religious tradition points to the temporal continuity of religious practices. It may refer to a religion's own claims about which practices and beliefs are essential to maintain for the religion to remain "orthodox" (for example, the need to believe in a Trinitarian

55. Many social scientists prefer the term "religiosity," but that strikes me as a barbaric neologism, so I use the phonetically simpler and more linguistically natural "religiousness."

56. Here I follow Riesebrodt. *Promise of Salvation.* P. 76.

57. Ibid.

doctrine of God to be considered Christian). Tradition may refer to the key symbols, practices, persons, and sites belonging to different religions that help to make them distinct from one another (for instance, the centrality of the Qur'an, Muhammad, Mecca, and Salat, which help identify Islam as distinct from other traditions). Tradition may also refer to the way religious practices have always (at least allegedly) been done, as a way to explain authoritatively and so legitimate the ways they are practiced today (for example, Jewish Passover commemorating the Exodus of the Israelites from slavery in Egypt). The term tradition may be applied in other useful ways, too. For my purposes, the important conceptual distinction to maintain here is between "religion" as a theoretical category useful for analytical purposes, and "religious tradition" or "traditions" as references to actual practices, beliefs, symbols, and other elements that seem to help define the continuity of religious identity and activity over time.[58]

What I do *not* mean by traditions are static and immutable ways of practicing and believing. We can recognize temporal continuity in religions without fossilizing their cultures in our minds. Human traditions of all kinds are never fixed but fluid, mixing, adapting, and morphing, sometimes slowly and sometimes rapidly. Clusters of religious practices are always diverse, converging, and diverging. The boundaries of religious traditions are porous, the premises and practices themselves often contain glitches and unanswerable questions, and the human cultures prescribing and persons performing the practices are by nature creative. A realistic concept of religious traditions, therefore, must grasp that their temporal continuities are *relative*, so religious cultures and institutions are always located somewhere in the middle range of a spectrum between the extremes of absolute flux and permanent changelessness.

The fourth distinct concept, which I have already been using, is the adjective "relig*ious*." That term simply operates, as in ordinary use, to note that a person, place, or thing has to do with religion in some significant way. Thus, we speak of religious founders, religious pilgrimage destinations, and religious relics, for instance, to denote that the people, locations, and objects in question are importantly related to some complex of practices referencing superhuman powers.

Some other clarifications are important. First, the discussion above relies on a common sociological shorthand that can make it sound like traditions, cultures, and institutions are the active agents or actors of history.

58. Ibid. P. 77.

That is a mere convention to keep prose from becoming unmanageable. In fact, traditions, cultures, and institutions are not agents that act. Human persons are. This point the theory of personalism requires.[59] Living traditions, cultures, and institutions are emergently real social facts existing because of the activities of persons, on which they are continually dependent. As a result, they possess irreducible "downwardly causal" powers, but, again, only emergently because of and through the ongoing activities of human persons. So, when I write as shorthand in this book that "the culture prescribes" and "the tradition intends," what I always mean is something like the more accurate but verbose phrases, "some combination of the founders, leaders, spokespersons, promoters, interpreters, and other influential agents in the culture/institution/tradition within which they have some position, authority, or legitimacy and so represent and speak for prescribes" or "intends." Readers presumably are pleased that I have sacrificed such technical precision for the sake of clarity. But it must be remembered that human *persons*, not social units, are always and everywhere the causally capacitated agents of action in this theory, whether as distinct persons or through social processes of institutional action.

Second, definitions of religion notoriously struggle with certain ambiguous cases. Among them is the question of whether Buddhism is a religion. Some versions of Buddhism posit deities, while others posit none. So is Buddhism a religion or "only" a philosophy? The answer is determined by the response to this question: Does the ambiguous case involve *the premise of superhuman powers, whether personal or impersonal*, and *the performance of complexes of culturally prescribed practices seeking to help practitioners gain access to and communicate or align themselves with the powers?* If it does, then it counts as a religion. If not, then it does not count. (And if between those definite positions we wish to apply concepts like "quasi-religions," "para-religions," "identity transformation organizations," and so on, nothing in this theory objects, as long as we remember the definitional touchstone of superhuman powers.) The same is true when it comes to Confucianism, Reform Judaism, Unitarian Universalism, the liberal end of mainline Protestantism, new religious movements centered on charismatic human leaders, the self-declared "spiritual but not religious," Scientology, Alcoholics Anonymous, New Age movements, astrology, holistic health groups, Star Trek fandom, ghost hunters, or any other arguably ambiguous case.[60] Furthermore,

59. See discussion of personalism in Theoretical Influences section of the introduction.
60. See Michael Jindra. 2003. "Natural/supernatural Conceptions in Western Cultural

massive social conglomerations that include or involve religious traditions *can also be more than* religious traditions. As Riesebrodt observes:

> To the extent that Hinduism and Buddhism represent complexes of religious practices, they are religious. At the same time, we must not reduce them to the concept of religion. They may even be far more than religions or, in part, something other than religions. . . . It is not necessary to classify under the rubric of religion every reflection made by a Buddhist regarding human existence . . . simply because someone has described a priori that Buddhism is a religion.[61]

In short, the categories religion and something-other-than-religion need not be either/or but may be both/and. Thus, for another example, we can rightly understand Hinduism to be a religion and, in various aspects, a civilization, a worldview, and a philosophical tradition. Also, importantly, weighing whether some complex of practices constitutes a religion is not a value judgment. To be called "only" a philosophy and not a religion is not an insult. Things simply are what they are, and our analytical goal is to understand and categorize them properly. There is no need to jockey to classify something as religious when it is not. Clarity in discerning the difference is our main concern.

When trying to sort out whether some group is a religion, it is absolutely crucial to keep in mind the distinction described above between religion and religiousness. Religion is an abstract analytical category defined by a set of stipulated features. Religiousness concerns the actual, variable subjective meanings and intensities of practices of religious practitioners (certainty of beliefs, frequency of prayer, etc.). Religions are constituted not by practitioners' subjective intentions at a given time, but by institutional and publicly objective elements, such as traditions, cultures, sacred texts, and established "liturgies."[62] Not every practitioner in a group must accept the premises about superhuman powers behind every practice, but to be religious the practices themselves must be culturally institutionalized as oriented toward gaining access to superhuman powers. So for a type of action

---

Context." *Anthropological Forum*. 13: 159–166; Arthur Greil, 1993. "Explorations along the Sacred Frontier." In David Bromley and Jeffrey Hadden (eds.). *Handbook of Cults and Sects in America.* Greenwich, CT: JAI. Pp. 153–172; Christopher Bader, Carson Mencken, and Joseph Baker. 2011. *Paranormal America*. New York: NYU Press.

61. Riesebrodt. *Promise of Salvation*. Pp. 77, 78.
62. See Bernhard Lang. 1997. *Sacred Games*. New Haven, CT: Yale University Press.

to count as a religion does not require that all or even any of the practitioners at any given time understand and affirm the premises behind their religious practices.

For example, a congregation of highly secular American Episcopalians, most of whom, let us suppose, worship not to get something from God but for social, aesthetic, and family reasons, still counts here as a religious community, since, regardless of their subjective beliefs and intentions, their practices of worship conform to our definition of religion. If, however, that congregation proceeded to eliminate the *Book of Common Prayer*, all liturgical formulas, sacramental practices like baptism and Eucharist, and so on, then eventually they would shift from being religious to a local community group. A similar logic would apply, for example, to a Reform Jewish congregation. Likewise, if a member of the clergy conducts a funeral using established religious rubrics, that counts as religion being practiced, even if everyone in attendance is agnostic, angry, or distracted.

By contrast, a "human potential" group led by a highly charismatic leader teaching esoteric ideas, whose members regularly report experiencing meaningful insights, transports of reverie, and a strong sense of the sacred unity of all things, would probably not count as religion if its leader did not claim to represent, possess, or control superhuman powers that the group sought to access through complexes of practices. Religion, in short, is not defined here by apparent signs of religiousness, however intense. Whether something is a religion is known by public, institutional features stipulated in the definition of religion. *Religiousness* then follows as a matter of practitioners' variable, subjective beliefs, as well as how often they perform and how meaningful they find religious practices (figure 1.4).[63]

63. Take the case of Spanish speakers saying goodbye, "Adios," which literally means, "To God," commending someone into the hands of God until they meet again. Is that religious? The question is answered by first recognizing that it does not concern religion (as conceptualized social ontology) but religiousness (as empirical practice)—it asks about what people do and why they do it, not what religion is. For questions about religiousness, subjective meanings and intentions matter. So whether bidding "Adios" is a genuine religious practice or a secularized shard of some former religious practice depends on the meanings and motives of the persons involved and the cultural context informing them. It may well belong to the religious practice of a devout Catholic who says it to another "meaningfully," but not for many others who say it casually. Thus, *religiousness* comes in degrees and can be plotted on continuums. Pentecostalism does not represent "more religion" than liberal Presbyterianism because it tends more obviously to be oriented toward seeking help from superhuman powers. Both are religions in their own right. But Pentecostals may express more reli*giousness* than liberal Presbyterians, according to this distinction.

FIGURE 1.4. Vietnamese American Loan Pham Thai proudly displays her Buddhist shrine in her California home, where she makes offerings, lights candles, and says prayers. For many people from most religious traditions, the regular performance of religious practices is more important than correctly professing the "right" religious doctrines. Photographer, Christina Tran. (Copyright: Vietnamese American Oral History Project at University of California–Irvine and UC Irvine Libraries Southeast Asian Archive.)

A Basic Illustration: Sunni Islam

The discussion thus far has been abstract. To help make the theory more concrete, I offer an example of how one widely accepted representation of one particular religious tradition, Sunni Islam, illustrates the ideas I have presented.[64] In Sunni Islam, the *superhuman power* of absolutely crucial importance is the One, Eternal, and Absolute, all-powerful, all-merciful, all-knowing God, Allah. Angels and Jinn (genies) may also play a role in Islam as other, less crucial superhuman agents. The *complex of practices* prescribed centers around the Five Pillars of Islam. These include, first, *Shahada* (faith), the declaration of faith and trust that there is only one God—Allah—and that Mohammad is his messenger; second, *Salat* (prayer), prayers offered five times a day, according to appointed times—at dawn, at noon, in the afternoon, in the evening, and at night; and third, *Zakāt* (charity), the practice of alms-giving in amounts based upon accumulated wealth. The fourth pillar is *Sawm* (fasting), abstaining from eating, which comes in three types: ritual fasting during the month of Ramadan, fasting as compensation for repentance, and ascetic fasting. Fifth is the *Hajj* (pilgrimage to Mecca), a pilgrimage to the holy city of Mecca that every able-bodied Muslim is obliged to make at least once in his or her lifetime, which occurs during the Islamic month of Dhu al-Hijjah. In addition, good Muslims are expected to follow *Sharia*, Islamic law, of which the Sunni tradition represented here comprises four main schools: the *Hanafi, Maliki, Shafi'i, Hanbali*. They are also supposed to observe certain hygienic, dietary, greeting, and burial practices. Sunni Muslims must not consume alcohol, pork, or blood, and male Muslims must be circumcised. Other practices related to family life, sex, and economic behaviors—such as obedience to parents and the prohibition of usury and polyandry—are expected to be observed in Sunni Islam as well (figure 1.5). More generally, Sunni Muslims are expected to avoid all sins defined by the tradition and instead to practice goodness.

Knowledge of this superhuman power and prescribed practices are *based on premises about the existence and nature of* Allah and his will for humanity, which are known through revelations of God to prophets of the past, including Adam, Noah, Abraham, Moses, and Jesus, but most definitively to Mohammad, through the archangel Gabriel, revelations that took

---

64. "Sunni Islam" encompasses massively different self-understandings and expressions, so I present this as "one widely accepted representation."

FIGURE 1.5. An Iraqi Sunni Muslim family gathers at home for *Iftar*, the breaking of the daily fast, to share an evening meal during the Islamic holy month of Ramadan, during which time adult Muslims abstain from eating food, drinking liquids, smoking, and having sexual relations from dawn to sunset. (Copyright: AP photo/Hadi Mizban)

written form in the Qur'an. Some of the *hoped-for goods and deliverances* promised by the practice of Sunni Islam include, perhaps most importantly, to be raised from the dead in body on the "Day of Resurrection" and judged by Allah according to one's deeds and rewarded with the joy, bliss, and physical pleasures of *Jannah*, that is, paradise, and to be delivered from the punishments and pains of *Jahannam*, hell. Meanwhile, in this life, devoted Muslims, in faith and obedience to Allah and belief in his messenger, Mohammad, are promised the blessings and protection of God, the merciful forgiveness of sins, justice for good works and repentance, and the assurance of knowledge that all things that transpire are decreed by Allah. Further, faithful Muslims hope to enjoy as a result of their religious practices happiness, inner peace, satisfaction of knowing one is obeying the true God, and the goods of an orderly and just civilization. Obedience as a Muslim also produces in the faithful the many this-worldly goods resulting from self-discipline, self-control, and self-restraint, including improved health, personal character, and tranquility. These in turn promise to curb individuals' destructive impulses and temptations, and form in them life-enhancing virtues, such as hospitality, generosity, and humility.

The collective result of the faithful practice of the whole Islamic community will be the suppression of exploitation, disease, and other social problems—all of which will culminate in the enjoyment of the fellowship of a transnational brotherhood of Muslims. At bottom and in the end, however, simply to know and obey the true God, Allah, is its own best and highest reward. As the Qur'an (13:28) teaches, "Truly, in remembering God do hearts find rest."

Another Illustration: American Protestant Evangelicalism

Consider as a second example American Protestant evangelicalism, about which my greater familiarity allows me to elaborate more. From the "emic" perspective of many of its practitioners, evangelicalism seems to be one of the least practice-oriented religious traditions in existence. True, American evangelicalism stands out among religions for its emphasis not on behavioral rituals and practices but on certain correct cognitive beliefs, words, and spiritual attitudes, and on having the right, informal, not culturally prescribed, relationship with God. Performing religious practices—repeatedly carrying out actions fraught with religious significance, especially any that are "ritualistic"—may on the inside seem very un-evangelical. Indeed, some evangelicals do not consider themselves "religious" at all; they see themselves as simply believers in the gospel truth, as opposed to followers of (other) religions who, though it probably should not be said in polite company, worship false gods. Evangelicalism thus provides a more challenging case with which to "test drive" my definition of religion.

The *premised superhuman power* of modern American evangelicalism is the Trinitarian God of Christianity, as presented in the Bible and defined in the first four ecumenical councils of the Christian church (even if many evangelicals are not aware of them), and focused through the theological lens of the Protestant Reformation, Christian pietism, and frontier and urban revivalism. For some evangelicals, Jesus Christ is in practice the primary agent of divine power, while for others it is the Holy Spirit. All, however, are (or at least are supposed to be) formally not only theistic in believing in a personal God, but properly Trinitarian, believing in God the Father, Son, and Holy Spirit.[65]

---

65. In the everyday practice of evangelical folk religion—especially as it is worked out in lay soteriology, in which the loving Son intervenes and "takes the bullet" of the punitive Father—

Among the *culturally prescribed religious practices* in the American evangelical tradition, the absolute necessities are believing in the Christian gospel, repenting from sin, accepting Jesus Christ as one's personal Lord and Savior, trusting in God's unmerited grace, and learning to follow God's commands. Required but perhaps not absolutely necessary practices in evangelicalism include regularly attending and worshipping at church, affirming the infallibility if not inerrancy of the Bible and reading scripture faithfully, praying regularly, giving money to one's church and other Christian organizations, and generally growing in personal "sanctification" (sinning less). Good evangelicals are also supposed to "share their faith" in personal evangelism by "witnessing" to non-believers.[66] Very important, too, is living an adequately righteous life that follows the Ten Commandments and other moral teachings of the Bible.

The list of optional or advanced practices that either foster more essential ones or add to them is lengthy. Typically it would include praying as a family before meals, having regular private "devotions," attending a weekly Bible study, "getting more involved" at church (by volunteering on committees or serving in the nursery, for instance), and reading Christian books to advance one's spiritual growth or theological knowledge. Resting on Sundays, going on short-term mission and service trips, supporting "para-church ministries," listening to edifying Christian music or radio preachers, learning about and supporting "world missions," and attending occasional Christian learning seminars are also applauded. Living a traditional family-centered life (valuing marriage and children, avoiding divorce, opposing abortion, and so on), tithing one-tenth of one's income, memorizing Bible passages, serving as an elder or deacon at church, attending an evangelical college, reading evangelical magazines, participating in a "prayer chain" team, voting in political elections to promote Christian values, purposefully working to strengthen one's marriage and family by "making God the center" of them, and other practices could be added to this list. Anthropologist Tanya Luhrmann has also identified six "emotional practices" that some kinds of evangelicals perform to evoke "the feeling of being loved by God."[67] They are "crying in the presence of

---

some if not many evangelicals live as practical tritheists, not Trinitarians, but that is another matter.

66. Although personal evangelism happens much less than the normative idea would commend.

67. On the important topic of emotions and religion generally, see Ole Riis and Linda Wood-

God," "seeing from God's perspective," "practicing love, peace, and joy," relating to "God the therapist," "reworking God the father," and enjoying "emotional cascades."[68] Evangelical "virtuosos"[69] may go even further and lead worship in church praise bands, consistently and confidently "share the gospel" with their non-Christian friends, learn some formal theology, go on extended missions or service trips overseas, and make spiritual retreats.

In addition to these positive or constructive religious practices, American evangelicalism also prescribes "negative practices," those that involve avoiding or abstaining from actions. Some of these are more "spiritual," like never trusting in one's own "good works" to earn one's salvation and not questioning the divine truthfulness of the Bible. They also include religious behaviors, such as not dropping out of Christian fellowship or ceasing to worship God. Evangelical negative practices also entail moral and relational (especially sexual) issues, like avoiding marrying a non-evangelical, not having sex outside of marriage, not talking dirty with swear words, and not viewing pornography. Avoiding these is necessary because they are believed in evangelicalism to compromise one's spiritual well-being and prospects of receiving the goods of evangelical life practice.

What are the *goods and deliverances* that evangelical practices promise? According to the American Protestant evangelical tradition, the most important blessings that result from these practices are personally to experience the grace, mercy, and love of God, to receive the complete forgiveness of one's sins by the substitutionary atonement of Jesus Christ on the cross, to live in daily fellowship with God, and to know the blessed assurance that one day one will live with God in heaven for eternity. Those promises concern both this world and life after death, and involve both positive and negative outcomes. Blessings from God include love, mercy, grace, forgiveness, fellowship, guidance, and eternal life in heaven. Troubles and catastrophes averted include living in guilt and spiritual darkness, being alienated from one's divine maker and redeemer, and enduring the torments of hell. These are the most important consequences of engaging

---

head. 2010. *A Sociology of Religious Emotion*. Oxford: Oxford University Press; Douglas Davies. 2011. *Emotion, Identity, Religion*. Oxford: Oxford University Press; Christian Smith. 2007. "Why Christianity Works: An Emotions-Focused Phenomenological Account." *Sociology of Religion*. 68: 165–178.

68. Luhrmann. *When God Talks Back*. Pp. 111–131.

69. Riesebrodt (*Promise of Salvation*) focuses on "virtuosos." Pp. 84–149.

(or not) in evangelical religious practices, according to that tradition's dominant cultural system.

Evangelical faith and practice are not only or even primarily about justification by faith, spiritual growth, and the promise of heaven, however. Often they concentrate on much more worldly and therapeutic concerns. The best place to learn about them is to listen to people's prayer requests in evangelical religious services and small groups. Then tune in to the blessings and goods that are named in contemporary worship songs, sermons given in pulpits and radio programs, and even many older traditional hymns. Pay close attention, too, to evangelicals talking in Bible studies about what certain scripture passages "mean to them" when it comes to their "practical application." Then peruse the shelves of evangelical bookstores and book publishers' catalogues. Doing so, what does one discover? Certainly, a great deal about Jesus, salvation, God's love, and eternal life—but much more as well.

Performing evangelical practices is also expected to yield an abundance of immanent blessings, including inner peace, security, comfort, stability, encouragement, courage, perseverance, and joy. Practicing evangelicalism is believed to grant access to divine guidance and powers to heal sickness, provide employment, resolve marital conflicts, overcome addictions, aid the skill of doctors, raise one's children well, make good decisions, ease the difficulties of major life transitions, exercise patience in trying situations, help courtroom judges make just decisions, reconcile neighbors, bring order to family chaos, turn wayward children home, ease the suffering of aging parents, and much more. Evangelicalism bathes its devoted practitioners in uplifting songs of praise and worship, envelops them in communities of personal care and support, and surrounds them with words of hope, affirmation, sustenance, encouragement, and the promise of subjective well-being. The charismatic movement and the therapeutic turn in American evangelicalism have amplified these tendencies since the 1960s and '70s,[70] yet they have been part of the evangelical tradition for centuries.

In short, like every other religion, American evangelicalism prescribes complexes of religious practices that are premised on the existence and na-

---

70. James D. Hunter. 1983. *American Evangelicalism*. New Brunswick, NJ: Rutgers University Press; Todd Brenneman. 2013. *Homespun Gospel*. New York: Oxford University Press; Kimon Howland Sargeant. 2000. *Seeker Churches*. New Brunswick, NJ: Rutgers University Press; Thomas Bergler. 2012. *The Juvenilization of American Christianity*. Grand Rapids, MI: Eerdmans.

ture of a superhuman power and that are oriented toward realizing human goods and averting bads, often including, for example, receiving blessings, avoiding misfortunes, and being delivered from or coping with crises and catastrophes.[71]

Is This Reductionism?

Is the account of religion advocated here reductionist? Reductionism could signify three different things, it seems to me. It might mean disallowing

71. Here is the question of whether "believing" can be considered a religious practice. The answer is: It depends on the particular tradition. In the case of American evangelicalism, believing is definitely one of its religious practices, as defined here. American evangelicalism appears to prioritize believing over doing, trusting over rituals, and the right subjective stance over bodily practices. Relative to most other religions, evangelicalism is quite cognitive, abstract, and subjective—even if that often plays out in highly relational terms and is activist in certain ways. Evangelicalism's account of itself insists that good practices always *follow* right beliefs, that anything good people do is a *response* to a prior inner transformation accomplished by correctly believing, accepting, and trusting. Anything else evangelicalism would consider "salvation by works," the heresy over which Martin Luther broke with Rome to launch the Protestant Reformation, from which American evangelicalism descends. Allowing human practices to take a place logically and chronologically prior to correct beliefs is theologically anathema in evangelicalism. In strictly formal, theological, and spiritual terms, evangelicalism's (emic) account of itself may be somewhat valid. But I think (theologically informed) sociological insight also challenges its formulation, and not simply by offering a relativistic, alternative perspective, but by more accurately describing the actual operation of religious beliefs vis-à-vis practices in evangelical life on the ground. I do not intend here to categorize every human belief as a practice. Some beliefs are just that, mere beliefs, and not practices. But in some cases, including, I think, American evangelicalism, repeatedly emphasizing the centrality of the need to believe in certain ways itself becomes part of the tradition's religious practice, in two senses. As a first-order fact, the very activities of believing in Jesus, trusting God, accepting forgiveness, believing the Bible, and so on, as they are continually performed by evangelicals, are themselves enacted as what is rightly described as a core practice in that religious tradition. They are also signified or instantiated by empirically observable actions, such as saying "the salvation prayer," raising a hand, walking down the aisle, making a "profession of faith," or giving public testimony. Then, as a second-order fact, evangelicalism's discourse about rightly believing, trusting, confessing, and professing becomes a higher-order core practice in that tradition. That is, the act of responding to the essential need to correctly believe as an evangelical is one evangelical practice, and the need then to continually talk about the need to correctly believe is a second evangelical practice. Stated differently, American evangelicalism has taken what begins as the volitionally oriented cognitive act of "having faith" and transformed it into a genuine religious practice that is sociologically central to its tradition. Recall that practices are culturally meaningful behaviors that are intentionally repeated over time. That is what believing in Jesus, having faith, trusting in God, accepting forgiveness, believing the Bible, trusting God's promises, and so forth are in American evangelicalism. They are obviously cognitive and affective behaviors: acts of assent, affirmation, commitment, and confession. They are accompanied by other behaviors, such as reciting prayers, responding to "invitations," and making public professions. They are clearly culturally

religious claims that superhuman powers really exist (*metaphysical* reductionism, an error of unwarranted denial). It might mean ignoring key features of religion that are essential for defining its ontology[72] (*conceptual* reductionism, an error of analytical omission). Or it could mean unacceptably violating the real complexities of religion by describing it in simplistic or one-dimensional terms—an error that usually sounds like "X is really *nothing but* Y," when in fact X through emergence is a lot more than Y[73] (*explanatory* reductionism, an error of superficial theoretical description). So, in any of these ways is my account of religion reductionist?

My theory is not *metaphysically* reductionist because it does not deny the possibility that the truth claims of any religious tradition are correct. This book's theory of religion concerns the ontology of objects in the human social world, not ultimate reality. It neither says nor implies that religious premises about superhuman powers are true or false. Making such a claim

---

meaningful. And they are indeed very intentionally repeated over time. Once we grasp this, it becomes hard to imagine *not* seeing the imperative of right believing in evangelicalism as a religious practice (many non-evangelical readers of my early manuscript said this was so obvious that I did not even need to explain it). The same is true of evangelicalism's thick and widespread discourse about the imperative to rightly believe. Not only is correct believing in evangelicalism a practice; so too is talking about correct believing. Furthermore, these two orders of evangelical religious practice organized around believing are mutually reinforcing. The ongoing work of believing by evangelicals is promoted by the continual discourse about the need to rightly believe, and vice-versa. Crucial to my case here is the fact that, in evangelical culture, it is never sufficient to believe in Jesus once and then to stop believing, to shift into neutral. One cannot simply trust God and then set that aside to focus on other things. Belief, trust, and acceptance must be ongoing, ever-renewed experiences. One must persistently believe, always trust, never stop having faith. Believing in Jesus, having faith in God, accepting forgiveness, believing the Bible, and the rest are life-long imperatives—even if the burden of those imperatives is said to be light and joyful. That belief must be ongoing and continually reaffirmed in evangelicalism, which transforms it from a mere one-time volitional-affective-cognitive act of "conversion" or "personalization" into a genuine practice. American evangelicalism's religious practices—including believing, trusting, and accepting Jesus—are therefore not exempt from the general category of practices in this book's definition of religion. In Riesebrodt's terms, believing, in American evangelicalism, is a "discursive practice," but also, I suggest, an "interventionist practice," in that both believing and talking about believing are crucial to having a right relationship with God in that religious tradition.

72. See footnote 8 in the introduction.

73. Applied to a theory of human minds, for instance, explanatory reductionism might assert that human consciousness is merely the physical activity of brain neurons, nothing more. Extending that logic to explain (away) the "you" of human personhood, for example, Francis Crick, the co-discoverer of DNA structure, declared in his book *The Astonishing Hypothesis* that, "You're nothing but a pack of neurons" (1994. New York: Charles Scribner's Sons. Pp. 3, 11). What is really astonishing is not Crick's hypothesis but his philosophical naiveté.

would be unwarranted, as it is beyond the capacity of the social sciences to know either way.[74]

I do not believe that this book's theory of religion is *conceptually* reductionist either. To understand why, we must distinguish between (1) key features of religion that are *essential* for *defining* its ontology, on the one hand, and (2) *important* aspects of religion that help us generally to *understand* and *explain* it well, on the other. Defining is not the same as understanding and explaining. I believe that my definition of religion includes the key features essential for naming religion's social ontology.[75] That does not mean, however, that my definition includes all important aspects of religion needed to understand and explain it well. *Of course it does not.* No definition of anything does. Definitions do not include every feature, property, and capacity of an object one might wish to know in order to comprehend it. Definitions tell us what things *are*. They do not tell us everything about what things *are like*, how they *work*, or what they are *good for*. That my definition does not aim to describe everything of importance about religion does not make it reductionist.[76] It only means we need more than a mere definition to understand and explain religion adequately.

The question of *explanatory* reductionism is more complicated. Does my theory unacceptably violate the real complexities of religion by describing it in simplistic or one-dimensional terms? I do not believe so. First, let us remind ourselves of the truism that any theory is descriptively simpler than what it theorizes. The whole point of theory is to help make an overwhelmingly complex reality comprehensible. Theory inherently reduces an object to the conceptual and explanatory necessities in order to clarify, enlighten, and explain. The relevant problem is not simplification per se—which is not only unavoidable but necessary and good—but unacceptable violations of complexities through the disregard of conceptual and explanatory necessities, which produces simplistic or one-dimensional descriptions. That is explanatory reductionism.

---

74. See footnotes 32 and 33 in the introduction.

75. If that is wrong, we will only know it if someone demonstrates its analytical omissions with good evidence and arguments. No definition is immune from potential improvement. Meanwhile, I take this book's definition to be fully adequate.

76. Part of the perceived problem here could be the "clinical" feel of social science definitions. For many people, religion is a uniquely personal, spiritual, or ineffable matter, so simply defining it social scientifically may feel reductionist. But that itself does not make such a definition reductionist.

I imagine my theory could be accused of explanatory reductionism for three possible reasons. First, that my account neglects the subjective experience in religion that is vital to many people's engagement in it. Second, that my account is really just warmed-over rational choice theory. Third, that my account is too instrumental or transactional. I take each of these claims and explain why I think they are incorrect.

The first is that my account neglects the subjective experience in religion that is vital for many people. My theory indeed does not make subjective experience the defining feature of religion. But neither does it neglect it. Subjective experience is in my account crucially important for understanding religion. Analytically, however, it concerns the issue of relig*iousness*, not relig*ion*, as differentiated earlier. In fact, most of the rest of this book explores various aspects of religious experience—subjective, cognitive, emotional, and otherwise. Subjective experience plays an important role in my account. It simply is not the key to defining religion's ontology. Whether or not that position is valid is an open theoretical question. But it does not count as explanatory reductionism.

The second anticipated objection is that my account is a version of rational choice theory, which it takes to be explanatorily reductionist.[77] That claim is not incomprehensible, since a broad "family resemblance" between the two is admittedly discernable. But my theory descends from an entirely different intellectual lineage than rational choice. The latter derives from the utilitarianism of Jeremy Bentham and market-exchange theorists like Adam Smith and Gary Becker, and so has a strong individualistic bent. My account descends from the "*eudaemonian* teleology" of the Greek philosopher Aristotle, mediated through a twentieth-century personalism that has always explicitly opposed utilitarianism and individualism. Some may *read into* my account rational choice's emphasis on the rational acquisition of benefits, the calculated exchange of goods, and the avoidance of costs and maximization of rewards. But my theory proposes nothing about rational deliberation, calculation, exchange, acquisitiveness, strategy, markets, or religious compensators. Although I do believe and have written elsewhere that all humans are oriented toward the realization of certain natural goods,[78] which here I say are crucial for motivating religion, "natural goods" as conceived

77. Which would especially surprise readers who know that I have spent my career criticizing utilitarian-based rational choice theory, "materialist" accounts of human motivation, and exchange-based views of social relationships, and stressing instead the importance of identity, morality, solidarity, and normative culture.

78. Smith. *What Is a Person?*; *To Flourish or Destruct.*

in personalism are radically unlike the chosen "benefits" and "rewards" of utilitarianism.[79] Furthermore, rational choice explains religious practices as individuals' choices among alternatives that solve their problem of preference maximizing or satisficing. My theory, by comparison, insists that, while religion may do that, it more importantly helps solve people's bigger "axiological meta-problem" of knowing even what they *ought to* want and "*how to rank* the relative values" of the incommensurate goods that humans face and trade off in life.[80] In the end, it is fair to say that both my account and rational choice theory belong to the theoretical genus of "purposive action theory." But within that common genus—to which I am more than pleased to belong—my theory and rational choice belong to two very different species. It cannot rightly be said, then, that my account is just warmed-over rational choice theory and so guilty of its explanatory reductionism.

The third anticipated claim about my theory's purported explanatory reductionism—that my account is too instrumental or transactional—is the most interesting and arguably plausible. This claim alleges that my theory wrongly characterizes religion as merely or primarily an instrument, a tool, that people use in order to get things they want (too instrumental); and that the relationships and interactions religious people have with superhuman powers are only or essentially deals arranged in order to trade mutually beneficial goods (too transactional). If my theory characterizes religion in these ways, then it is indeed guilty of explanatory reductionism. Does it?

As a preliminary observation, let us note that, while not all religions are instrumentalist or transactional, some are. Some unapologetically prescribe

79. A phenomenological approach (for those who put stock in it) also distinguishes my theory from rational choice. The human existential concerns with human goods and bads, with the blessings, misfortunes, and crises that my theory references, cannot be reduced to instrumental costs and benefits. Many religious concerns about human goods and bads are matters of profound hope and anxiety, emotional elation and upheaval, identity affirmation and crisis, and relational solidarity and alienation—which cannot be re-described in utilitarian terms without doing them violence. In many people's religious experiences, possible calculations of benefits are overwhelmed by the yearnings, tears, godsends, terrors, pleadings, and resolutions that accompany them. All of that can be forced through the meat grinder of academic utilitarian-based theories and squeezed into the casings of rational choice terminology, if that is what one is determined to do. But it violates not only the integrity of the critical realist personalism undergirding my account but also the nature of people's professed experiences of the human goods and bads that my theory references.

80. Schilbrack. *Philosophy and the Study of Religions.* P. 124—"religions typically function to legitimate comprehensive, all-inclusive paths, highest values, or ultimate norms" (P. 125). Recognized here is the fact that religion is often not merely a choice, but also a prescribing, governing, and controlling tradition, institution, and authority that governs choices.

practicing religion "in order to," "so that," and "to get." Some religious read-ers ought not to universalize their perhaps less instrumental and transac-tional religious experiences to all times and places. They also ought not to underestimate the semi-instrumental or quasi-transactional elements of their seemingly less instrumental and transactional religions. Beware the ostensible nobility of seemingly selfless religious faith. Many religious peo-ple today are loath to say that they essentially use their religion as a tool to get things from superhuman powers. But that is the least flattering way to put it. Better versions can be expressed. And a close inspection of many people's actual religious practices reveals a lot more interest in receiving goods through religion than many may be comfortable admitting.[81] That is not cynicism, just empirical observation.

Nonetheless, seeing why this book's account of religion is not reduction-ist on instrumental or transactional grounds requires understanding things like blessings sought, crises managed, and misfortunes averted in inclusive, agreeable, and legitimate terms. We have no need to code the goods that religion offers in narrow, negative, or stigmatized ways—as if most religious people are simply manipulating, jockeying for advantage, and brokering bargains with stingy superhuman powers for their own selfish ends. That my theory does not suggest.[82] In fact, many of the goods for which religious practitioners hope are, when understood inclusively, perfectly legitimate. Is there anything wrong with someone praying for healing from sickness, if they believe superhuman powers can and do heal? Why should not a person want to go to heaven instead of hell, if they believe in them? Ought people wishing to receive blessings in life and the ability to cope with crises really be judged to be bad? I think not. I would be happy to receive blessings and to be able to cope with crises, and I am sure most readers would be, too. So what is the problem?

81. One possible explanation of modern people's aversion to seeing themselves as practicing religion in order to obtain goods is that idea's association with "primitive" religions, magic, and anthropomorphized gods, which moderns want to believe they have risen above (perhaps echo-ing an outdated evolutionary model of religious progress leading to contemporary religion as "Man's highest spiritual achievement"?). I do not claim that all religions are similar with regard to the character of their superhuman powers or the goods their practitioners hope for. But recall that one of modernity's favorite conceits is how very different moderns are from traditional, pre-modern peoples. Let us not flatter ourselves too much. Historical continuities in the basic nature of religions are stronger, I suggest, than discontinuities.

82. My account, for instance, does not say that religious practitioners are strategists, plan-ners, managers, or salespeople; or that superhuman powers are resistant, passive, or manipulable targets of their interests.

I suspect the problem is my theory's perceived threat to the following kinds of self-understandings: "I practice religious faith just because I want a personal relationship with God, not to get anything out of him." "I am religious because I believe my faith is true and I wish to know how God wants me to live." And "I am not a religious person because of what it does for me but because of powerful subjective encounters with divine love that I experience." (In fact, these are verbatim quotes from some readers of an early version of this book's pre-publication manuscript.) I do not deny the truth of such statements. I simply note that they entail the very kinds of goods my theory discusses. To have "a personal relationship with God" is itself a blessing that some religions offer their practitioners. But to enjoy such a relationship, one must engage in certain practices, such as praying, worshipping, and reading scripture. No religious tradition says otherwise. Likewise, knowing what "is true" in life and "how God wants me to live" are also benefits this person's religion offers, as well as a means of avoiding misfortunes (that would result from believing untruths and not knowing God's will). Enjoying these too requires performing some religious practices. Similarly, the experience of "powerful subjective encounters with divine love" is also clearly a blessing enjoyed as a result of practicing a religion.[83]

For whatever reason, some people seem to fear acknowledging that they receive something as a result of engaging in religious practices. But why? Again I ask: What is so bad about that? Human persons, as I explain further in chapter 4, are well equipped to practice religion and have many good reasons to do so. And what would be the alternative, anyway? A theory that says people practice religion for no reason at all? Or do so for reasons that bring them no human goods? Or a theory that says that religious goods are automatically enjoyed or guaranteed without their recipients ever having to perform any practices? Those make no sense. Real religions are not like that. Human beings are not like that. The theory proposed in this book accurately describes the reality of human religions. Whether or not it feels too instrumentalist or transactional—and I do not think it should—it is not guilty of explanatory reductionism on this account.[84]

83. Note that this does not stretch the ordinary meaning of "blessings" to a breaking point (as rational choice recurrently does to rescue itself from internal inconsistency); those goods very reasonably count as blessings.

84. Theories that are fundamentally instrumental or transactional tend to involve a highly "voluntaristic" account of human action, giving people more credit for strategizing and directing their actions and their consequences than they deserve. But my theory is clear that religions and

This objection of reductionism seems to be animated by a desire to experience, understand, or protect religion as fundamentally revolving around a *relationship*, not a giving-and-getting arrangement with superhuman powers. But that objection assumes a false dichotomy, namely, that authentic relationships and arrangements of giving and getting are mutually exclusive. All human relationships, including the most authentic—marital, parental, filial, fraternal, sororal—involve giving and receiving. They are not only about that, but they involve it. (Mind experiment: Try to imagine an authentic, valuable personal relationship that involves no giving or receiving.) That is true even of the religious traditions whose superhuman powers bestow gifts gratuitously, without practitioners needing to earn them. "And can it be that I should gain an interest in the Savior's blood?"[85] Giving and receiving need not mean selfish gain; they can readily involve love, grace, mercy, mystery, kindness, reciprocity, and unconditionality. That wide range of possibilities is what I intend my theory to include, in which case, the objection of explanatory reductionism fails.

Critical Empirical Scholarship

This theory of religion is deployable for empirical research programs not only about established religious traditions understood from the perspective of their own institutional centers, but also for critical scholarship focused on power, subordination, exclusion, and dissent within and around religious traditions. (Such concerns are part of what the "critical" in critical realism means.) While my theory of religion centers on the interaction of human and superhuman powers, its broader emphases on power, institutions, traditions, and communities spawn questions for understanding the power-laden interactions *between humans* played out in religious contexts. In particular, since performing "culturally prescribed complexes of practices" to access superhuman powers is the crux of religious activity, a set of important empirical questions emerges about authority and control in the prescription of those practices.

---

believed-in superhuman powers often, in fact usually, influence, possess, govern, and sometimes overwhelm religious practitioners (see chapter 2). By my account, people are not only the controlling subjects but also the receiving and dependent objects of religion's emergent social powers. That also contradicts allegations of instrumental and transactional reductionism.

85. Charles Wesley. 1738. *And Can It Be that I Should Gain?* Skeptical readers might also ponder the biblical idea of a "covenant."

FIGURE 1.6. US Roman Catholic bishops vote on a "zero tolerance" policy on clergy sexual abuse at their 2002 meeting in Dallas, Texas. The social scientific study of religion can focus on issues of institutional and communal authority, power, influence, inclusion, exclusion, voice, silencing, empowerment, and marginalization. (Copyright: Rick Wilking/AFP/Getty Images)

Who are the gatekeepers of the practices of religious traditions and communities? How is authority in religious communities structured, and whom does that structure privilege and deprive? Who has the authority to prescribe which practices may be performed by whom, in what ways, and under what conditions? Whom do various religious groups empower and disenfranchise (purposefully or de facto), how is that achieved, and what are its consequences (figure 1.6)? How and why do different types of religious communities negotiate, manage, or suppress differences in practices and beliefs, both among their religious specialists and ordinary practitioners? What kinds of formal and informal sanctions do religious actors use to maintain the continuity of acceptable practices and beliefs in particular communities over time, and with what consequences for different (potential and actual) members of those communities?

In more concrete terms, how do religious institutions, cultures, and practices interact and help reproduce social inequalities based on social class, race and ethnicity, gender, sexual identities, age, and other markers of human difference?[86] Why do various religious groups in diverse times

86. For example, Michael Emerson and Christian Smith. 2000. *Divided by Faith.* New York: Oxford University Press.

and places emphasize and de-emphasize different unacceptable behaviors—for example, economic ("greed") versus sexual ("promiscuity")—when their larger tradition condemns them all? Who recurrently is silenced or shut out of membership of religious communities, under what conditions, why, and with what results? What are the practical consequences in different religious contexts of being poor, female, a foreigner, a racial or ethnic minority, gay or lesbian, elderly, mentally disabled, or physically malformed? This theory of religion should animate these and many related empirical research questions.

Conclusion

To understand and explain religion requires first knowing what religion *is*. Partly, we want to know how to identify a religion when we see it, so as not to confuse religious and non-religious entities and muddle our later analyses. Categorizing entities well requires a clear, accurate, and discriminating definition that carefully matches its concepts to features of the real world. Beyond that and equally importantly, we need to grasp the essential character of religion, its particular social ontology. Only by theorizing religion's core distinguishing features well—by carefully formulating concepts that both include religion's essential elements and exclude "accidental" and superfluous characteristics—can we adequately comprehend its nature, causal capacities, and importance in human social life. I hope that is what the definition above accomplishes.

As a final reminder, let us underscore some key distinctions in this theory's terms that are easy to confuse: the differences between what religion *is* (ontology), what religion *can do* (causal capacities, addressed in the following chapter), and *why* people practice their religions (personal motivations); and the distinction between relig*ion* (a conceptual, analytical category) and relig*iousness* (an empirical variable). We must keep these distinct. Yet my definition of what religion *is* includes ideas about what religion *can do* (help people realize goods and avoid bads) and what *motivates* religious practices (seeking to gain access to and communicate or align oneself with superhuman powers). This is all theoretically coherent only when we remember that the meanings and purposes behind the prescribed religious practices in this analytical definition should be understood as institutional, not personal; that what matters for defining "religion" here are the public, institutionalized meanings and purposes of the cultures and traditions that prescribe religious practices, not the subjective, private, and variable interests of the people performing them.

Appendix to Chapter 1:
Situating This Account Theoretically

Finally, it may help some readers, especially scholarly readers, to understand the definition of religion advanced in this chapter if I compare and contrast it with other theoretical accounts. What follows is not an exhaustive comparison with all other definitions and theories of religion, but merely a comparison with enough relevant theories to situate my approach more clearly. Readers less interested in details of theoretical comparison can skip this appendix.

The late sociologist Daniel Bell, one of my mentors in graduate school, described religion as "a set of coherent answers to the core existential questions that confront every human group," such as "how one meets death, the meaning of tragedy, the nature of obligation, the character of love . . . recurrent questions which are . . . cultural universals." Religion, then, is "the codification of these answers into creedal form that has significance for its adherents, the celebration of rites which provide an emotional bond for those who participate, and the establishment of an institutional body to bring into congregation those who share the creed and celebration, and provide for the continuation of these rites from generation to generation."[87] One can recognize in Bell's definition elements of the approach of this chapter, including his emphasis on humans' existential problems and the celebration of practices and rituals by believers. However, differences are apparent, too. From my perspective, Bell's defining religion as "codified answers to questions" is too cognitive, cerebral, intellectualist. Religion is not at heart a set of replies to existential questions, even if it often involves this. Instead it often places more emphasis on mundane, this-worldly concerns. Bell's account clearly excludes religions that have strong elements of magic involved. His definition also lacks any reference to the superhuman (or supernatural, sacred, or other substantive term). Any number of secular philosophies or worldviews could count as religions by his account, which is a problem. Furthermore, Bell's emphasis on "codified creedal forms" seems to privilege certain kinds of text-based religions, neglecting less systematic religions often practiced in non-literate cultures. And the stress his definition places on emotionally bonded congregations and intergenerational continuity conflates the concept of religion with the distinct notion of a religious tradition, which I differentiated above. From my perspective, Bell hits the target

---

87. Bell. 1980. "The Return of the Sacred?" In Bell. *The Winding Passage*. New York: Basic Books. Pp. 333–334.

but misses the bull's-eye. His definition lets in too much that is not essential and excludes some key points that are essential.

More recently, the political scientists Pippa Norris and Ronald Inglehart have advanced an account of religion that seems closer to the one I am advocating. Their book, *Sacred and Secular*, actually never defines religion, as it focuses primarily on the question of secularization in modernity. Nevertheless, their theory does imply a particular view of religion that we can rationally reconstruct from their discussion. They write:

> Virtually all of the world's major religious cultures provide reassurance that, even though the individual alone can't understand or predict what lies ahead, a higher power will ensure that things work out. . . . Religious . . . ideologies assure people that the universe follows a plan, which guarantees that if you follow the rules, everything will turn out well, in this world or the next. This belief reduces stress, enabling people to shut out anxiety and focus on coping with their immediate problems.[88]

They then run this commentary:

> Without such a belief system, extreme stress tends to produce withdrawal reactions. Under conditions of insecurity, people have a powerful need to see authority as both strong and benevolent—even in the face of evidence to the contrary. Individuals experiencing stress have a need for rigid, predictable rules. They need to be sure what is going to happen because they are in danger—their margin of error is slender and they need maximum predictability.[89]

Again, this approach includes numerous elements that parallel those of this book, including the emphases on human reliance on "higher powers" for help in trouble, the need for people to perform practices that are something like "follow[ing] a plan," and the promise of security and coping with problems. But, like Bell, Norris and Inglehart are too specific in some places and not precise enough in others. In reality, religion is about more than mere psychological "reassurance," stress reduction, and anxiety management. This definition of religion is too psychological. It also neglects religion's positive side of promising blessings. Few religions see the universe as "following a plan," not to mention one that "guarantees" that "if you follow the rules, everything will turn out well, in this world or the next." The idea

---

88. Norris and Inglehart. 2004. *Sacred and Secular: Religion and Politics Worldwide.* Cambridge: Cambridge University Press. P. 19.

89. Ibid.

of a "plan" is too schematic and mechanical. Most religions offer promises and hopes, not guarantees. The idea of things "turning out well" is too optimistic and vague. Also, some religions do not believe in "the next world" at all, and in any case it is unclear how that world relates to this account's focus on "immediate problems." Furthermore, this view's emphasis on the human desire to "understand and predict" the future, "to be sure what is going to happen," reflects an overly constricted idea of the range of concerns that animate religious practices. In addition, not all religions conceive of their superhuman powers as "authorities," and not all that do view them as necessarily "strong and benevolent." Some religions' superhuman powers are finite, fickle, or malicious. Moreover, not all religions involve "rigid, predictable rules." Religions involve varying degrees of flexibility and customization in the application of prescribed practices—not to mention that "rules" are not the same thing as practices. Overall, while parts of it point in the right direction, Norris and Inglehart's account of religion is sloppy and ill-informed. The definition offered in this chapter is more careful, precise, and widely applicable.

Rodney Stark and Roger Finke have proposed a different approach to religion using a framework oriented around rational choice theory and social exchange. Their more complex approach defines religions as "very general explanations of existence, including the terms of exchange with a god or gods."[90] They expect there to exist "an extensive collection of ideas, principles, myths, symbols, images, and other elements of religious culture built upon this base" of "general explanations of existence." According to their view, "explanations are conceptual simplifications or models of reality that often provide plans designed to guide action." In general, humans attempt to make rational choices that increase or maximize their "rewards." "Because explanations help humans to maximize, in and of themselves explanations constitute rewards and will be sought by humans." Rewards, however, are scarce and not available to all. Therefore, people tend to invent theories, both secular and religious, about rewards in the future that cannot presently be verified. Religious explanations and rewards are those that involve "the capacity to postpone the delivery of the rewards to an otherworldly context. . . . The truly potent religious resource is otherworldly rewards." Those "are obtained only in a nonempirical (usually posthumous) context," so it is "extremely difficult, if not impossible, for living humans to discover whether or not the rewards [will] arrive as promised." Such otherworldly

---

90. Stark and Finke. *Acts of Faith.* Pp. 87–107 are the pages from which the quotes in this paragraph are taken.

rewards postulate the existence of "a supernatural being." Therefore, "religion is concerned with the supernatural; everything else is secondary." Supernatural "refers to forces or entities beyond or outside nature that can suspend, alter, or ignore physical forces." In the pursuit of rewards, "humans will seek to utilize and manipulate the supernatural." Many supernatural beings are personal gods, which may be good, evil, or inconsistent. They vary in how responsive to human exchanges they are, and differ in the diversity and scope of their powers. Religious commitment refers to "the degree to which humans promptly meet the terms of exchange with a god or gods as specified by the explanations of a given religious organization." Participating in religious rituals—that is, "collective ceremonies having a common focus and mood in which the common focus is on a god or gods, while the common mood varies"—increases people's confidence in religious explanation.

Stark and Finke's approach and my own are broadly similar in focusing on people engaging powers that are somehow above or beyond humans in order to realize some desired outcome that they believe they are unable to obtain on their own. Both also foreground substantive definitional elements (superhuman, otherworldly, supernatural) that provide content differentiating things religious from non-religious. And both emphasize human activities (practices, exchanges, rituals) that are required to obtain desired outcomes from the above-and-beyond powers. Past these broad parallels, however, the similarities break down and Stark and Finke's approach proves problematic. By now the reader should recognize the main points of difference. "Superhuman" is the only term that captures the full range of religious premises, while "otherworldly" and "supernatural" apply to only some religions—again, other religions understand the superhuman powers they postulate as belonging entirely to the natural world. Religious practices also involve much more than exchanges, the latter being only one form of human interaction among others, not all of which are reducible to exchange.[91] Also, it is not really possible to make an exchange with an impersonal superhuman power. The term "explanations of existence," furthermore, sounds—like Bell's definition above—too cognitive and intellectualist to represent all religions.

Moreover, the full breadth of things that humans seek from religion is not captured by the single concept of "rewards," which tends in meaning

---

91. See Alan Fiske. 1993. *Structures of Social Life: Four Elementary Forms of Human Relations.* New York: Free Press.

toward either a narrow utilitarian emphasis on physical pleasure or else a tautologically vague notion of "whatever people want." It is better, I suggest, to go beyond the limited range of rational choice vocabulary and rely on the fuller array of concepts that better represent real people's actual interests. This means, in part, emphasizing concerns like blessings, misfortunes, and crises instead of "scarce rewards." In any case, as I have already stated, religion is not only or even primarily about "other-worldly" rewards, but also everyday concerns. Thus, contra Stark and Finke, not all of religion's promises are "nonempirical." Some, such as healing from a disease or achieving peace of mind, are empirically verifiable to religious practitioners. Finally, Stark and Finke's view of participating in religious rituals is misguided in multiple ways. Rituals are only one kind of religious practice, as noted above. The "ceremonies" of which rituals are said to consist need not be "collective," since some religious practices are properly performed by individuals or very small groups. Religious rituals or practices may or may not increase people's confidence in religious explanations—we should consider that an open empirical question, not take it as a theoretical presupposition. Even when they do increase people's confidence in religious explanations, rituals are carried out not, in the main, for that purpose, but to access superhuman powers to solicit their blessings and help. While in some ways Stark and Finke are on the right track, on other important particulars their theory does not represent the reality of religion well.

Daniele Hervieu-Leger's 2000 book, *Religion as a Chain of Memory*, offers a creatively different view of religion.[92] After spending 80 pages thoughtfully exploring existing definitions of religion and their problems, Hervieu-Leger proposes this approach: "A religion is an ideological, practical, and symbolic system through which consciousness, both individual and collective, of belonging to a particular chain of belief is constituted, maintained, developed, and controlled." This agrees, she says, with proposals "to apply the term 'religious' to the form of believing whose distinguishing mark is to appeal to the legitimizing authority of a tradition." For Hervieu-Leger, religious *beliefs* are central to defining religion. But she is weary of the established arguments between substantive and functional definitions of religion, and so recommends changing the basic terms of the debate. "I propose," she writes, "to abandon the traditional markers—the content and function proper to religious belief—and concentrate on the

---

92. Daniele Hervieu-Leger. 2000. *Religion as a Chain of Memory*. New Brunswick, NJ: Rutgers University Press. Pp. 82, 83.

type of legitimation applied to the act of believing, in order to attempt to specify religious believing itself. The assumption I shall make is that there is no religion without the *authority of a tradition* being invoked (whether explicitly, half-explicitly, or implicitly) in support of the act of believing."[93] A religion is thus a system of beliefs continuing across time as a "chain of memory" that is legitimated specifically by the authority of tradition.

Readers will realize that by the account I am advocating, this definition is seriously deficient, however intelligent and original Hervieu-Leger's book is generally. Not only must practices and not beliefs take center place in a widely applicable definition of religion, but also, her shift of focus away from the substance or function of religion to a "type of legitimation" creates more problems than it solves. Most crucially, there are all kinds of cultural forms that are legitimated by the authority of tradition that are not remotely "religious." Hervieu-Leger's account is indiscriminately inclusive in this way. Furthermore, far from grounding their authority on the weight of tradition, some new religious movements ground it on a new revelation of charismatic leadership. So her account is, on the other hand, too exclusive on this point. While I admire much of Hervieu-Leger's theoretical reflections on religion in modernity, when it comes to defining religion, we must conclude that she confuses the question of religion's ontology with that of its legitimation. What something *is* turns out to be a quite different matter than what gives it legitimacy, a point that Hervieu-Leger obscures. Besides keeping those subjects analytically distinct, I, again, following Riesebrodt, propose underlining the conceptual notions of religious *practices* and *superhuman* powers, which Hervieu-Leger also neglects.

The fifth theory of religion that helps situate my own theoretical account comes from Steve Bruce, one of the few remaining advocates of traditional secularization theory. He defines religion as "beliefs, actions, and institutions predicated on the existence of entities with powers of agency (that is, gods) or impersonal powers or processes possessed of moral purpose (the Hindu notion of karma, for example), which can set the conditions of, or intervene in, human affairs."[94] This definition resembles the one advocated in this chapter, and shares several of its strengths. It is substantive but avoids the notions of "supernatural" and "transcendent." By my lights, however, Bruce's definition lacks clarity on a few key points. First, in some religions, the beings that have "powers of agency" are not limited to "gods," but con-

---

93. Ibid. P. 76.
94. Steve Bruce. 2002. *God Is Dead: Secularization in the West*. Malden, MA: Blackwell. P. 2.

tain a variety of types of agents, including spirits, demons, devils, angels, ghosts, deceased ancestors, and more. "Gods" is too narrow. Second, Bruce's language of "beliefs, actions, and institutions" is good, but that ordering may privilege "beliefs" over "practices," which is a misstep to be avoided. And the term "actions" fails to convey the culturally prescribed and repeated character of practices, which is important for understanding religion. Third, Bruce rightly notes that the personal and impersonal powers and processes can "set the conditions of" and "intervene in" human affairs; however, his definition does not explain why people predicate such powers and processes on which to build beliefs, actions, and institutions. I think a better definition overtly includes the idea of realizing goods and avoiding bads, especially seeking blessings and avoiding and coping with misfortunes and crises.

Sixth and finally, some early readers of this book's manuscript asked me prior to its publication to explain how the definition of religion advanced above differs from the definition I proposed in my 2003 book, *Moral, Believing Animals: Human Personhood and Culture*. In that book, I defined religion as "sets of beliefs, symbols, and practices about the reality of superempirical orders that make claims to organize and guide human life."[95] How the definition of religion that I currently advocate differs from this one is clear: It prioritizes practices over beliefs and symbols, it centers on the superhuman instead of the superempirical, it replaces "orders" with "powers," and it shifts the purpose of religion away from moral order and instead toward deliverance and blessings. These changes do not signal an abandonment of my previous book's concern with moral order (which shows up again in the next chapter of this book)—only a reconceptualization of moral order (as derived from religions) as framed within premises about the existence and nature of superhuman powers and the human interest in gaining their help. Emphasis shifts away from moral order and cognition and toward navigating the problems and promises of everyday life. The revisions in my definition also reflect the growing influence of the philosophy of critical realism on me since 2003. My turn toward critical realism was in fact primarily spurred by inadequacies that I recognized in my own reasoning in parts of *Moral, Believing Animals*, particularly around the unacceptable consequences (namely, total cognitive and perhaps moral relativism) of my arguments concerning presuppositional epistemology (chapter 3) and the

95. Christian Smith. 2003. *Moral Believing Animals*. New York: Oxford University Press. P. 98.

foundational character of cultural narratives (chapter 4). Critical realism met and overcame those problems, and has significantly influenced my work since then. More simply and straightforwardly, in 2012 I read and re-read Martin Riesebrodt's book *The Promise of Salvation*, and his argument persuaded me that his approach was theoretically the best way to proceed. It was both more careful and robust than my previous thinking and the available alternatives, and thus caused me to revise my understanding of religion in ways that closely follow Riesebrodt's approach, as advanced in this chapter.

2

What Causal Powers Does Religion Produce?

Intuitive understanding, wisdom, cleverness,
glory, beauty, pleasure, wealth and honor,
all comforts, bliss, happiness, and salvation,
O Nanak, appear by chanting the Name of God.

—SIKH SCRIPTURE (GURU GRANTH SAHIB JI, 1323)

The kingdom of heaven is like a mustard seed,
which a man took and planted in his field.
Though it is the smallest of all seeds, when it grows,
it is the largest of garden plants and becomes a tree,
so that the birds come and perch in its branches.

—JESUS OF NAZARETH (MATTHEW 13:31-32)

The feature of religion that distinguishes it from other human doings is its engagement with postulated superhuman powers through complexes of prescribed practices in hopes of realizing human goods and avoiding bads, such as receiving blessings, protection, and deliverance from troubles both small and immense. But religion is surely about more than that. What about ecstatic experiences of the divine? Fellowship among believers? How do things like the identities people draw from religious faith or the appreciation of sacred beauty fit into this theory?[1] Are they not essential parts of religion, too? Are these not also or even mainly the reason why many people are religious?

The basic answer to these inquiries is this. Practices to access superhuman powers for things like blessings and help are the core, the essence, the deepest wellspring of religion. All of the many other features of religion are secondary outgrowths and supports. None of them are unique to religion. At their origin, all of them ultimately depend upon the energy generated by core religious concerns. In the long run, few of them are sustainable in religious contexts apart from religion's essential purpose to access the help of superhuman powers. For these reasons, the various capacities and characteristics of religion that do not directly involve seeking through prescribed practices the help of superhuman powers we should theoretically consider secondary to, derivative of, and dependent on the core of religion. That does not make them unimportant in religious people's lived experience. They are often crucial. But they are not what religion *is* conceptually. Rather, they grow out of and usually strengthen religion.

Secondary Products, Features, and Powers

What are some of the important secondary products, features, and powers that religion can generate? The list that follows is not comprehensive. It is schematic, its organization is somewhat artificial, and some of its categories overlap. But I think it does the job needed here. Not every religion engenders all of the items. Exactly which of the following a religion produces depends on the interaction of the content and character of the religious tradition itself with the particular social and historical context in which it is set. The same religious tradition can also generate and emphasize different things at different points in time. That said, we can observe that many religions at various times and places engender many of the following.

Identity

1. *Personal identity*: distinct persons' particular self-concepts that exhibit continuity across time.
2. *Group identity*: distinct persons' understanding of their characteristic selves derived directly from memberships in delineated social groups or institutions.

---

1. For example, Robert Wuthnow. 2003. *Creative Spirituality*. Berkeley: University of California Press; Robert Wuthnow. 2003. *All in Sync*. Berkeley: University of California Press.

3. *Social identity*: a social group's collective sense of belonging, which involves joint self-definition, common social location, and shared emotional investment.[2]

Community

4. *Community belonging*: membership in a relationally significant social group.
5. *Social solidarity*: the cohesion and integration derived from a place in affectively significant social networks of relatively homogenous groups.
6. *Social support*: being cared for, assisted, and comforted by others in social relationships.

Meaning

7. *Moral order*: normative systems specifying and organizing good, right, and proper relations among persons and groups.
8. *Cosmic or life meaning*: understandings of the larger or ultimate significance or purpose of life and the universe.
9. *Theodicy*: explanations of suffering, injustice, and death.

Expression and Experience

10. *Artistic creation*: the crafting or building of aesthetically expressive or attractive objects or performances.
11. *Aesthetic expression*: the outward expression of subjective feelings, ideas, and desires through singing, dance, shouting, speaking, drama, facial countenances, distinct postures, and so on.
12. *Transcendent experiences*: encounters or events of joy, awe, enlightenment, terror, rapture, the sublime, the ecstatic, divine union, and the like that surpass the limits of the ordinary or normal.

Social Control

13. *Internalized self-regulation*: voluntary compliance with established norms of thought and behavior through the subjective acceptance of their importance and legitimacy, usually through socialization.

2. This parsing of identity is slightly different from that of many social psychologists (e.g., Jan Stets and Richard Serpe. 2013. "Identity Theory." In John DeLamater and Amanda Ward (eds.). *Handbook of Social Psychology*. New York: Springer. Pp. 31–60).

14. *Interpersonal controls*: compliance with established norms of thought and behavior achieved through the informal rewards and sanctions communicated through relational interactions.
15. *Formal social controls*: compliance with established norms of thought and behavior achieved through institutionalized standards, expectations, monitoring, and systems of rewards and punishments.

Legitimacy

16. *Institutional legitimation*: acknowledgment of the acceptability or right of established social practices and organizations that exercise authority in social settings.
17. *Political legitimacy*: the acceptance of the rightful authority of a state or political regime to govern.
18. *Legitimacy of dissent*: belief in the right or justification of opposition, resistance, or protest against what is believed to be an illegitimate practice, organization, or regime.[3]

Many of these powers, features, or products are related in some ways to the essential core of religion. For instance, beautiful music—one type of artistic creation—is often composed for use in liturgies of worship, which belong to the prescribed practices seeking the help of superhuman powers. Likewise, following a religious commandment in order to live properly within a larger moral order is often understood as an essential religious practice. Nonetheless, all of the listed items also frequently involve important aspects of religion that are not directly linked to practices oriented toward superhuman powers. Enjoying friendships at church, for example (community belonging, solidarity, and support), may be described as "Christian fellowship," which is related to a prescribed practice oriented toward pleasing and obeying the Christian God, but it is sometimes simply a nice experience enjoyed for its own sake, and not motivated directly or indirectly to seek God's blessings or help.[4]

In fact, sometimes religion generates characteristics, opportunities, and happenings that aren't just irrelevant to but actually violate a religious tradi-

---

3. Including in sometimes very subtle ways—See, e.g., Saba Mahmood. 2011. *Politics of Piety: The Islamic Revival and the Feminist Subject*. Princeton: Princeton University Press.

4. Such secondary powers of religion then result in further consequences—for example, the fact that the community belonging, solidarity, and support involved in regular religious service attendance have the same magnitude of effect on reducing mortality as not smoking one pack of cigarettes a day. Robert Hummer, Richard Rogers, Charles Nam, and Christopher Ellison. 1999. "Religious Involvement and U.S. Adult Mortality." *Demography*. 36: 273–285.

tion's own prescribed practices oriented toward the help of superhuman powers. For instance, the social status and privileges of religious leaders (community + legitimacy) may engender relatively secure opportunities for illicit sexual advances on minors. Members of a church youth group might use the social network created there (community) to buy and sell drugs on the side. Businesspeople may exploit the familiarity and trust in their religious congregations (identity + community + legitimacy) for their personal commercial advantage. Religious clergy may use their careers (identity + community + legitimacy), which draw to them attention, authority, and deference, to stroke their own egos. Parents may drop off their children at religious education classes (community + meaning + social control) as a way to enjoy quiet time at home alone over coffee and the newspaper, rather than as a means to attend religious services themselves. Phenomena such as these are possible only because religious people and organizations are performing core religious practices. Yet none are part of the defining practices of religion, but can controvert and abuse them.

In short, when we consider all that religion not only is but does, involves, produces, and makes possible, we see that religion can be "about" a lot more than seeking through prescribed practices to access superhuman powers. We need to distinguish these capacities from religion's essential social ontology, in relation to which they are secondary, derivative, and dependent. In what ways?

Secondary, Derivative, and Dependent

Unlike seeking the help of superhuman powers, none of the 18 items listed above are unique to religion. All are routinely found in various non-religious activities and institutions. Non-religious spheres of life offer many sources of identity, community, meaning, expression, social control, and legitimacy. Superhuman powers are not required to generate or obtain them. Identity can be drawn from a profession, for example, community from a sports association, meaning from a secular philosophy, aesthetic expression through a community choir, social control through culture and law, and legitimacy through tradition or rational authority. Religions often generate all of these things, too, yet they are not crucial to religion's social ontology.

Furthermore, these secondary products depend in their origin, when they are religious, upon the energy and relations generated by the core of religion. The identities, community, and meanings found in religious settings only arise because of religion's fundamental concern with accessing superhuman powers for blessings and help. The same is true of expression, social control, and legitimacy. There would be no bar and bat mitzvah parties or doctrine of the divine right of kings or mystical experiences of sublime oneness with the cosmos if Judaism did not worship God, medieval Catholicism did not proclaim the Holy Trinity, and various religious traditions did not create the ground out of which such mystical experiences grow.

Metaphorically, one might think of religion's engagement with superhuman powers as the roots and trunk of the tree, and the secondary products as the tree's branches and leaves (see figure 2.1). The latter's existence and health depend on the roots and trunk, which supply them structural grounding and nutrients. They always branch off from the more basic concerns of religion. At the same time, the life of the trunk and roots also depends upon the leaves on the branches to absorb sunlight and accomplish photosynthesis. But the roots and trunk are more vital to the tree than the branches and leaves. If the roots and trunk are severed and cut, the branches and leaves inevitably die. However, if the branches and leaves are shorn away, and the trunk even cut down to a stump, the tree might still retain life and, through the process of "regeneration," grow back to health.[5]

In the long run, as I just suggested, few of the secondary products of religion are sustainable in religious contexts if religion's core prescribed practices to access the help of superhuman powers are not performed. One can find all 18 of the secondary and dependent products of religion named above in non-religious contexts. But, I suggest, they will not flourish in religious environments indefinitely when a religion abandons its defining purpose, especially when alternative sources for the offshoots of religion are available. Historical and contemporary empirical evidence, I propose, validates this observation: The kinds of secondary products of religion described above are most robust and dynamic in religious settings when the essential concerns of religion are treated as real and important. Conversely, when religious traditions cease to focus on entreating superhuman powers

---

5. Jenny Leonardsson and Frank Götmark. 2015. "Differential Survival and Growth of Stumps in 14 Woody Species after Conservation Thinning in Mixed Oak-rich Temperate Forests." *European Journal of Forest Research.* 134: 199–209. Thus, in the ancient story of Job, the tale's protagonist observes that, "At least there is hope for a tree: If it is cut down, it will sprout again, and its new shoots will not fail. Its roots may grow old in the ground and its stump die in the soil, yet at the scent of water it will bud and put forth shoots like a plant" (Job 14:7–9). And so the eighth century (BCE) Hebrew prophet, Isaiah, used this same image to foretell that, "A shoot will come up from the stump of Jesse; from his roots a branch will bear fruit. . . . In that day the Root of Jesse will stand as a banner for the peoples; the nations will rally to him, and his resting place will be glorious" (Isaiah 11:1,10).

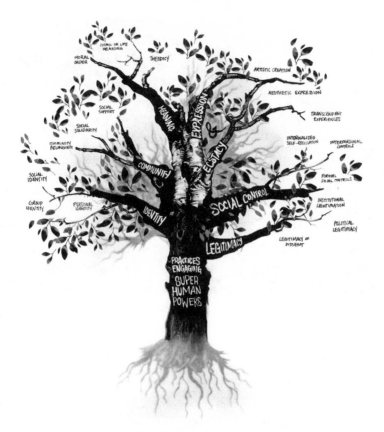

FIGURE 2.1. Tree metaphor of religion's secondary features and capacities

for blessings and help through prescribed practices, the secondary phenomena that religion also generates tend to languish. More systematic, comparative research is needed on this question. For now, suffice it to suggest that major aspects of religion not directly related to its core concern of accessing superhuman powers should be viewed theoretically as not only secondary and derivative but also dependent on religion's essential concerns (figure 2.2). They may be vital parts of actual religious life in a particular tradition and community, but they are not the essence of what religion *is*. Even if highly visible and valued, theoretically they are always secondary, derivative, and dependent.[6]

6. My claim here concerns religion's ontology—what religion *is*—but *not necessarily* its *phylogeny*, that is, its evolutionary or (pre-)historical origins and development as a "species" of human action. Meaning, some of what I count as secondary for purposes of defining religion (such as the collectivistic nature of religious identities) might in religion's phylogenetic history actually have been fundamental and generative. But that is not my concern here.

FIGURE 2.2. Shinto practitioners purify themselves at the purification basin, *te-mizuya*, of the Nishinomiya Shrine in Hyōgo, Japan, during *Shōgatsu*, the Shinto New Year. Like religions generally, Shinto not only promises the help of superhuman powers but also provides personal, communal, and national identity, solidarity, belonging, meaning, aesthetic expression, and political legitimacy. (Copyright: Jeremy Sutton-Hibbert/Alamy stock photo)

The Emergence of Religious Causal Powers

Stated differently, once religion is born in human life—by virtue of practitioners seeking to access superhuman powers—it comes to possess causal powers to engender secondary products, features, and capacities. Analytically speaking, when no one in a group of people seeks the help of superhuman powers, religion does not exist and thus cannot exercise any powers of its own. Once religion begins to be practiced, however, it becomes real in existence and generates capacities to make things happen in the world. A newly existent religion can confer on people religious identities that they could not have had before, for example. It can provide previously nonexistent theodicies to explain suffering. And so on. All of this generates new powers or capacities that religion can exercise or express.

This development is an instance of what critical realists call "emergence."[7] By relating and interacting in a particular way (in this case, engaging in

7. Smith. *What Is a Person?* Pp. 25–97; Philip Clayton and Paul Davies (eds.). 2006. *The Re-Emergence of Emergence.* New York: Oxford University Press; R. Keith Sawyer. 2002. "Durkheim's Dilemma: Toward a Sociology of Emergence." *Sociological Theory.* 20: 227–247; Geoffrey Hodg-

practices oriented toward believed-in superhuman powers), people bring into being as an "institutional fact" something new that possesses characteristics, capacities, and powers that did not previously exist. Something real (religion's new features and powers) is literally brought into existence at a "higher level" of reality simply by other already-existing entities (religious people) interacting together in particular ways (engaging in particular practices). This emergence of new religious powers is of course only one occurrence among many of humans bringing all kinds of social institutions with powers into being, just by interacting together in particular ways. But it is crucial to grasp the emergence of new religious features and powers, and their relationship to religion's core ontology, in order to understand the nature and influence of religion.[8]

The key point here is not just that humans can invent things, but rather that the new things humans invent become real themselves and bring into being with them new causal capacities and powers. The latter remain completely dependent on the human activities that, through emergence, give rise to them. But, once they have come into being, they are then themselves entirely real, possessing their own new capacities and features that are *irreducible* to the activities that gave and continually give rise to their

---

son. 2000. "The Concept of Emergence in Social Science." *Emergence.* 2: 65–77. Emergence involves: First, two or more entities that exist at a "lower" level interact or combine. Second, that interaction or combination serves as the basis of some new, real entity that has existence at a "higher" level. Third, the existence of the new higher-level entity is fully dependent upon the two or more lower-level entities interacting or combining as they have and could not exist without them doing so. Fourth, the new, higher-level entity nevertheless possesses characteristic qualities (e.g., structures, qualities, capacities, textures, powers) that cannot be reduced to those of the lower-level entities that gave rise to the new entity possessing them. When these four things occur, emergence has happened. The whole is more than the sum of its parts. Emergence is anti-dualistic and anti-monistic: It explains the existence of different qualities and features in a reality that is understood to be unified, not dualistic (though not a singular monad, either).

8. The failure to understand emergence often leads to "reductionism," a ruinous move claiming that an emergent entity can be best explained by reducing it to its lower-level component parts and proposing a description referencing only those parts and not the emergent whole. Reductionism asserts that an emergent reality is *nothing but* the parts from which it came into being and can only be explained in terms of them. It takes this standard form: "I know that you normally think that P is really a complex matter of A, B, C . . . X, Y, and Z. But I, as a scientist who knows the real truth of the matter, tell you instead that P is really nothing but e." Reductionism squashes complicated, emergent complexity into simple, pre-emergent components. Its fatal mistake is to *fail to see all of the new properties, capacities, and tendencies that come into being at higher levels of reality through processes of emergence*, which do *not* exist at the lower levels of reality from which the higher comes into being. Reductionism *proceeds as if emergence does not happen*, stripping reality of its upwardly emergent features, powers, and operations. Critical realism is resolutely anti-reductionistic, since reductionism makes no sense within a realist ontology.

existence. This is the power of emergence. Engage in practices that seek the help of superhuman powers that you believe in, and you and your fellow practitioners emergently bring something new into being: a religion. It did not exist before, but it does now, and it possesses powers that cannot be reduced to the religious practices that brought it into being. In creating religion, people generate in it new, irreducible causal powers that did not exist before, including those involved in the items named above. (Again, these may also be found elsewhere, as emergently generated by other human activities, but not as they particularly exist here in religion, as powers and capacities grounded specifically in religion.) In this way, the creation of religion in human life entails the creation of many *other* new powers and capacities—aside from the matter of accessing blessings and help from superhuman powers—which exert strong and widespread causal influences in life and the world.

Note the irony in this situation. Religion exists because humanity lacks causal powers, but religion itself brings into being an immense array of new causal powers. That is, precisely because humans do not (believe that they) themselves have the capacities to realize some goods and avoid some bads, especially to gain certain blessings and avoid and cope with misfortunes, they engage in practices to enlist superhuman powers to achieve what they cannot. In so doing, through the process of emergence, they bring religion into reality. Once religion exists among humans, it comes to possess, at least in potential, a host of new causal capacities and powers that humans can use and that religion exercises "back upon" humans. Religion, the reality that is born of humanity's incapacities and limits of power, thus ironically has the secondary effect of expanding through emergence new capacities and powers among, for, and over humans. In short, the human recognition of powerlessness produces new, real powers in human life. This insight helps to explain religion's causal influence in human societies, which I discuss below.

Important to recognize here is the fact that the new powers that religion generates are not only those available to religious people to use for their purposes. Some can be used in this way. But more commonly, these powers and capacities come to exert causal influences *on, over,* and *within* religious people. In short, religious people are often the objects, not the masters, of the exercise of the causal influence of those powers and capacities. Those new capacities frequently end up shaping the thinking, feelings, desires, experiences, and actions of religious people more than religious people use them—despite the fact that they derive entirely from the practices of those same people.

In other words, that the new powers of the secondary features of religion are generated emergently through the practices of religious people does not mean that those practitioners can control those powers as they wish. That is because, like every other social structure, those secondary features and their capacities become ontologically real social facts existing at a level in reality's ontologically "stratified" order "above" personal being and often above their control.[9] Critical realists call this "*downward* causation": emergently real, higher-level entities possess the capacities to influence the lower-level entities that brought them into being through their relations or interactions. Such is the causal power of the realm of "the social," which social science studies: The social world as a whole exerts causal powers greater than the sum of its parts, so that the very people whose activities give rise to social worlds are also then "downwardly" influenced in powerful ways by the social worlds they created. That happens in social life everywhere, all the time, including in religion.

An Example: Mormonism

The religion of the Church of Jesus Christ of Latter Day Saints (LDS), popularly known as Mormonism, came into being in western New York in 1820, a time of intense religious ferment in the United States known as the Second Great Awakening. The founder of Mormonism, Joseph Smith, claimed that an angel directed him to the location of buried golden plates containing writings in an ancient language, which Smith translated and dictated "by the gift and power of God" into *The Book of Mormon*.[10] Smith and his followers later moved to various locations in the American Midwest and eventually to Utah, the current geographic center of Mormonism.

Like all religions, Mormonism engages in complexes of prescribed practices to establish and maintain contact with postulated superhuman powers to realize goods and avoid bads, to obtain blessings and avert and handle misfortunes and crises. These include the "ordinances" of baptism by immersion, confirmation, reception of the gifts of the Holy Ghost, ordination to the Aaronic and Melchizedek priesthoods for males, "sealing" in

9. Smith. *What Is a Person?* Pp. 25–89, 317–383.

10. Richard Bushman. 2008. *Mormonism*. New York: Oxford University Press. P. 21; Douglas Davies. 2010. *An Introduction to Mormonism*. Cambridge: Cambridge University Press; Rodney Stark and Reid Neilson. 2005. *The Rise of Mormonism*. New York: Columbia University Press; Jan Shipps. 1985. *Mormonism*. Chicago: University of Illinois Press; Eric Eliason. 2001. *Mormons and Mormonism*. Chicago: University of Illinois Press.

marriage, baptism for the dead, the "sacrament" of the Lord's Supper, the naming and blessing of children, the anointing and blessing of the sick, participation in prayer circles, serving on missions, the setting apart of persons who are called to church leadership, and ongoing repentance from sin and obedience to God's commands. These are believed to lead to eternal salvation, and to many and various blessings in life on earth.

The founding and spread of Mormonism, however, did not only establish new religious practices and the goods believed to spring from them. Along with them emerged a host of secondary, derivative, and dependent personal and social realities with their own causal powers. First is the formal organization of the Church of Jesus Christ of Latter Day Saints, in all of its local, national, and global expressions. This institution then gave rise to myriad meetings, activities, and relationships not directly tied to the performance of religious practices.[11] Mormonism endows its adherents with very strong identities, for instance: the capacity to know and say that, "I am a Mormon," "I belong to the Mormon church," "We together are the LDS." The history of Mormon persecutions and the LDS's story of the "handcart pioneers," believed to have been assisted by divine miracles during the church's great migration on foot to Utah, reinforce the sense of faithfulness, sacrifice, and perseverance that are central to Mormon identity.[12]

Mormonism is also well known for the intense community it engenders, providing its adherents a potent sense of belonging, solidarity, and communal support.[13] LDS doctrine, cosmology, scripture, and prophetic teachings give practitioners powerful senses of moral order, meaning in life, and explanations of suffering, injustice, and death. Mormonism says that God the Father is the progenitor of the spirits or "intelligences" of all people, which existed before being born as mortal humans on earth, and that all people can become exalted and glorified, as joint heirs with Jesus Christ, receiving all that God possesses, becoming like Christ as a God. Life on earth, by the Mormon view, is only a brief part of eternal existence, in which humans can advance toward salvation by learning to choose good over evil.

11. Marie Cornwall, Tim Heaton, and Lawrence Young (eds.). 2001. *Contemporary Mormonism*. Chicago: University of Illinois Press.

12. Among the vast literature on this history, see, for instance, Andrew Olsen. 2006. *The Price We Paid: The Extraordinary Story of the Willie and Martin Handcart Pioneers*. Denver, CO: Deseret Books; History of the Saints. 2014. *The Mormon Wars: Early Persecutions, Hawn's Mill, Nauvoo War, Johnston's Army, War on Polygamy*. American Fork, UT: Covenant Communications.

13. Rick Phillips. 2014. *Saints in Zion, Saints in Babylon*. CreateSpace Publishing; Richard Ostling. 2007. *Mormon America*. New York: HarperOne.

In the process, Mormons believe they participate in the "restoration" of the true Christian church, which fell into a "Great Apostasy" not long after Jesus's ascension into heaven. This belief system affords Mormons a clear framework of purpose in life, moral guidance, and understanding of suffering and death.

At first glance, Mormonism does not appear to emphasize artistic creation and aesthetic expression, but in fact the LDS church has produced a distinctive style of art, architecture, furniture, and other forms of material culture.[14] For LDS adherents who are steeped in Mormon culture and experience, these artistic and material objects evoke mental and emotional responses that express and fortify the faith and confirm religious identity, commitment, and solidarity. The LDS faith also may generate powerful personal religious experiences of divine presence, confirmation, and assurance through adherents' participation in worship, reading the Book of Mormon, serving on a mission, and many other practices.[15] Many Mormons testify, for example, that "God our heavenly Father" or "the spirit of Christ" has "confirmed in my heart the assurance of the truth of the Book of Mormon."

In part as a result of all of the above, Mormonism engenders all kinds of causal capacities to regulate how its practitioners think, feel, and behave. Mormons internalize through socialization capacities for strict self-regulation in the name of repentance from sin, obedience to God, and the faithful practice of religion. They likewise monitor and influence each other through positive and negative sanctions toward the same ends and often with the same results. The LDS church also controls behavior through many institutional means. Mormons, for instance, are not permitted to "shop for" and attend the congregation to which they most want to belong, which they feel best meets their needs, but are assigned to their "wards" by church leaders according to the geographical location of their home. For another example, once a year, Mormon ward members meet in person with their bishop (the lay leader of their local ward) to review the faithfulness of their

14. Richard Oman and Robert Davis. 1995. *Images of Faith: Art of the Latter-Day Saints.* Denver, CO: Deseret Books; C. Mark Hamilton. 1995. *Nineteenth-Century Mormon Architecture and City Planning.* New York: Oxford University Press; John Welch and Doris Dant. 2009. *The Book of Mormon Paintings of Minerva Teichert.* Provo, UT: BYU Studies; Marilyn Conover Barker and Scott Peterson. 1995. *The Legacy of Mormon Furniture.* Layton, UT: Gibbs Smith; Thomas Carter. 2015. *Building Zion: The Material World of Mormon Settlement.* Minneapolis: University of Minnesota Press.

15. Melvyn Hammarberg. 2013. *The Mormon Quest for Glory.* New York: Oxford University Press; Phillips. *Saints in Zion*; Ostling. *Mormon America.*

behavior—including whether or not they had tithed 10 percent of their financial income to the church during the previous year. Important practical consequences are meted out depending on the answers, such as the ability to enter LDS temples and benefit from the ordinances practiced in them. The LDS church also works to control the ideas of intellectual dissenters within the fold.[16]

Institutional social controls are not all about monitoring and negative sanctions, however. Through a combination of strong, positive normative expectations and the high social status afforded Mormon youth who serve on missions, large proportions of LDS males ages 18 to 25 spend two years proselytizing for the faith with an assigned partner in foreign settings (and often foreign languages) that they did not choose. This practice produces more than 85,000 full-time foreign LDS missionaries and more than 30,000 "church service" missionaries in the field at any given time.[17] Mormon missions demand a major sacrifice of time, focus, and energy during the prime of life—requiring the meeting of "standards of worthiness" and the delay of marriage—but it is a sacrifice the LDS church voluntarily elicits (figure 2.3).

Finally, the LDS religion provides formal and informal legitimacy to many social institutions and practices beyond its core religious exercises, including heterosexual marriage, democratic government, capitalism, and public and private schools. But not all practices Mormonism approves have been culturally mainstream. For more than half of the nineteenth century, the LDS church also legitimized polygamous marriage, or "plural marriage" as they called it—so that between 1852 and 1890, approximately 20–30 percent of Mormons practiced polygamy. Some sectarian LDS fundamentalists continue the custom today.[18] Mormons also have a long history of engagement in American politics, with an influence disproportionate to the size of its membership.[19] And the LDS church has been a base of political protest

16. Philip Lindholm. 2011. *Latter-Day Dissent*. Draper, UT: Greg Kofford Books.

17. http://www.mormonnewsroom.org/article/2014-statistical-report-for-2015-april -general-conference. Young LDS women also serve on missions, but in lower proportions, due to historical precedents. The percentage of youth from any other religious tradition who serve on equivalent kinds of missions is paltry by comparison.

18. Kathleen Flake. 2004. *The Politics of American Religious Identity*. Chapel Hill: University of North Carolina Press. Pp. 65, 192; Richard S. Van Wagoner. 1989. *Mormon Polygamy*. Salt Lake City: Signature Books; Jessie Embry. 1994. "Polygamy." In Allan Powell (ed.). *Utah History Encyclopedia*. Salt Lake City: University of Utah Press; Cardell Jacobson. 2011. *Modern Polygamy in the United States*. New York: Oxford University Press.

19. David Campbell, John Green, and J. Quin Monson. 2014. *Seeking the Promised Land*. Cambridge: University of Cambridge Press.

FIGURE 2.3. New Mormon missionaries in training gathered on the first day of their formal preparation at the Latter-Day Saints Missionary Training Center in Provo, Utah. The training campus, one of 15 around the world, has 19 buildings on a 39-acre site and a capacity to house and train 3,700 missionaries at one time. Offering instruction in 55 languages, the Provo center has trained more than 600,000 missionaries from nearly every country in the world. (Copyright: Robert Huber)

and dissent, from its early insistence on its legal right to practice "plural marriage" to its active 2008 campaign for Proposition 8 to make same-sex marriage unconstitutional in California.[20]

In short, the Mormon religion does more than establish a complex of practices by which its members can attain the knowledge and help of super-human powers—such as God the Father and Jesus Christ—for salvation, earthly blessings, and other forms of assistance and comfort. Mormonism has also created a host of emergent, powerful social facts, which are not always directly related to the promise of help from superhuman powers. These facts are not the essence of Mormonism, but secondary, derivative, and dependent offshoots. Still, the identity, community, meaning, expressive modes, social control, and legitimacies that Mormonism brings into

20. Brooke Adams. "California's Prop 8: LDS Leader Calls for Healing the Gay-Marriage Rift." *Salt Lake Tribune*, November 5, 2008.

existence are real, important, and potent; they bestow on adherents many emergent powers, and exercise powers over them. We cannot understand Mormonism and its influence without accounting for them.

Religion's Causal Powers in Human Life

Many of us want to understand why and how religion influences people and social life in spheres beyond religion. It is important to understanding religion for its own sake. But religion also matters because it often makes a difference in the wider world. Religion shapes people's lives. It influences groups and movements. It forms whole cultures and societies. We need to understand how and why it does so. Related to this is a theoretical question: Is there something unique about religion that produces particularly *religious* effects in human life? Scholars disagree. Some think religion contributes particular forms or intensities of influence on the world. Others think religion is no different from other human institutions in the way it works, so that for analytical purposes, religion can be folded into broader categories of explanation, such as culture or organizations.

I suggest that religion exerts causal influences in, on, and through people and social life by nearly all the same *processes* that other social practices, institutions, and types of cultures do, but that religion sometimes does so in particular *ways* because of the unique content of beliefs and practices that define religion's social ontology. The means by which religion shapes the human world normally resemble those of most non-religious factors—they are standard processes well known to social scientists—but the substance of the beliefs, practices, and institutions that are unique to religion make religious influences, under certain conditions, particularly intense and prolonged. Thus, religious influences are mostly ordinary in *how* they work, but they can be quite distinct in *why* they work and sometimes the *ways* they work, because of what religion uniquely is.

To elaborate on the first point, that religious influences are mostly ordinary in how they work: Religion exerts causal forces in, on, and through people and social life mainly through the same *generic formations* of beliefs, perceptions, assumptions, desires, emotions, habits, interests, goals, rewards, costs, networks, reinforcements, commitments, identities, opportunities, constraints, monitoring, sanctions, repertoires of action and practice, and so on. Through the resulting human activities, whole new social and institutional powers emerge at a level "above" that of the personal—at the social level—which possess their own capacities that can operate "downwardly" on persons and communities. Those religious powers like-wise shape human life through the same kinds of means and processes as many non-religious social structures and institutions. Thus, when it comes to the *means* and *processes* by which religion influences people and societies, religion is not unlike non-religious institutions and dynamics.

However, when it comes to why religious influences are operating in the first place, religion is different and so its causal influences can be distinctive. When we examine the content of religious practices and their results, in-cluding many emergent religious powers, we find a particular kind of be-liefs, motives, and interests: those that presuppose and seek to access su-perhuman powers. That is what sets religion apart from everything else human, and it has implications for the particular character of religious influ-ences. In most times and places, religion's power to shape life operates at an intensity no stronger, deeper, or longer-lasting than many other influences in life. Although religion's powers to affect different outcomes in personal and social life are often significant, they are usually rivaled by many non-religious influences, like those involved with earning a living, family life, politics, sexuality, and so on. However, sometimes religion's causal powers stand out among all causal influences; they intensify and become more ac-tive. This can happen for a variety of reasons, but my point here is general: In certain situations, religious influences in human personal and social life become particularly galvanized, energized, activated. In those settings, it becomes especially vital to understand religion.

Of course, many parts of human social life can under certain conditions become particularly influential. That is not unique to religion. What mat-ters for this discussion are the potential implications of the fact that religion alone is about accessing the help of superhuman powers. Under certain social circumstances, the unique character of the human interest in religion and things superhuman can generate a level of *intensity, depth, and persis-tence in people's motivations, commitments, and endurance* not often seen in non-religious life. Religious visions, I suggest, can transcend the mundane world in ways that non-religious imaginations rarely do. Religious motiva-tions can provide a depth and determination that are seldom matched by motives grounded in non-religious life. Religious activities can exhibit de-grees of commitment, sacrifice, and determination that surpass those ordi-narily found in non-religious human activity. Religious premises about superhuman powers and the belief systems that often develop from them are frequently of such a foundational and sometimes comprehensive nature that they more readily help form the bedrock categories, assumptions, and dispositions of entire cultures and civilizations than do non-religious beliefs.

Religion, in short, possesses—not always, but under certain conditions—particular capacities to shape people and social life in ways that are truly exceptional, that stand out from causal influences derived from non-religious factors. (By this I do not mean that the strongest of religion's causal capacities are more powerful than the strongest of non-religious causal capacities, such as those involved in nationalism—not that religion and nationalism can usually be so easily separated and compared—but simply that religious influences can stand out as exceptionally powerful in certain social contexts.[21]) Again, the means and processes by which religion exerts force are similar to those operating in most other areas of human social life, but, I suggest, the depth, intensity, and persistence of religious motives can be extraordinary. And that can make a big difference in the type and force of influences that religion exerts on people and societies.[22]

Why would religion's unique concern with accessing the help of superhuman powers provide, under the right social circumstances, religious visions, beliefs, motivations, and actions with unusual force? The very premises about superhuman capacities upon which religion is based pivot human beliefs and interests away from mundane life and toward a believed reality of *greater power*. That reality may or may not be understood as transcendent, sacred, ultimate, holy, eternal, or inescapable. But it clearly involves an ability to bring about desired outcomes that people do not believe they possess. Superhuman powers by definition (are believed to) exercise superior causal capacities that can provide people with goods. Depending on the circumstances and the desire of the religious practitioners to realize their purposes—which, they believe, only the superhuman powers can accomplish—this fact may produce among humans the kind of extraordinary motivations and actions mentioned above. Especially when some humans badly want what they believe only superhuman powers can provide, when the concerns involved are emotionally fraught, or when the situation in-

21. My approach here seeks to counter the unbalanced view of many scholars in various fields concerned with religion and politics, namely, that religion is either uniquely powerful in its violent and destructive tendencies, on one extreme, or else that religion possesses no particular causal powers and so can be reduced to non-religious categories, such as culture, ethnicity, organizations, or networks, at the other extreme. A realistic account requires a more balanced, nuanced, and contextualized perspective.

22. Christian Smith. 1996. "Correcting a Curious Neglect, or Bringing Religion Back In." In Smith. *Disruptive Religion*. Pp. 1–25.

volves questions of the afterlife, eternal destinies, and final judgments, human motivations and actions can indeed become intense and concerted. Thus the extraordinary character of some capacities of religion springs from the heart of religion's social ontology, the centrality of superhuman powers, and what people believe they can provide.

The demands of the practices that are believed to be required to access, please, or align with the superhuman powers in question can also produce the kinds of intense and steadfast activities mentioned above. This is particularly true of "behavior-regulating" practices. In religions, if one wants the help of superhuman powers, one must perform the practices that are prescribed as necessary and effective for doing so. Sometimes these practices are simple, even perfunctory, and many religious people shirk or take shortcuts in their performance. But in other cases, religions demand and manage to elicit impressive expressions of devotion, discipline, and surrender. These may take the form of piety, self-mortification, self-discipline in worldly matters, or something else. Religious behavior-regulating practices concern bringing ordinary behaviors in line with superhuman powers, often understood as living righteously and morally, fulfilling the will of a superhuman power, or upholding some version of what several religions call The Way (the Dao; in Shinto, "kannagara")—by adhering to the truths, commands, virtues, laws, or paths that religiously regulate behavior. At the heart of religiously prescribed behaviors often lies some kind of sacrifice, whether of possessions, such as animals or money, or of one's own self, such as one's pleasures, indolence, or willfulness. Sacrifice is a basic element of many religious practices—so basic that some scholars think it the most universal feature of religions.[23] I do not take a position on that question, but merely observe that sacrifice is one key religious practice among others that can, under the right conditions, take intense and extraordinary forms.

The capacity of superhuman powers to offer faithful religious practitioners help beyond ordinary human abilities can also serve to *relativize the negative* risks and consequences of faithful religious life and *heighten the positive* promised outcomes. Compare religious promises and threats to non-religious ones, those of the immanent, human world. In the latter, positive and negative consequences are normally modest. On occasion they can be momentous: one may gain or lose a job or a spouse or even one's life. At

23. See René Girard. 2011. *Sacrifice*. Lansing: Michigan State University Press; René Girard. 1989. *The Scapegoat*. Baltimore: Johns Hopkins University Press; Nancy Jay. 1994. *Throughout Your Generations Forever: Sacrifice, Religion, and Paternity*. Chicago: University of Chicago Press; Moshe Halbertal. 2015. *On Sacrifice*. Princeton: Princeton University Press.

the extremes, one may suffer excruciating tortures or luxurious gratifications, depending on one's fate and fortunes. But the threats of the immanent world are limited. The worst they can inflict is physical and emotional suffering, loss, and death. Humans can imagine fates worse than these—fates superhuman powers are often believed to control. One may suffer endless rebirths into an unbroken cycle of suffering and futility. One may be eternally embraced by an incomprehensibly loving God. One may have not just one's body broken but one's very soul compromised and damned.

The ancient Hebrew psalmist wrote that "Better is one day in your [God's] courts than a thousand elsewhere; I would rather be a doorkeeper in the house of my God than dwell in the tents of the wicked."[24] The Muslim Qur'an teaches:

> Did you think you would enter Heaven without Allah testing those of you who fought hard [in His cause] and remained steadfast? . . . Gardens of perpetual bliss they shall enter there, as well as the righteous among their fathers, their spouses, and their offspring; and angels shall enter unto them from every gate [declaring]: "Peace unto you for that ye persevered in patience! Now how excellent is the final home!"[25]

Jesus of Nazareth instructed, "Do not be afraid of those who kill the body but cannot kill the soul. Rather, be afraid of the One who can destroy both soul and body in hell" (Matthew 10:28). The Apostle Paul wrote to early Christian believers in Rome that, "I consider that our present sufferings are not worth comparing with the glory that will be revealed in us" (Romans 8:18). "If a man has not discovered something that he will die for, he isn't fit to live," preached the Baptist minister Martin Luther King, Jr.[26] The Tibetan Buddhist teacher Chogyal Namkhai Norbu writes, "All the visions that we see in our lifetime are like a big dream. . . . If we can finally liberate ourselves from the chains of emotions, attachments, and ego by this realization, we have the possibility of ultimately becoming enlightened."[27] Relativizing of the good and bad in life in this way, something many religions do, holds the potential to motivate extraordinary commitments and actions in this world that transcend what most people are willing to do in everyday life. The work of activists in the American civil rights movement of the 1950s and '60s,

---

24. Psalm 84:10.

25. Qur'an, sura 3:142, 13:23.

26. King. Speech at the Great March on Detroit. Cobo Hall. June 23, 1963.

27. Chogyal Namkhai Norbu. 2002. *Dream Yoga and the Practice of Natural Light*. Boston: Snow Lion. P. 49.

which was grounded in the black church, is but one case.[28] Other examples abound.[29]

The unique social ontology of religion thus involves particular features that under certain conditions can endow human commitments and actions with a depth, intensity, and tenacity normally not found in non-religious contexts—even when the means and processes by which religion inspires those actions are similar to those in non-religious contexts. Understanding more clearly when, why, how, and among whom these "extra" religious dynamics work is one of the tasks of the empirical study of religion.

I must immediately offer four caveats and clarifications. First, by repeating the phrase "under the right social conditions," I mean to suggest that religion's natural capacity to act as a distinctively powerful force must be understood as a result not simply of the work of the impressive will or genius (or pathology, as the case may be) of religious humans but of complex combinations of forces, usually both religious and non-religious. When religion becomes especially "strong" in human social life, religious factors are usually interacting with complexes of related influences, like those related to nationalism, ethnicity, politics, and social class.[30] I am *not* claiming that religion is routinely "used" as a "front" by cynical secular forces. Sometimes

28. Aldon Morris. 1986. *The Origins of the Civil Rights Movement*. New York: Free Press; Charles Marsh. 2006. *The Beloved Community*. New York: Basic Books.

29. For example, focusing only on religion, social movements, and politics, see: Kraig Beyerlein. Forthcoming. *Flooding the Desert: Faith-Based Mobilizing to Save Lives along the Arizona-Sonora Border*; Christian Smith. 1996. *Resisting Reagan*. Chicago: University of Chicago Press; Robert Woodberry. 2012. "The Missionary Roots of Liberal Democracy." *American Political Science Review*. 106: 244–274; Sharon Erickson Nepstad. 2008. *Religion and War Resistance in the Plowshares Movement*. Cambridge: Cambridge University Press; Smith. *Disruptive Religion*; Tristan Anne Borer. 1998. *Challenging the State: Churches as Political Actors in South Africa, 1980–1994*. Notre Dame, IN: University of Notre Dame Press; Christopher S. Queen. 1996. *Engaged Buddhism*. Albany: State University of New York Press; Michael Nojeim. 2004. *Gandhi and King*. Westport, CT: Praeger; Christophe Jaffrelot. 1998. *The Hindu Nationalist Movement in India*. New York: Columbia University Press; Gilles Kepel. 1993. *The Revenge of God*. State College: Pennsylvania State University Press; Martin Marty, R. Scott Appleby, Nancy Ammerman, Robert Frykenberg, Samuel Heilman, and James Piscatori (eds.). 1994. *Accounting for Fundamentalisms*. Chicago: University of Chicago Press; Lawrence Wright. 2007. *The Looming Tower: Al-Qaeda and the Road to 9/11*. New York: Vintage; Helene Slessarev-Jamir. 2011. *Prophetic Activism*. New York: NYU Press; Ziad Munson. 2009. *The Making of Pro-life Activists*. Chicago: University of Chicago Press; Rodney Stark. 2010. *God's Battalions*. New York: HarperOne; Michael Barkun. 1996. *Religion and the Racist Right*. Chapel Hill: University of North Carolina Press.

30. Gabriel Almond and R. Scott Appleby. 2003. *Strong Religion*. Chicago: University of Chicago Press; Monica Duffy Toft, Daniel Philpott, and Timothy Shah. 2011. *God's Century*. New York: Norton.

that occurs, but in the sort of cases to which I refer, an authentic religious dynamic is involved.

Second, the long arm of religion's causal influence in the world can reach well beyond the realm of explicitly religious spheres. Many secular ideals, institutions, and movements have religious origins, but became secularized over time. Some of the particular depth, intensity, and persistence generated by religion, as previously described, can "migrate" along with them in their move away from religion. So ideas and movements that are actually post-religious or quasi-religious can, under certain circumstances, residually embody aspects of religion's uniquely "strong" character. One example is twentieth-century Marxism, which, though explicitly anti-religious, was influenced by the deep cultural categories, exacting religious ethics, and utopian millenarianism of the faltering Western Christendom in which Marx lived. Marx embraced, secularized, and infused that utopianism with a moral passion that drove the intensity of many "strong" communist movements.[31] One can make a similar argument about the twentieth-century human rights movement.[32] This perspective requires us to take a long view of religion's influences, not merely focusing on a given point in time. This capacity of religion to shape the world, in ways well beyond its defining purposes and direct influence, must be kept in mind if we wish to understand religion's significance for society and history.

Third, I have emphasized unusual times when religion's causal influences stand out against the backdrop of normal social life. Not all of religion's significant causal effects happen in such extraordinary situations, however. Arguably most religious influences are modest. Sometimes religion only

31. Daniel Chirot observes: "In the modern world, the two most apocalyptic, millenarian, and fanatical new political ideologies of the twentieth century, namely Marxism and Fascism, came out of the Judeo-Christian world. . . . [Marx's] was a view of history that was quite similar to the Christian vision. In the beginning, said Marx, there was perfect equality and a strong sense of community, a kind of Garden of Eden. Then, with the coming of agrarian societies, there was the invention of private property, of social stratification, and of inequality and oppression. . . . Capitalism was making the situation even worse and destroying what was left of community and social solidarity by intensifying competition and greed. But then a prophet, Karl Marx, would come to show the way to a better future. Eventually, there would be a great battle between the forces of good and evil, a kind of apocalyptic Armageddon. The struggle would be won by the forces of good, that is, the Marxist socialists, and humanity would be saved" (*How Societies Change*. 2012. Los Angeles: Sage. Pp. 32, 90). Raymond Aron succinctly noted, "Marxism is a Christian heresy." Aron. 2002. *Le Marxisme de Marx*. Paris: Librairie Générale Française. P. 203. Also see Scott Montgomery and Daniel Chirot. 2015. *The Shape of the New*. Princeton: Princeton University Press. Pp. 101–103.

32. Hans Joas. 2013. *Sacredness of the Person*. Washington, DC: Georgetown University Press.

nudges human attitudes and behaviors to be a bit different from the norm. A great deal of "variables social science" demonstrates statistically significant differences between religious adherents and others, and often those differences are only moderately strong. Not all important causal influences operating in the world are spectacular. We must keep in perspective the fact that religion exerts significant causal influences in ordinary human social life even when its expression is not radical, heroic, "strong," fundamentalist, or violent.

Finally, religion sometimes fails to produce the kind of effects in the world that one might expect. Sometimes its moral demands are affirmed in speech but are accompanied with little action. Sometimes the clear implications of theological doctrines and imperatives are ignored. More than infrequently, the causal influences of non-religious interests and forces neutralize or override religious intentions and ideals. No force in human life is consistently causally efficacious, certainly not religion.[33] This is aided by the fact that humans can realize that their desired outcomes might be achieved through human means without the help of superhuman powers. Or religion's effects may be compromised by the uncertainty of people's belief in superhuman powers or their reliability, or by basic human distraction and weakness of will. So we must keep in mind the full range of religion's causal powers, from null effects to world-historic transformation.

Religion's Multiple Mechanisms of Causal Influence

Religious influences work through a variety of causal mechanisms, which differ in their immediacy, depth, and type of operation. The idea that religious teachings may shape people's ethical or devotional behaviors is not hard to imagine. But religion also influences the social world in other ways than that. To appreciate adequately the scope of religion's impact on human life and society, we need to broaden our vision of the diverse means by which religion exerts causal powers. Here I will briefly describe some of them.[34]

33. Mark Chaves. 2010. "Rain Dances in the Dry Season: Overcoming the Religious Congruency Fallacy." *Journal for the Scientific Study of Religion.* 49: 1–14.

34. In reality, the categories I distinguish often overlap with and reinforce each other; for instance, that Sikh men do not shave their beards is the result not only of their following religious teachings, but also of their being encouraged, essentially demanded, to avoid shaving by the social influence of intra-religious network ties.

Prescriptive Teachings. Perhaps the most obvious way that religion influences people and institutions, as I just mentioned, is by promulgating specific teachings that their practitioners follow. Jains believe in the doctrine of *ahiṃsā* (to cause no harm to any living being, except the lowest of plants) and so Jains go to great lengths to avoid killing even insects. Sikh men are taught not to shave their facial hair, and so they grow beards. Muslims are enjoined to fast during the daylight hours of Ramadan and so they do. Christian Science teaches that sickness, suffering, and pain have no objective reality, so their faithful eschew mainstream medicine. Amish tradition teaches not to use the modern technologies of "the English," such as automobiles and electricity, so they ride horses and buggies instead. The Reverend Sun Myung Moon's Family Federation for World Peace and Unification (aka, "Moonies") teaches that marriages blessed by their church provide a means of salvation, so the church repeatedly presides over mass-wedding ceremonies in which tens of thousands of Moonie Koreans and others marry. Hinduism prescribes the celebration of a variety of festivals, such as Holi, which involves huge bonfires, the playful splashing of bodies with brightly colored powders and water, and the temporary suspension of rigid norms of social hierarchy. Most Hindus celebrate instead of working on festival days. Such influences represent the fairly routine following of the ritual, social, and moral teachings and norms prescribed by religions. And that following in turn shapes the lifestyles, institutions, and cultures surrounding those religious practitioners, often both within their religious communities and beyond.

Social Influence of Network Ties. Besides following the formal teachings of their religions, religious practitioners are frequently swayed by the influences of the social network ties that their religious communities establish. One thing that can differentiate this type of influence from the one above is that the resulting behaviors or outcomes may not be formally promulgated by religious traditions. We know that social network ties exert powerful influences on people's thinking, desires, feelings, and behaviors generally, and certainly also take place in religious circles.[35] For example, as a result of hearing their preacher endorse a particular politician from the pulpit on Sunday, many members of a black Protestant church may go to the polls and vote for that politician the next Tuesday. Their denomination's formal teachings say nothing about voting for any particular politician, but the pas-

---

35. Nicholas Christakis and James Fowler. 2011. *Connected: The Surprising Power of Our Social Networks and How They Shape Our Lives.* Boston: Back Bay Books.

tor's social influence and authority over his flock can produce that outcome nonetheless. Similarly, families who join certain evangelical Protestant churches or traditionalist Catholic parishes in the United States may become interested in home-schooling their children—not because either of those traditions teach "Thou shalt home-school thy children," but because so many families in their new congregations home-school. The practice of home-schooling children in those churches is rooted in certain conservative religious sensibilities and values (again, even if the religions themselves do not officially advocate home-schooling and, in fact, might prefer another option, such as Catholic schools), so the inclination of new families to consider home-schooling is a specifically *religious effect*, albeit one operating through social influences instead of formal religious teachings.

Contextual Effects. Social network, historical, and institutional influences can all exert religious effects in other ways. One of them, too often ignored by scholars of religion, is through what sociologists call "contextual effects." The causal powers of religion in this case operate not through individual beliefs or face-to-face promptings, nor the ongoing influence of religiously founded social institutions. Rather, religion here shapes a larger social context at the level of an entire community or population of people, and the context then—through what critical realists call "downward causation" from the social to the personal levels—exerts causal influences on the people living within it. The formal religious properties of that larger social context exert an influence on the people in that community, doing so (and here is the key point) *independently of the religious characteristics of the people themselves*. That is, whatever the religiousness or religious affiliation of any given person in that context, the entire group is susceptible to the influences of the shared structural religious features of that collective environment. The religious causal mechanisms at work, in other words, operate on persons through the religious features of collectives, rather than directly through networks of individuals.

Two examples drawn from the United States aptly illustrate this type of religious influence. Research on regional differences in the United States (by yours truly and colleagues) has shown that, apart from the religious characteristics of the persons involved, a change in the character of one's religious environment can alter the intensity of one's religious practices. Specifically, moving to the American South has the causal effect of significantly *increasing* people's religiousness, independent of what religion they practice (after statistically controlling for the possible confounding effect of many other variables), whereas moving *out* of the American South to any other US region has the effect of *decreasing* people's religiousness.[36] We know that the American South is more religious by most measures than the rest of the country. But the point here is that just residing in a specific religious contextual environment can modify the intensity of people's religious practices, apart from their individual religious characteristics. Something about the religious ecology of the American South encourages people who move there to behave significantly *more* religiously than they did before they moved, regardless of their personal religion and how much they practiced it previously. Likewise, something about the religious ecology of other US regions tends to push people moving there from the South to behave significantly *less* religiously than they did when they lived in the South, independent of their personal religious characteristics. That means that even non-religious people who move to the American South are potentially susceptible to the region's religiousness-boosting effect. The key theoretical point here is that changes in people's religiousness are sometimes explained not by the traits of the individuals in question, but by the collective religious environments in which they live.

Other research on religious contextual effects has shown that US counties' population mortality rates—which tell us the likelihood of people dying at various ages—are significantly shaped by their religious composition.[37] Specifically, in US counties where mainline Protestants and Roman Catholics tend to predominate, mortality rates are lower than in counties dominated by conservative Protestants (statistically independent of relevant control variables). Again, religion's effect on mortality is not that members of various religious traditions display different mortality rates; it is about certain religious *contexts* shaping everyone living in them, whatever their individual religion. The religious influence, in other words, is *ecological*.[38] Comprehending the full range of ways that religion can influence

36. Christian Smith, David Sikkink, and Jason Bailey. 1998. "Devotion in Dixie and Beyond." *Journal for the Scientific Study of Religion*. 37: 494–506.

37. Troy Blanchard, Troy, John Bartkowski, Todd Matthews, and Kent Kerley. 2008. "Faith, Morality, and Mortality: The Ecological Impact of Religion on Population Health." *Social Forces*. 86: 1591–1620.

38. How does that contextual effect arise? The study hypothesized that the individualistic and other-worldly orientations of American conservative Protestantism dampen that tradition's commitment to public health, which negatively affects long-term investments into health institutions, such as hospitals, and thus produces demonstrably different outcomes in mortality. In comparison, mainline Protestantism and Catholicism put more emphasis on teachings about social justice and human development in this world, spurring greater investment in health institutions, which translates over time into lower county-level mortality rates.

human life (and death) requires taking into account contextual effects such as these.[39]

Social Service Programs. Religious communities make a massive impact on the world of a different nature through the countless organized religious social service programs that provide material resources and other forms of help to people. Of course, religious congregations and meetings of every religion are their own kinds of community organizations. But here I mean the organizations that go beyond churches, temples, and mosques. Such religious organizations can be local, regional, national, or worldwide in focus, ranging from neighborhood soup kitchens to global organizations, such as Catholic Relief Services and Buddhist Global Relief. Sometimes the programs are extensions of local religious groups (such as a neighborhood volunteer tutoring program), sometimes they are organized by religious associations or denominations (like Mennonite Central Committee and American Friends Service Committee), and sometimes they are independent, global non-profit groups (such as World Jewish Relief, Habitat for Humanity, Islamic Relief Worldwide, and American Hindu World Service).[40] Not only "progressive" but also traditional, religiously conservative groups run such social services.[41] The areas in which religious programs provide services are many, including education, food security, recreations, literacy, homelessness, job assistance, refugee housing, prison reform, computer skills training, crime watches, personal mentoring, clean water, racial and ethnic understanding, economic development, and emergency and crisis relief.[42]

The effects of such religious social service organizations are impossible to measure, but undoubtedly enormous. The amount of "social capital"

39. Examples of other studies demonstrating religious contextual effects include: Chaeyoon Lim and Carol Ann MacGregor. 2012. "Religion and Volunteering in Context." *American Sociological Review.* 77: 747–779; Francesca Borgonovi. 2008. "Divided We Stand, United We Fall." *American Sociological Review.* 73: 105–128; Tim Huijts and Gerbert Kraaykamp. 2011. "Religious Involvement, Religious Context, and Self-Assessed Health in Europe." *Journal of Health and Social Behavior.* 52: 91–106; Stijn Ruiter and Nan Dirk De Graaf. 2006. "National Context, Religiosity, and Volunteering." *American Sociological Review.* 71: 191–210.

40. Robert Wuthnow. 2010. *Boundless Faith.* Berkeley: University of California Press.

41. Including, for instance, Pentecostal and charismatic churches and denominations; Donald Miller and Tetsunao Yamamori. 2007. *Global Pentecostalism.* Berkeley: University of California Press.

42. Ram Cnaan and John DiIulio. 2002. *The Invisible Caring Hand.* New York: NYU Press; Stephanie Boddie and Ram Cnaan (eds.). *Faith-Based Social Services.* New York: Routledge; Ram A. Cnaan, Robert Wineburg, and Stephanie Boddie. 1999. *The Newer Deal.* New York: Columbia University Press.

involving "bridging" social network ties generated through these religious organizations' activities is immeasurably vast.[43] The total material value of resources distributed by such programs worldwide may exceed $100 billion each year. Just one Christian organization, World Vision International, operates with a budget of $2.8 billion, serving scores of millions of people in myriad ways in more than one hundred nations. For every one such big organization, there are thousands of modest ones around the world. One careful study of the collective "replacement value" of the social services provided by all Philadelphia-area religious congregations calculated the total dollar value as one-quarter of a billion dollars ($256,348,958).[44] Obviously Philadelphia is just one city. We cannot estimate the total value of all religious social service provisions in the world, but such services need to count among the ways that religion exerts causal influences.

Generating Social Capital. Religious influences in life and the world also appear in the form of "social capital." The social service programs that create social capital are only part of the picture. Social capital is related to social networks, also discussed above, yet its effects are distinct enough to merit its own discussion here. For present purposes we can think of social capital as *social relationships of trust and reciprocity.*[45] Social capital comes in different types. "Bonding" social capital refers to solidarity within and between groups made up of similar people, whereas "bridging" social capital concerns relational ties between groups that differ in important ways.[46] Like financial capital, social capital can grow or dwindle, depending on the character of the social ties and institutions that gave rise to it. Although it is intangible, social capital entails real causal powers capable of affecting a host of social outcomes, such as fostering greater civic engagement, community development, public health, social cooperation, democratic participation, public safety, and educational achievement.[47] Social capital is valu-

43. Heidi Unruh and Ronald Sider. 2005. *Saving Souls, Serving Society.* New York: Oxford University Press; Robert Wuthnow. 2004. *Saving America?* Princeton: Princeton University Press; but see Omar McRoberts. 2005. *Streets of Glory.* Chicago: University of Chicago Press.

44. Ram A. Cnaan, Stephanie Boddie, Charlene McGrew, and Jennifer Kang. 2006. *The Other Philadelphia Story.* Philadelphia: University of Pennsylvania Press. Pp. 98–100.

45. The relevant literature is vast, but for starters, see Robert Putnam. 2001. *Bowling Alone.* New York: Touchstone; Robert Putnam and Lewis Feldstein. 2004. *Better Together.* New York: Simon & Schuster; James Coleman. 1988. "Social Capital in the Creation of Human Capital." *American Journal of Sociology.* 94: s95–s120; John Field. 2008. *Social Capital.* London: Routledge.

46. Putnam. *Bowling Alone.* Pp. 22–24, 358–414.

47. David Halpern. 2005. *Social Capital.* Malden, MA: Polity. Social capital can also pro-

able because its positive effects enhance not so much individual interests but the common good, the welfare of the whole community.

Relevant for the present discussion is religion's immense capacity to generate social capital. The production of social capital is difficult to quantify; however, careful attempts to do so reveal religion's importance. According to Robert Putnam, for example,

> Faith communities in which people worship together are arguably the single most important repository of social capital in America. . . . Nearly half of all associational memberships in America are church related. . . . Churches provide an important incubator for civic skills, civic norms, community interests, and civic recruitment. . . . In sum, religious involvement is a crucial dimension of civic engagement.[48]

We should expect religion's capacity to cultivate social capital to operate similarly in other contexts, depending on the extent of religious practice and type of religious organizations involved. As with many of the other forms of religious causal influence discussed in this section, religion's generation of social capital does not operate through individual means, nor does it shape only those who are religious. Its effects are genuinely emergent, social, and ecological.

Religious Institutions Secularized. With at least partly religious motives, religious practitioners from previous generations established and built many social institutions that, over time, survive but lose their religious character. Thus there exist secularized religious institutions with significant roles in society that are no longer obviously religious. Those (now secular) social institutions exist for clearly *religious* reasons: It was *religious causes* that established and built them. Had religion not exerted causal influences in the past, those social institutions would not exist. And so such social institutions, many of them well known, are rightly considered the results of *religious* causal powers; their existence and influence in the present day are partly *religious effects*, even if the role of religion in creating them is no longer evident.[49]

---

duce less positive outcomes, such as criminal gang activity and the reproduction of socioeconomic inequalities (see, for example, Pierre Bourdieu and Jean-Claude Passeron. 1990. *Reproduction in Education, Society and Culture.* Thousand Oaks, CA: Sage; Putnam. *Bowling Alone.* Pp. 350–362).

48. Putnam. *Bowling Alone.* Pp. 66, 69. By "churches" here, Putnam really means religious congregations of all traditions, although most of them do happen to be Christian churches.

49. Critics may counter that those institutions would have been founded by secular actors

Many social institutions today exemplify this form of religious influence, even though many people are unaware of their religious origins. In the United States, countless people exercise and play sports at the YMCA, probably without knowing that it was founded and spread across many countries as the "Young Men's *Christian* Association" in 1844, as "a refuge of Bible study and prayer for young men seeking escape from the hazards of life on the streets."[50] Harvard, Yale, Princeton, Oxford, and Cambridge universities and most other non-government colleges and universities were founded as religious institutions of higher education, often with the express purpose of training young Christian men to become clergy.[51] The right of conscientious objection to military service, which is now an official part of the international human rights regime, was conceived and fought for by religious pacifists, particularly Mennonites and Quakers, during the modern era.[52] The International Committee of the Red Cross, whose mission statement today makes no reference to religion, was founded in 1863 in Geneva, Switzerland, by social service activists (Henry Dunant and Gustave Moynier) who were impelled by their devout Calvinist faith to alleviate suffering.[53] The American social reform movement, the model of organized activists advocating for social and political change in the United States, was first conceived and institutionalized by early nineteenth-century evangelical activists fighting vice and promoting temperance, abolition, and moral reform. The movement was later embraced by less religious activists for more secular causes (feminism, anti-war, civil rights, etc.).[54] When one pays attention to the origins of organizations, examples of this type of religious influence turn up far and wide.

Secular Transpositions of Religious Dispositions and Practices. Religion can shape the lives of even the most seemingly secular people in yet another

had their religious founders not established them first; but that argument is speculative, not empirical, and does not erase the fact that historically it was religious interests that founded them.

50. http://www.ymca.net/history/founding.html. The story is similar for the YWCA.

51. George Marsden. 1996. *The Soul of the American University*. New York: Oxford University Press.

52. UN Commission on Human Rights (March 8, 1995). http://www.ohchr.org/EN/ProfessionalInterest/Pages/CCPR.aspx; United Nations High Commissioner for Human Rights (April 22, 1998). http://www.refworld.org/cgi-bin/texis/vtx/rwmain?page=topic&tocid=4565c22523&toid=4565c25f2c9&docid=3b00f0d220&skip=0.

53. Caroline Moorehead. 1998. *Dunant's Dream*. New York: Carroll & Graf. P. 12; http://www.ifrc.org/en/who-we-are/history/; http://www.christianitytoday.com/history/2008/august/compassionate-in-war-christian-in-vision.html.

54. Michael Young. 2007. *Bearing Witness against Sin: The Evangelical Birth of the American Social Movement*. Chicago: University of Chicago Press.

way. A religion may promote particular dispositions and habits among practitioners, which over time become "transposed" into less overtly religious
expressions. The form and much of the content that was religiously generated is sustained, often with a zeal resembling that of religion, even while
some of the explicitly religious rationales fade. This type of influence parallels the secularized religious institutions described above, except it operates
not through institutions but through people's enduring, culturally formed
habits, mind-sets, and dispositions.

The classical sociological example of this form of causal influence is described in Max Weber's *The Protestant Ethic and the Spirit of Capitalism.*[55]
Modern capitalism, Weber suggested, was born in part of the (mostly secular) dispositions and practices of a strong work ethic, delayed gratification,
and the saving and reinvestment of financial assets. But these, Weber argued, originally arose out of the religious beliefs and motivations of Reformed Calvinists centuries earlier. They, for their part, developed these
habits because they were anxious to validate their predestined election to
salvation through the reassuring "outward signs" of material prosperity,
which required the practice of self-discipline and denial. The Calvinists'
original intentions were fundamentally religious, Weber pointed out, but
the cultural complex of bourgeois temperaments and routine behaviors to
which they gave rise eventually lost their religious motivations. The complex endured in form and expression with a quasi-religious moralism and
intensity—as reflected, for example, in Benjamin Franklin's teachings in
Poor Richard's Almanac. In this way, the story goes, some of the roots of
modern, secular capitalism lie in what were in fact religious beliefs, motivations, and practices.

More recently, Phil Gorski has advanced a similar argument about the
ways that Reformed Calvinist religious concerns with self-discipline were
over time transposed and harnessed by European political leaders for the
(secular) purpose of nation-building.[56] In which case, analogously, modern,
secular nation-states are the result in part of what were originally intensely
religious beliefs, dispositions, and practices. When we train ourselves to
recognize transpositions like these, we recognize that many of our non-
religious orientations and practices sprang at least in part from causal influences that were initially religious. For example, activists in modern, secular

---

55. Max Weber. 2002. *The Protestant Ethic and the Spirit of Capitalism.* New York: Penguin.

56. Philip Gorski. 2003. *The Disciplinary Revolution.* Chicago: University of Chicago Press.
On the role of British Methodism in the "making" of the English working class, see E. P. Thompson. 1963. *The Making of the English Working Class.* New York: Vintage.

American political and social movements plead for social change with rhetorical structures that are transposed versions of Puritan jeremiads.[57] The "simple living" earnestly sought by some modern environmentalists and countercultural hippies carries forward the ideal "Christian simple life" established by early American Puritans, Quakers, Anabaptists, and Pietists, and later passed on to our contemporaries through the quasi-religious Transcendentalists.[58] Contemporary evangelical Protestants help to reproduce their structurally racialized American society by transposing the individualistic "relationalism" with which they interact with God to be applied to the problem of "racial reconciliation."[59] Environmentally minded suburbanites treat curbside recycling with all the seriousness of moralistic Puritans.[60] In these and analogous ways, we see that religion still shapes (albeit indirectly) many realms of human life and society, far more than most moderns recognize.

Institutional Legal Codes. Another subtle way that religion exercises enduring causal powers over human life and society is through laws and regulations that were originally adopted thanks to the influence of earlier religious sensibilities, moral beliefs, and movements. Bodies of law in human societies generally reflect the mainstream moral and cultural sensibilities of the people they govern. Whether or not nation-states are formally religious, many adopted laws more or less obviously reflect certain religious values, assumptions, and ethics that undergird the society's larger culture. Oftentimes, the majority of a population continues to practice (or at least concedes legitimacy to) the religion(s) reflected in their society's legal codes. Other times, the majority of citizens are not as religious as their forebears. Yet legal codes rarely change as quickly as religious demographics and opinions; often a "lag" between laws and contemporary conditions sustains the intentions of earlier (more religious) authorities. As a result, seemingly secular societies can remain regulated by legal systems with deeply embedded religious influences, even if most contemporary citizens neither practice those religions nor are aware of their influences.

57. Sacvan Berkovitch. 1978. *The American Jeremiad.* Madison: University of Wisconsin Press; also see Berkovitch. 1975. *The Puritan Origins of the American Self.* New Haven, CT: Yale University Press.

58. David Shi. 1986. *In Search of the Simple Life.* Salt Lake City: Peregrine Books; David Shi. 2007. *The Simple Life.* Athens: University of Georgia Press.

59. Emerson and Smith. *Divided by Faith.*

60. David Brooks. 2001. *BoBos in Paradise.* New York: Simon & Schuster. Pp. 192–193, more generally 189–217.

Most societies present examples of this legalized form of religious influence. Because many religions are especially preoccupied with marriage, sexuality, fertility, gender relations, divorce, religious freedoms, and death, laws governing these realms are especially likely to have been shaped by religion. Very diverse laws and quasi-legal codes of various nations concerning who may marry, the rights of religious proselytization and conversion, access to legal abortion, the participation of women in public life, the conditions of lawful divorce, and so on are usually grounded, at least in part, in the religious traditions that have historically dominated or still dominate those countries. A moment's contemplation of the comparative law of the Taliban-ruled Afghanistan, post-Lutheran Sweden, and Hindu-saturated India makes this point clear.

Islam, for instance, strongly influences the laws of many Muslim societies, which is not surprising, given, among other factors, the fact that Islam draws no sharp boundaries between religion and government, mosque and state.[61] Although India is a formally secular state, Hinduism still holds significant sway over its laws and their applications.[62] Similar influences of religion on laws in many other countries are evident as well.[63] In the United States, numerous laws that were partly justified on religious grounds have been repealed.[64] Yet many laws with ultimately religious foundations continue to govern American life, including tax advantages for married filers, prohibitions of most forms of public nudity, restrictions in certain states and counties on the sale of alcohol on Sundays, tax exemptions for religious property and certain religious incomes, the near absolute right of parents to inculcate their children in whatever religion they choose, and

61. Frank Vogel. 2000. *Studies in Islamic Law and Society, Islamic Law and Legal System.* Leiden, Netherlands: Brill; Tim Lindsey and Kerstin Steiner (eds.). 2012. *Islam, Law and the State in Southeast Asia.* London: I.B. Tauris; Wael Hallaq. 2009. *An Introduction to Islamic Law.* Cambridge: Cambridge University Press.

62. Gerald Larson (ed.). 2001. *Religion and Personal Law in Secular India.* Bloomington: Indiana University Press; J. Duncan Derrett. 1999. *Religion, Law, and the State in India.* London: Oxford University Press; Timothy Lubin, Donald Davis, and Jayanth Krishnan (eds.). 2010. *Hinduism and Law.* Cambridge: Cambridge University Press.

63. For example, Merike Blofield. 2006. *The Politics of Moral Sin.* New York: Routledge; Rebecca French and Mark Nathan (eds.). 2014. *Buddhism and Law.* Cambridge: Cambridge University Press; Gideon Sapir, Daphne Barak-Erez, and Aharon Barak (eds.). 2013. *Israeli Constitutional Law in the Making.* Oxford: Hart Publishing.

64. Including the Prohibition laws of 1920, which were repealed in 1933; many (but not all) "blue laws" that restricted or banned certain commercial and recreational activities on Sundays; and laws enshrining only heterosexual marriage that are being replaced (as of this book's writing) by the legalization of same-sex marriage.

proscriptions against polyamorous and consenting adult-child sexual relationships. Whenever laws are on the books at least in part because of religious motivations, religion exerts influence on everyone governed by those laws, whether or not they recognize or like it.[65]

Direct Interventions by Religious Authorities. Religion can also affect the world through the direct public and private interventions of religious leaders in political, economic, military, and other affairs.[66] Religious leaders can exercise great influence in these spheres when the religious institutions they represent are powerful or when their personal moral authority is highly respected by the other actors involved, whether political authorities, masses of people, or other institutional leaders.[67] Famous examples of this kind of religious intervention spring readily to mind (figure 2.4). They include Mahatma Gandhi's non-violent confrontation of British colonial authorities in India and his leadership of the independence movement,[68] the Reverend Martin Luther King, Jr.'s vital role in the US black civil rights movement that produced major legislative and regulatory reform,[69] Jerry Falwell and Pat Robertson's mobilization of the US Christian Right starting in the late 1970s,[70] Pope John Paul II's key role in the fall of communism in the late 1980s and early 1990s,[71] the activism of religious leaders such as Desmond Tutu in the 1980s anti-apartheid movement in South Africa,[72] the Ayatollah Khomeini's decisive intervention in the Iranian Revolution of 1979,[73] the "Saffron Revolution" against the Burmese military regime led by Buddhist monks in 2007,[74] and the worldwide activism of the Buddhist Dalai Lama

---

65. Also see Paul Johnson and Robert Vanderbeck. 2014. *Law, Religion, and Homosexuality*. New York: Routledge; John Witte. 2006. *God's Joust, God's Justice*. Grand Rapids, MI: Eerdmans; John Witte and Frank Alexander (eds.). 2008. *Christianity and Law*. Cambridge: Cambridge University Press.

66. Scott Hibbard. 2010. *Religious Politics and Secular States*. Baltimore: Johns Hopkins University Press.

67. Anna Grzymala-Busse. 2015. *Nations Under God*. Princeton: Princeton University Press.

68. Mohandas Karamchand (Mahatma) Gandhi. 1993. *Gandhi: An Autobiography*. Boston: Beacon Press.

69. David Garrow. 2004. *Bearing the Cross*. New York: William Morrow.

70. Michael Lienesch. 1993. *Redeeming America*. Chapel Hill: University of North Carolina Press.

71. Jonathan Kwitny. 1997. *Man of the Century*. New York: Henry Holt; also see Eamon Duffy. 2011. *Ten Popes Who Shook the World*. New Haven, CT: Yale University Press.

72. Tristan Borer. 1998. *Challenging the State*. Notre Dame: University of Notre Dame Press.

73. Stephen Hughes. 2015. *The Rise of the Islamic Republic of Iran*. Denver, CO: Outskirts Press.

74. Benedict Rogers. 2008. "The Saffron Revolution." *Totalitarian Movements and Political Religions*. 9: 115–118; Kyaw Yin Hlaing. 2008. "Challenging the Authoritarian State: Buddhist Monks and Peaceful Protest in Burma." *Fletcher Forum of World Affairs*. 32: 125–144.

FIGURE 2.4. Polish Roman Catholic Pope John Paul II meets Polish military officer, Communist politician, and prime minister of the People's Republic of Poland General Wojciech Jaruzelski, June 17, 1983. News film footage showed Jaruzelski's knees shaking upon meeting the pope, whose moral authority with the Polish people and Catholic opposition to totalitarian political regimes helped bring the end of Communist rule in Poland in 1989. (Copyright: Henri Bureau/ Corbis/VCG via Getty Images)

against China's occupation of Tibet.[75] Similar lesser-known instances of such religious interventions are innumerable.[76]

Thinking typologically, we see that sometimes these religious influences take the form of public opposition and *protest*.[77] At other times, religious leaders play public roles as central *mediators* between contending

75. Daniel Goleman. 2015. *A Force for Good*. New York: Bantam.

76. For example, see Helen Hardacre. 1989. *Shinto and the State, 1868–1988*. Princeton: Princeton University Press. Pp. 123–124; John Faupel. 2011. *African Holocaust*. Whitefish, MT: Literary Licensing; Maura Shaw. 2003. *Thích Nhất Hạnh: Buddhism in Action*. Woodstock, VT: Skylight Paths; James Brockman. 2005. *Romero: A Life*. Maryknoll, NY: Orbis; Felix Bautista. 1998. *Cardinal Sin and the Miracle of Asia*. Manila: Reyes Publishing; Reinaldo Sapag. 2014. *El Cardenal Raúl Silva Henríquez y los Derechos Humanos*. Edición Digital; Eric Metaxas. 2007. *Amazing Grace*. New York: HarperOne; Laszlo Terray. 1997. *He Could Not Do Otherwise: Bishop Lajos Ordass, 1901–1978*. Grand Rapids, MI: Eerdmans; Charles Marsh. 2015. *Strange Glory: A Life of Dietrich Bonhoeffer*. New York: Vintage; Dean Stroud. 2013. *Preaching in Hitler's Shadow*. Grand Rapids, MI: Eerdmans; Dom Helder Camara with Francis McDonagh (ed.). 2009. *Dom Helder Camara*. Maryknoll, NY: Orbis Books.

77. Christian Smith. 1991. *The Emergence of Liberation Theology*. Chicago: University of Chicago Press; Smith. *Resisting Reagan*.

parties.[78] In certain cases, religious leaders confront situations they deem unacceptable by circumventing laws through *direct action* and *civil disobedience*.[79] In yet different conditions, religious leaders intervene in conflict situations as *neutral observers* of elections or peace-accord implementations,[80] or operate *covertly* in private negotiations over policy decisions.[81] Such interventions do not always succeed, and they can result in the religious leaders' deaths, whether intentionally[82] or not. But sometimes they do succeed. Activist religious leaders have even achieved world-historical influences over entire political regimes, societies, and empires. Interventions by religious leaders may not be the first kind of religious causal influence we think of, but it can be a potent method for promoting and preventing social change.

Deep Culture and Invisible Religion. The final form of religious influence I note here is best described as religion operating through "deep culture." Sometimes religion's effects are not immediately evident on the "surface" of life, culture, society, or discourse—but they are nevertheless powerful. That is because human cultures have a *depth* that is often more determinative than what is happening on the surface. So if we want to understand the big picture of religious (or other cultural) causal powers, over the *longue durée*,[83] we must plumb below the surface to examine the cultural currents operating at greater depths.[84] To use a marine analogy, the surface of ocean

78. Emelio Betances. 2007. *The Catholic Church and Power Politics in Latin America.* Lanham, MD: Rowman and Littlefield.

79. Beyerlein. *Flooding the Desert.*

80. For example, John Paul Lederach. 2010. "The Long Journey Back to Humanity." In Robert Schreiter, Scott Appleby, and Gerard Powers (eds.). *Peacebuilding.* Maryknoll, NY: Orbis. Pp. 23–55; David Little. 2007. "Men Who Walked the Streets." In David Little (ed.). *Peacemakers in Action.* Cambridge: Cambridge University Press. Pp. 53–96.

81. Kenneth Serbin. 2000. *Secret Dialogues: Church-State Relations, Torture, and Social Justice in Authoritarian Brazil.* Pittsburgh: University of Pittsburgh Press; Karrie Koesel. 2014. *Religion and Authoritarianism.* Cambridge: Cambridge University Press.

82. As with religious intervention protests of self-immolation, for example, when the Vietnamese Mahayana Buddhist monk Thích Quảng Đức burned himself to death while sitting in the lotus position in a busy Saigon road in 1963 to protest the persecution of Buddhists by the South Vietnamese government. Queen and King. *Engaged Buddhism.* P. 327; Sallie King. 2009. *Socially Engaged Buddhism.* Honolulu: University of Hawaii Press. Pp. 78–79.

83. I refer here to the French Annales School of history, which prioritizes the development and transformation of long-term historical structures over shorter-term events; see Fernand Braudel and Sarah Matthews. 1982. *On History.* Chicago: University of Chicago Press; Fernand Braudel and Richard Mayne. 1995. *A History of Civilizations.* New York: Penguin Books.

84. Most social scientists should be intuitively capable of thinking about culture as having *depth*, but critical realism is, I think, especially amenable to this image as a result of its belief in

water may be placid or it may be turbulent in a storm, depending on local conditions, and that difference would be notable to any observer. But at a deeper level, in a way hardly evident on the surface, a strong current may be sweeping the entire body of water to a completely different part of the globe, with major impacts on the climates of entire nations and continents.[85] That would be much more important than the state of the water's surface.

Likewise, over the long haul, human life and society are driven less by obvious current events and arguments—"this morning's news is this evening's recycling"—than by the forces of deep culture. By that concept I mean a culture's most basic categories, assumptions, beliefs, and intuitions. These are the primordial, enduring elements upon which all of the rest of culture and sometimes entire civilizations are built. Precisely because they are so deep, they often operate invisibly, unrecognized, taken for granted. But they are no less culturally powerful as a result.[86] They are simply *doxic*, the substrata of unreflective practical consciousness. And very often the elements of deep culture derive from religions, since most civilizations and societies were religious in their earliest days, however secular they may have subsequently become. Finally, despite being ordinarily unnoticed, deep culture is also often "sacred," in the Durkheimian sense[87]—such that we may not recognize its importance to us until it is contradicted or threatened, and thereby forced to the surface to be fiercely defended.[88]

"depth ontology" (as opposed to the "actualism" that dominates most social sciences) and its consequent appreciation for the complex, differentiated, and stratified nature of reality. It is possible to arrive at "deep culture" without critical realism, but the two fit together most coherently and elegantly within that school of thought.

85. I am here thinking of the Gulf Stream and North Atlantic Drift of the western and northern North Atlantic ocean, which are imperceptible to ordinary observers above, but are massively more powerful forces (the Gulf Stream runs between 800 and 1,200 meters deep, moving water at 30 million cubic meters per second past Florida, and increasing to 150 million cubic meters per second south of Newfoundland, Canada) than whatever is happening on the surface (calm, tempest, etc.), and which end up creating more temperate climates in what would otherwise be often frozen, nearly sub-arctic lands (Ireland, England, parts of Scotland and Scandinavia, etc.).

86. To use another metaphor, deep culture is like the unseen keel and rudder running below the waterline and guiding a ship this way and that.

87. Emile Durkheim. 1995. *Elementary Forms of the Religious Life*. New York: Free Press.

88. For example, as of the time of this writing, many western and central Europeans are struggling with the question of whether contemporary Europe should recognize and affirm its "Christian heritage" or insist on being simply "secular and liberal"—a question impressed upon European consciousness by the "threat" of a growing Muslim presence in Europe. See, for instance, Brent Nelsen and James Guth. 2015. *Religion and the Struggle for European Union*. Washington, DC: Georgetown University Press.

A few examples of differences in "deep culture" should help make the point. In some cultures, the cosmos is a marvelous order of meaning, relations, and purpose; while in others, the cosmos is aimless, impersonal, and empty. Such views do not change readily, but are normally entrenched, invisibly "obvious," and highly resilient. For some cultures, history is "going somewhere" by progressing through temporal stages to some appointed end; for others, history is an eternal cycle of futile repetition. Examples continue. In some cultures, nature is infused with spiritual beings and forces; in others, "the spiritual" does not exist. In certain cultures, humans are obviously not equal in most ways and so properly belong in a certain place within natural social hierarchies; in other cultures, the idea that all people are fundamentally equal, despite their apparent differences, is sacred. For some cultures, dogs are often family members and are treated with nearly as much sacredness as persons; in others, dogs are food.[89] For some, the physical world is chaotic, unpredictable, or illusory; for others, it is orderly, rational, and comprehensible. In certain cultures, one absolute truth must triumph over other false claims to truth, even if by force; in other cultures, truth claims are relative and considered suspect when asserted. These are the sorts of things I mean by "deep culture": any group's most fundamental assumptions, beliefs, and intuitions. I have set some out here in contrasting pairs to underscore how different elements of deep culture may be, and to suggest how obvious certain ideas may seem in one culture yet how inconceivable or repugnant they would be in another.

Taking a different approach to deep culture, consider how humans in various times and places conceive of reality through their most basic conceptual *categories*. Are the vast majority of people in a population peasants or citizens? Do humans occupy a natural cosmic hierarchy of being, or rather "socially construct" all of reality? Is the individual the most basic unit of society deserving of self-fulfillment, or an illusion needing to be "blown out" in nirvana and moksha toward cosmic unity with Brahman? Is human suffering "redemptive," or simply an unmitigated evil to be eliminated? Who or what has final authority in life: tribal elders or scripture or science or what? Is one's family an eternal center of belonging and kinship solidarity entailing life-long relations of respect, deference, and honor; or is family instead a launch pad for preparing autonomous individuals to leave it behind? Is slavery a normal part of society or a reprehensible moral evil? These are the kinds of categories and assumptions that comprise deep cul-

---

89. Hal Herzog. 2011. *Some We Love, Some We Hate, Some We Eat*. New York: Harper.

ture. At rare historical junctures, these questions may come up for debate and revision in cultures undergoing change. But at most points in history, the answers are settled and taken for granted.

How, then, does religion operate through deep culture to influence human life and societies? Answering this requires going beyond the standard social science narratives about religious influences and exercising some imagination, since deep culture is not normally reflectively considered. I offer two examples that I hope convey some sense of what I mean by the deep cultural influences of religion.

The caste system of social inequality in India—in which status, power, material wealth, and opportunity are stratified along the lines of caste (more properly, *varna* and *jāti*[90])—has proven extremely difficult to suppress, despite many legislative, social movement, and constitutional efforts in the post-colonial era to do so.[91] Articles of India's Constitution prohibit discrimination based on caste and declare "untouchability" to be illegal. A host of other laws, regulatory commissions, and affirmative action programs also attempt to undermine caste practices. Nevertheless, caste boundaries remain evident in disparities in ownership of wealth and land, access to jobs and housing, health and poverty status, mortality rates, and vulnerability to violence. One 2005 United Nations report found more than 165 million Dalits ("untouchables") continue to suffer segregation in housing, schools, and public services access in India; and counted 31,440 cases of violent acts against Dalits in 1996.

One factor contributing to the entrenched nature of the caste system of India is the way that until 1947, when India gained independence, British colonial rulers relied on caste as a central instrument of government and administration. But even a century of reinforcement of the caste system by

90. "Caste" is etymologically derived not from Indian languages but from the Portuguese word *casta*, meaning "race, lineage, breed," originally "pure or unmixed (stock or breed)," applied in India in the middle of the sixteenth century (Oxford English Dictionary, "caste," http://www .oed.com/view/Entry/28546?isAdvanced=false&result=1&rskey=gauzAq&). Indian languages contain no direct translations of "caste," making *varna* ("color") and *jāti* ("birth") the two closest Indian terms in functional meaning.

91. Nicholas Dirks. 2001. *Castes of Mind*. Princeton: Princeton University Press; Brian Smith. 1994. *Classifying the Universe*. New York: Oxford University Press; Susan Bayly. 2001. *Caste, Society and Politics in India*. Cambridge: Cambridge University Press; Mark Muesse. 2011. *The Hindu Traditions*. Minneapolis: Fortress Press; Louis Dumont. 1981. *Homo Hierarchicus*. Chicago: University of Chicago Press; Frank de Zwart. 2000. "The Logic of Affirmative Action." *Acta Sociologica*. 43: 235–249; Ian St. John. 2011. *The Making of the Raj*. Westport, CT: Praeger; http:// www.cbc.ca/news/world/un-report-slams-india-for-caste-discrimination-1.693195; http:// lawmin.nic.in/olwing/coi/coi-english/coi-indexenglish.htm.

the British cannot explain its seeming indestructability. British colonial rule was not beloved by Indians, and independence, now seven decades old, fueled many commitments to tear down its oppressive systems. More importantly, the practice of organizing society according to caste divisions long pre-dates the presence of the British in India. At least as far back as 1,500 BCE, early Vedic and Aryan tribes in the Indian subcontinent had established class divisions, prototypes of today's caste system. Most importantly for my point here, although social inequality in human societies is universal, the caste system that descended from these early tribes became rooted in and legitimated by sacred religious texts, especially the *Dharmaśāstras* and the *Laws of Manu* (composed 1–3 millennia BCE). The modern caste system ultimately embodies and ratifies a major tenet of one major interpretation of Indian, Hindu "deep culture": that people are not born equal but with innate differences according to how they lived in previous lives, outcomes that the unalterable force of *karma* determine. Everyone's place in life is therefore the consequence of their own previous actions, through reincarnation, so that present social inequalities are a just expression of cosmic moral order. To try to dismantle caste inequalities is thus to revolt in a futile and irrational way against the most basic forces of reality, inviting social chaos and destruction and disturbing the balance of cosmic order. Good and rational persons accept their present fate as deserved and seek to fulfill the obligations (*dharma*) of their caste, in order to try to improve their position in the next life, with the final goal of transcending this world and its endless cycles of reincarnation entirely. That is the force of deep culture at work.

Another example concerns the structure and ideology of European welfare states. In her book *Poverty and Eternity: How Religion Shapes Assistance to the Poor, from Early Church to Modern Welfare States*, Sigrun Kahl investigates the origins of striking cross-national variations in beliefs about the deservingness of the poor. She argues that European societies' varying responses to poverty depend on their dominant, long-term religious legacies. What modern governments do to help the poor, Kahl shows, actually depends on what early modern Catholics, Calvinists, and Lutherans believed about who was saved in the afterlife. Soteriology thus shaped social policy. How so? Sixteenth-century reformers institutionalized their beliefs in the form of programs to aid the poor, and these programs were later incorporated into and secularized by modern nation-states. Contemporary welfare regimes, in other words, which most people assume to be recent secular inventions, in fact have their origins in early modern religious reformations and the deep culture trajectories they generated.[92] Other illustrations of the often subtle ways that religion shapes social life and institutions through deep culture would include the fundamental assumptions that laid the groundwork for the rise of modern science,[93] the role of the Confucian tradition in ordering notions of authority, family, and even economic development in contemporary East and Southeast Asia,[94] the role of spirituality operating in the background of much of the modern environmentalist movement,[95] the invention of "the person" in the Christological doctrinal debates of the fourth century CE and its impact on the subsequent development of the notion of human dignity and rights,[96] and the ways ancient Catholic symbols resonated with and helped mobilize the Solidarity movement in Poland.[97]

Summary. The various forms of religion's causal powers in human life suggest an ironic situation. The irony is that some people today dismiss religion as an antiquated practice only marginally important for modern people and contemporary society, when, in reality, religion likely has many significant effects on and around those very people's lives, even though they do not recognize it.[98] Religion is far more influential in the world than most

92. Sigrun Kahl. Forthcoming. *Poverty and Eternity: How Religion Shapes Assistance to the Poor, from Early Church to Modern Welfare States*; also see Kahl. 2009. "Religious Doctrines and Poor Relief." In Kees van Kersbergen and Philip Manow (eds.). *Religion, Class Coalitions, and Welfare State Regimes*. Cambridge: Cambridge University Press. Pp. 267–295; Kahl. 2005. "The Religious Roots of Modern Poverty Policy." *European Journal of Sociology*. 46: 91–126.

93. Peter Harrison. 2001. *The Bible, Protestantism, and the Rise of Natural Science*. Cambridge: Cambridge University Press; Rodney Stark. 2003. *For the Glory of God*. Princeton: Princeton University Press.

94. For example, Cristobal Kay. "Why East Asia Overtook Latin America." 2002. *Third World Quarterly*. 23: 1073–1102; Lucian Pye. 1988. *Asian Power and Politics*. Cambridge, MA: Harvard University Press. Pp. 55–89; George De Vos and Walter Slote. 1998. *Confucianism and the Family*. Albany: State University of New York Press; Geert Hofstede and Michael Bond. 1988. "The Confucius Connection: From Cultural Roots to Economic Growth." *Organizational Dynamics*. 16: 6.

95. Justin Farrell. 2015. *The Battle for Yellowstone: Morality and the Sacred Roots of Environmental Conflict*. Princeton: Princeton University Press.

96. Joas. *Sacredness of the Person*; Samuel Moyn. 2015. *Christian Human Rights*. Philadelphia: University of Pennsylvania Press.

97. Maryjane Osa. 1996. "Pastoral Mobilization and Contention." In Smith. *Disruptive Religion*. Pp. 67–85.

98. A related irony is that when enough people, religious and otherwise, act under religious influences without realizing it, religion's causal power may obscure itself: People observe that religious and non-religious people are little different and conclude that religion has no effect on any of them. For example, if Hinduism animated everyone in an Indian village (Hindu and not Hindu alike) to participate in the celebration of the Hindu festival of Holi, Hinduism would be exerting a strong religious effect on all the celebrants; it would be nonsense to claim that there

people in the secularized West realize. That religion's impact goes unrecognized is partly because many people hold parochial and myopic perspectives on the matter of religious causal influences, and so fail to see the many and various levels, types, proximities, temporal horizons, and mechanisms of operation of religion's causal powers. By expanding our awareness of religion's wide-ranging causal capacities, we can better understand, analyze, and explain religion's importance in the world today.[99]

Religion's Multiple Directions of Influence— The Example of Engaged Buddhism

Religious causal effects in the human social world can move in many "directions," and not always those that we might look for based on what we know

---

was no religious influence on the grounds that non-Hindus were celebrating the same way as the Hindus. Just as religious practitioners can live lives not very shaped by their religious traditions, so non-religious people can be significantly shaped by the religion of their environments and social networks. If, at the height of the Protestant Establishment in the United States or the Victorian Age in England, most middle-class, non-religious people generally conformed to the dominant religious mores of their societies in order to be thought respectable, and so ended up not behaving much differently from their church-attending Protestant neighbors, the effect of being a church-attending Protestant may not be pronounced (or statistically significant if measured in a survey). But rather than concluding that religion had no effect, we should conclude that a strong religious effect operated: Religion was shaping both religious and non-religious people, so that the visibility of its effect was "swamped" by its own power.

99. Taking this analysis one step further, we might ask whether religion is not actually the basis of all human civilization. A growing number of scholarly experts on proto-human and early human social life representing various disciplines have recently suggested that religion is the basis upon which early human civilizations were built. Contrary to standard materialist and ecological accounts, these scholars argue that the founding of human civilizations did not give rise to religion as a secondary outcome, but instead that it was precisely early humans learning to practice religion that enabled and gave rise to workable human civilizations. By the emergence of human "civilizations," they generally mean the transition from humans living in small bands of mobile hunter-gatherers to founding the world's first settled village societies of farming and herding. Such a claim is somewhat extraneous to my central point here. But it seems worth considering on its own terms and, if it does have merit, it adds another layer to my larger argument, since, if this claim is true, then religion is "ontogenetically" an ultimate causal influence behind civilized human life, a developmental precondition of settled human societies. Here is not the place to unpack the case for this claim, but interested readers can pursue the question by reading Jacques Cauvin. 2007. *The Birth of the Gods and the Origins of Agriculture*. Cambridge: Cambridge University Press; Ara Norenzayan. 2013. *Big Gods*. Princeton: Princeton University Press; Ian Hodder. 2010. *Religion in the Emergence of Civilization*. Cambridge: Cambridge University Press. More broadly, see Colin Renfrew and Iain Morley (eds.). 2009. *Becoming Human*. Cambridge: Cambridge University Press; and Robert Bellah. 2011. *Religion in Human Evolution*. Cambridge: Belknap Press.

about the religious traditions. Religions can draw upon their native cultural resources to express themselves in a variety of outcomes and consequences. Casual observers, for instance, might suppose that (theologically) conservative Protestants will be conservative in all ways, politically and economically. But research shows that the views of conservative Protestants in the United States are more complicated than that; these Protestants sustain a capacity to apply their "moral cosmologies," rearrange their cultural "building blocks," and employ the tools in their "cultural toolkits" in various ways that can cause them, for example, to support more progressive economic policies than mainline Protestants.[100] Likewise, anyone familiar with the history of the Roman Catholic Church in Latin America up to the 1960s would have been confident that, with its long record of traditionalism, conservatism, alliances with elites, and anti-communism, it would remain conservative for a long time. However, in the late 1960s, 1970s, and 1980s, the Latin American Catholic Church (along with some Protestant collaborators) unexpectedly took a turn in progressive, leftist, and sometimes even pro-socialist directions with the emergence of "liberation theology" and activist "base ecclesial communities."[101] In retrospect, the reasons for that turn are explicable, but few standing on the cusp of those changes would have expected them.

One of the most interesting illustrations of religion's capacity for exercising its causal influences in multiple and, for some, unexpected directions is the movement of "Engaged Buddhism" that has emerged as a political force in much of the Buddhist world and somewhat in the West in recent decades.[102] Engaged Buddhism is a movement seeking to address situations of

---

100. Robert Robinson. 2009. "Two Approaches to Religion and Politics." *Journal for the Scientific Study of Religion*. 48: 650–69; Robert Robinson and Brian Starks. 2007. "Moral Cosmology, Religion, and Adult Values for Children." *Journal for the Scientific Study of Religion*. 46: 17–35; Stephen Hart. 1996. *What Does the Lord Require?* New Brunswick, NJ: Rutgers University Press; Christian Smith. 2000. *Christian America?* Berkeley: University of California Press.

101. See, for instance, Christian Smith. 1991. *The Emergence of Liberation Theology*. Chicago: University of Chicago Press; Madeleine Cousineau Adriance. 1995. *Promised Land*. Albany: State University of New York Press.

102. The following is based upon these works: Ian Harris (ed.). 2007. *Buddhism, Power, and Political Order*. New York: Routledge; Christopher Queen and Sallie King. 1996. *Engaged Buddhism*. Albany: State University of New York Press; Sallie King. 2009. *Socially Engaged Buddhism*. Honolulu: University of Hawaii Press; David Loy. 2003. *The Great Awakening*. Boston: Wisdom Publications; Ken Jones. 2003. *The New Social Face of Buddhism*. Boston: Wisdom Publications; Loretta Pyles. 2005. "Understanding the Engaged Buddhist Movement." *Critical Social Work*. 6(1); Damien Keown, Charles Prebish, and Christopher Queen (eds.). 2003. *Action Dharma*. New York: Routledge.

political, economic, social, and environmental suffering by drawing upon the resources of the Buddhist religious and philosophical traditions. This movement was first explicitly promoted by the Vietnamese Buddhist teacher Thích Nhất Hạnh, who coined the term "Engaged Buddhism" in his 1967 book, *Vietnam: Lotus in a Sea of Fire*.[103] After spending the early 1960s studying and teaching comparative religions in the United States, Hạnh returned to Vietnam in 1963 and, with the members of his Buddhist "sangha" (spiritual community) began working to extend the implications of their monastic meditation and mindful practices to alleviate the suffering around them caused by the Vietnam War. Hạnh and his fellow Engaged Buddhists considered such practical, this-worldly actions to be not at odds with their Buddhist beliefs and practices, but natural expressions of them. Years later, Hạnh summarized the teachings of Engaged Buddhism in "Fourteen Precepts," a somewhat abbreviated version of which instructs:

1. Do not be idolatrous about or bound to any doctrine, theory, or ideology, even Buddhist ones. Buddhist systems of thought are guiding means; they are not absolute truth.
2. Do not think the knowledge you presently possess is changeless, absolute truth. Avoid being narrow minded and bound to present views. Learn and practice nonattachment from views in order to be open to receive others' viewpoints. . . .
3. Do not force others . . . by any means whatsoever, to adopt your views. . . . Through compassionate dialogue, help others renounce fanaticism and narrow-mindedness.
4. Do not avoid suffering or close your eyes before suffering. Do not lose awareness of the existence of suffering in the life of the world. Find ways to be with those who are suffering. . . . Awaken yourself and others to the reality of suffering in the world.
5. Do not accumulate wealth while millions are hungry. Do not take as the aim of your life fame, profit, wealth, or sensual pleasure. Live simply and share time, energy, and material resources with those who are in need.
6. Do not maintain anger or hatred. Learn to penetrate and transform them when they are still seeds in your consciousness. . . .

---

103. Published in New York by Hill and Wang. Hạnh's own thinking about a Buddhism oriented toward this world was shaped in part by his admiration for a previous movement of "Humanistic Buddhism" promulgated by Buddhist reformers in China and Taiwan.

7. Do not lose yourself in dispersion and in your surroundings. Practice mindful breathing to come back to what is happening in the present moment. . . .

8. Do not utter words that can create discord and cause the community to break. Make every effort to reconcile and resolve all conflicts, however small.

9. Do not say untruthful things for the sake of personal interest or to impress people. . . . Always speak truthfully and constructively. . . . Have the courage to speak out about situations of injustice, even when doing so may threaten your own safety.

10. Do not use the Buddhist community for personal gain or profit, or transform your community into a political party. A religious community, however, should take a clear stand against oppression and injustice and should strive to change the situation without engaging in partisan conflicts.

11. Do not live with a vocation that is harmful to humans and nature. Do not invest in companies that deprive others of their chance to live. . . .

12. Do not kill. Do not let others kill. Find whatever means possible to protect life and prevent war.

13. Possess nothing that should belong to others. Respect the property of others, but prevent others from profiting from human suffering or the suffering of other species on Earth.

14. Do not mistreat your body. Learn to handle it with respect. Do not look on your body as only an instrument. Preserve vital energies (sexual, breath, spirit) for the realization of the Way.[104]

In recent decades, partly under the umbrella of the Engaged Buddhism movement, the Buddhist world has seen the rise of an activist and interventionist expression of Buddhism, especially in the political and environmental realms.[105] For instance, in the fall of 2007, Burmese (Myanmar) Buddhist monks—whose total number matches that of soldiers serving in the Burmese military—mobilized en masse to join the national protests against the military government's economic austerity policies and to support the opposition movement, the National League for Democracy.[106] The Alliance of

---

104. From Thích Nhất Hạnh. 1987. *Interbeing*. Berkeley: Parallax Press.

105. The nonviolent Engaged Buddhism movement is distinct from the sometimes violent nationalist Buddhist movements in Sri Lanka and Myanmar.

106. Rogers. "The Saffron Revolution."

All Burma Buddhist Monks condemned the military regime, an unprecedented act in Burmese history. The monks marched non-violently by the thousands in the streets, chanting sutras from the Pāli Canon (Theravadan Buddhist scriptures), and leading lay protesters. This uprising—dubbed the "Saffron Revolution," in reference to the color of the monks' robes—failed to overturn the government, and in fact suffered repression at the hands of the state (figure 2.5).[107] This awakening of the Buddhist sangha to protest economic and political suffering reflected a particular (and what to many Westerners seemed to be a new) face of Buddhism. Along similar lines, many Buddhists have recently entered public life in visible and decisive ways, through political organizing, protests and demonstrations, environmental activism, and work in social services, public health, and community organizing in Tibet, Thailand, Cambodia, Vietnam, India, Japan, Sri Lanka, and beyond. Sallie King, a scholar of Engaged Buddhism, describes it as:

> a large and powerful movement throughout Buddhist Asia . . . a vehicle capable of giving voice to the people's political aspirations and bringing down national governments. It became a path of psychological and practical liberation to oppressed peoples and of the economic development of impoverished peoples. . . . [It] engages actively yet nonviolently with the social, economic, political, and ecological problems of society. At its best, this engagement is not separate from Buddhist spirituality, but is very much an expression of it.[108]

But why does Engaged Buddhism seem so curious? Do not many religions engage in social service and sometimes political involvement for the larger good? The issue here concerns the multiple and sometimes unexpected directions of religious causal influences. Engaged Buddhism exemplifies this point because, first, most Westerners for at least a century would have considered that term an oxymoron; and, second, some Buddhists do teach and practice a more "other-worldly" version of Buddhism. In reality, "the Buddhist tradition" and its history are so vast, varied, and evolving it is impossible to generalize about it in any way—one wonders if anything holds "Buddhism" together other than a common reference to the Buddha.[109] But that is precisely the point here: Buddhism can, has, and does express itself

107. Paul Rowe. 2012. *Religion and Global Politics.* New York: Oxford University Press. Pp. 165–166.

108. King. *Socially Engaged Buddhism.* P. 1.

109. See Thomas Tweed. 2000. *The American Encounter with Buddhism, 1844–1912.* Chapel Hill: University of North Carolina Press; David McMahan. 2008. *The Making of Buddhist Mod-*

FIGURE 2.5. Buddhist monks in the "Saffron Revolution" lead a street protest against the military government in Yangon, Myanmar, September 24, 2007. About 100,000 anti-government protesters led by a phalanx of Buddhist monks marched in the largest crowd to demonstrate in Myanmar's biggest city since a 1988 pro-democracy uprising that was brutally crushed by the military. (AP photo)

in many kinds of directions, including some that are unexpected, given certain interpretations.

Consider first an other-worldly version of Buddhism. Some Buddhist communities, teachings, and practices interpret their tradition in a way that largely disengages them from worldly concerns. This is the version of Buddhism that has especially impressed itself upon the Western imagination. According to this version, Buddhism is about *disengaging* from the worries and needs of this material world to focus on individual enlightenment. This understanding of Buddhism teaches that the apparent individuality of souls and material entities are delusions, false perceptions of reality. Suffering (*dukkha*) itself is caused by incessant human striving after desires, pleasures, and self-affirmation, which produce anxiety, stress, and disappointments. Through enlightenment and devotion we may come to see that true happiness is achieved by letting go of our desires, struggles, and egos. Release from the futility and suffering of endless rebirths in this world is achieved in nirvana, the "blowing out" of the individual self for absorption into the Absolute, which is totally beyond and unlike anything in this world.

---

ernism. New York: Oxford University Press, among other works stressing the pluralism within and recurrent reinterpretation of Buddhism especially in the West.

In this interpretation, Buddhism is therefore an "other-worldly" or a "world-denying" religion. Its goal is not to repair or save what is lost or broken in this world—as is the case in, say, much of Judaism and Christianity—but rather to see beyond, to dissolve the illusions of, and finally to transcend and escape this world. What is required is not the salvation of humanity or society or history, but personal enlightenment. For such reasons, Max Weber famously described Buddhism as an "anti-political status religion, more precisely, a religious 'technology' of wandering and of intellectually schooled mendicant monks" for whom "the most radical form of salvation-striving conceivable . . . is a solely personal act of a single individual."[110] Many other scholars have assessed the political and social implications of Buddhism similarly.[111] This view of Buddhism is not absolutely false. Some Buddhists have opposed Engaged Buddhism as too this-worldly because they subscribe to something like it. But the above is only one interpretation or expression of Buddhism, not a representation of its "essence," and so as a general account is inadequate.

Consider next Engaged Buddhism, which insists that its very this-worldly service and activism are not aberrations but rather spring directly from Buddhist teachings. How can that square with the "Weberian" version of Buddhism just described? To do so, we need to take seriously the "multivocality" and "polysemy" of religious traditions, and the "loose coupling" they afford between a religion's beliefs and their potential social, political, and economic implications. Multivocal means having the capacity to speak in "many voices." Polysemy means possessing "many meanings." Most religious traditions that endure over long periods of time involve collections of ideas and narratives—scriptures, myths, histories, proverbs, heroes, interpretive corpuses, prayer books, etc.—that are rich, complex, and flexible. Among other things, this helps those religions adapt to changing conditions and provides maximum flexibility in making religious attributions (chapter 3) to make sense of life's difficulties. Religions whose traditions' resources are instead thin and rigid may thrive for a time but struggle to adapt to environmental change and to interpret through attributions the work of superhuman powers, and eventually die out. Those conditions that help some religions to adapt and prosper in the face of environmental change—richness, complexity, and flexibility—are precisely those that entail multivocality and polysemy. They can enable the same religious tradition to exhibit

110. Max Weber. 1958. *The Religion of India*. New York: Free Press. P. 206.
111. See Queen. *Engaged Buddhism*. Pp. 17–18.

certain other-worldly orientations, for instance, while under other conditions to engage instead in this-worldly activities. Thus the "coupling" between the beliefs of a religious tradition and their possible social, political, and economic implications can be "loose."

How does this work for Engaged Buddhism? I cannot delineate all possible ways that Buddhist multivocality and polysemy might enable an Engaged Buddhism, so I will focus on one aspect of Buddhist teachings that works to that effect. Buddhism in many of its forms is broadly interpreted as fundamentally anti-dualist, teaching that the distinction between ego and other, to take one example, is a delusion. Nobody possesses a distinct entitive self, an eternal soul, a bounded personhood with substantial continuity through time and space. The separate ego is a chimera. Our persistent belief in the human self is deluded. This is one common interpretation of the Buddhist doctrine of "anatman," or "no-self." Not only in the final end, but even now, everything is changing, shifting in form, slipping away. To try to preserve ourselves is an impossibility that only brings *dukkha*: suffering, disappointment, and frustration. Liberation from the clinging to self and the futility of striving requires an abandonment of self, indeed, a rejection and transcendence of the dualisms of self and other, subject and object, ego and alter. It demands embracing the truth that all being is ultimately one.

What are the implications of this understanding of Buddhist beliefs for social, political, and economic life in this world? Religion's multivocality and polysemy tell us that there is more than one possible set of implications. In the "Weberian" version of Buddhism, the implications are world-rejecting, apolitical, other-worldly. If one considers all of the distinctions perceived in this world to be illusions, and if our only good end as humans is release from the suffering of this life through the blowing out of our apparent individual selves, then logically, one should turn away from seeking political and economic improvement in this world and devote oneself to personal enlightenment, good karma, and nirvana. That is one common interpretation of Buddhist social ethics, which leads in a particular implicational "direction."

But Engaged Buddhism shows us that the very same ideas in the very same religious tradition can be reinterpreted in a way that instead very much attends to the good of society here and now.[112] How so? Engaged Buddhists say that the *fundamental non-duality* of all reality means not that I as an individual should escape this world as soon as possible, but that what

112. Loy. *The Great Awakening.*

I take to be myself is fundamentally one with all other human selves and all other beings, both in ultimate reality and in this life. Thích Nhất Hạnh called this "interbeing."[113] Therefore, the true good of any one person is finally identical with the true good of all other humans and all creatures. And since I am not an ego opposed to others, subject to the conflicts that arise from competing interests of contrasting selves, I am free to seek the true good of all humans without fear and need for self-protection. Through such a "self-less universalism," every enlightened person is thus liberated not only for themselves but to help others realize their true good of enlightenment, liberation, and right vision. And in fact there is, with the light of the truth, nothing to lose, only much for all to gain. Furthermore—and here is introduced one element that seems largely absent from traditional Buddhist teachings of most interpretations—we in the modern world now realize that all that Buddhism takes to be evil and delusional (striving, greed, anger, malice, etc.) not only arises in misguided individual persons but has also become *institutionalized* in political systems, economies, military regimes, and environmentally destructive processes. For this reason, overcoming *dukkha* and pursuing right Buddhist living requires more than personal transformation: it also means actively confronting and overcoming those immoral and delusion-perpetuating institutions. Finally, because the Engaged Buddhist understands the non-duality of being, he or she can confront those evil institutions without taking sides, harboring ill will, or seeking revenge, which is always debilitating. Who is guilty, to blame, and deserving punishment simply does not matter. The point is not to vanquish one's enemies, but to respond non-violently to the suffering of all, wherever suffering is found and whatever caused it, to help all people to "awaken together," to shed our destructive illusions, and to move toward our final destiny of absolute oneness.

In this way, the very same Buddhist doctrine of the fundamental non-duality of reality can produce a Buddhism that is involved in the world as well as one that is world-rejecting.[114] Max Weber was a master at describing the worldviews of various religious traditions and explaining their social,

---

113. Hạnh. 1987. *Interbeing.* Berkeley: Parallax Press.

114. The question of why Buddhism is at times expressed in one (other-worldly) form and other times in another (engaged) form is an important but separate issue. The general answer is that particular configurations of complex social, political, and economic conditions will tend to give rise to different expressions of the same religious tradition. How and why religious traditions in particular cases end up moving in different directions in the expression of their causal powers is one of the crucial questions that the social sciences exist to explain.

political, economic, and military consequences. But his approach sometimes failed to appreciate the ways that conceptual nuances, ambiguities,
and complexities in religious belief systems can offer many meanings. Were
he alive today, Weber would no doubt be amazed and fascinated and enlightened by Engaged Buddhism.

Religion as Social Control

One of religion's crucial causal powers that operates commonly in human
social life is the exercise of social control. This means that religions have
the capacity to regulate the thoughts and behaviors of persons and groups
in ways that produce their compliance with and sometimes support for the
norms and laws of specific cultures and subcultures. Social control can be
formal or informal, sanctioned positively or negatively, and internally
regulated or externally imposed. A requirement for the maintenance of
any social order, social control is ubiquitously deployed by persons, institutions, and states to produce agreement and conformity with certain desired outcomes. Interpersonally, people routinely influence others—
whether consciously or not—through various mechanisms of social
control in order to get the others to think and behave as they want them
to. Social institutions and governments do the same, as they are able. People also often work to control themselves, to think the kinds of thoughts
and perform the kinds of behaviors that they desire. Religion is one
important means by which humans exercise such control over themselves
and each other. Religion involves power and access to superhuman
powers. And given that humans routinely organize their social institutions
in ways that involve status hierarchies, control, and exclusion, it often
happens that—no matter how egalitarian or ethically correct their official
teachings are, and whatever other good they may do—religions often
engage in subtle and obvious forms of silencing, disempowerment, and
marginalization.

Religion's capacities to provide leverage for social control are many. Recall that one of Martin Riesebrodt's four major categories of religious practices was *behavior-regulating practices*, which "pertain to the religious reshaping of everyday life with respect to superhuman powers." These, he
said, "concern the avoidance of sanctions or the accumulation of merits."[115]
Thus, one major kind of practice that religious people perform to access the

115. Riesebrodt. *Promise of Salvation.* P. 76.

help of superhuman powers directly involves the regulation of behavior, that is, the exercise of social control. The promise of help from superhuman powers is related to the performance of practices that promote social control, usually of oneself but sometimes also of others.

The motivation behind these forms of social control is not merely group pressure but the desire to make religious practices effective. That raises the stakes, since most superhuman powers have the ability to monitor and reward (or punish) fidelity to behavioral regulations more closely and accurately than do other humans. It is harder to fool an all-knowing deity, or one not limited by physical and spatial barriers, than it is to fool ordinary humans, so religious social controls can be more consistently effective. That, combined with the fact that people are engaging in religious practices in the first place because they do not feel sufficient control over things like the blessings and misfortunes at stake, often affords religion immense powers of social control.

Sociologists and political scientists have long noted that the costs of controlling populations by force is much higher—usually unsustainably so over time—than the costs of fostering internalized social control, setting agendas, and issuing implicit threats of punishment for non-conformity. "Internalized social control" makes those being controlled the agents of their own regulation; their own beliefs and commitments inspire them to conform voluntarily. Agenda-setting means limiting the very assumptions and terms by which people tend to think about issues of concern, so that they are often unable to frame or advance rival approaches successfully. And implicitly issuing threats to deter non-conformity relies on people's shared tacit understandings of the punishment and perhaps violence that would be inflicted for breaking the rules, which usually produces sufficient amounts of conformity that no such force proves necessary. Only in unusual circumstances—such as institutionally sponsored doctrinal inquisitions or religious wars—does religion use overt force to exercise social control.

Religion's most potent tools for facilitating social control are not force and violence, however, but internalization, agenda-setting, and admonitions about the costs of disobedience. Religious practitioners are usually internally motivated to think and behave in certain ways; have had their moral and intellectual horizons formed by the cultural worldviews and ways of life that belong to their religions; and understand without testing the boundaries the negative consequences of thinking and behaving incorrectly, in ways that conflict with group norms. This is one of religion's "comparative advantages" over other, more overtly force-based institutions of social control, such as the military, police, and judicial system.[116]

Furthermore, nearly all of the emergent causal powers that religion often generates readily lend themselves to the exercise of social control, not only those (capacities 13 to 15, as listed above) that are explicitly about social control. Personal, group, and social identity, for example, all involve a sense of association with some social group, the community of religious practitioners and their religious tradition. That kind of identification often touches people's senses of self so deeply that it entails strong motivations to show conformity and obedience. The same is true of community belonging and social solidarity. Moreover, the giving and receiving of social support in religious settings creates ties of reciprocal benefit, gratitude, and obligation that generate opportunities for the parties involved to exercise social control over each other, however subtly and benevolently that may occur.

Likewise, the moral orders, cosmic and life meanings, and theodicies that religion is expert at providing offer ample material by which to construct the directives and motivations required to exercise social control. In addition, religion's capacity to provide legitimacy to institutions and governments also easily reinforces their ability to exercise social control over the people whose lives they shape. It is true, as I noted above, that religion can legitimize dissent against institutions and governments believed to be unjust. But various forms of social control operate even in protest movements, since it is impossible to carry out a simple demonstration, much less a revolution, without coordination, compliance, and conformity to the views and needs of the dissenting cause.

Concrete examples of religion's involvement in social control should immediately spring to mind, so I will not belabor the point.[117] This is also not the place to elaborate a full-blown theory of religion and social control.[118]

116. See Dominic Johnson. 2016. *God Is Watching You.* New York: Oxford University Press.

117. In the literature, however, see, for example, Stephen King. 2007. *Reggae, Rastafari, and the Rhetoric of Social Control.* Jackson: University of Mississippi Press; Gordon C. Zahn. 1988. *German Catholics and Hitler's Wars.* Notre Dame: University of Notre Dame Press; Mordechai Rozin. 1999. *The Rich and the Poor.* Sussex, UK: Sussex Academic Press; Austin J. Shelton. 1971. *The Igbo-igala Borderland.* Albany: State University of New York Press; Aaron Menikoff. 2014. *Politics and Piety.* Eugene, OR: Pickwick Publications; Dominic Bryan. 2000. *Orange Parades.* London: Pluto Press.

118. But see, relying on a different framework, Rodney Stark and William Sims Bainbridge. 1997. *Religion, Deviance, and Social Control.* New York: Routledge.

For present purposes suffice it to note that religion's exercise of social control through various processes is pervasive in human society, and that religion's unique social ontology—its interest in accessing the help of superhuman powers—can endow its methods of social control with great power.

Finally, we should observe that religion's capacities for social control are neither always pernicious nor always commendable. Members of liberal, individualistic societies tend to assume that social control per se is bad because it coerces people to do things they do not want to do. Sometimes that is true. Not all social control is coercive, however, since some of it takes the form of mere influence. Furthermore, in some situations, social control encourages people to do what their "best selves" really want to do; it assists them in realizing their desired ends. Moreover, social control can produce results that most people judge to be not pernicious but good and necessary, even when the socially controlled persons wish to behave otherwise. For instance, most of us are likely happy when society's forces of social control—including religious influences—help to restrain the anti-social and destructive tendencies of thieves, rapists, murderers, thugs, white-collar criminals, corrupt government officials, and other social deviants and offenders. The point is simply that, even if some kinds of social control are coercive in problematic ways, not all are.

Religion's "Dark Side"

I have tried in this book so far to provide a variety of examples of religion's impact in the world that most people consider both positive and negative. Religion clearly can produce good things and bad. That includes its role in the exercise of social control, as I just said. But it is worth mentioning a further note about the bad side of religion and the related "politics" of its study before closing this chapter. Much of twentieth-century social sciences—influenced by the skeptical Enlightenment and later critical thinkers like Marx and Freud—viewed religion as irrational if not pathological. Much research on religion presumed it to be naturally aligned with intolerance, neurosis, "the authoritarian personality," psychological dependence, and other morbid traits. That tendency continues in academia.

But in the United States, a subset of social scientists turned in a different direction in the latter part of the twentieth century. For three reasons, I think—because the United States is itself a more religion-friendly country, because well-endowed foundations congenial to religion funded research, and because American social science is rather more empiricist than that across the Atlantic—there was something of a pendulum swing away from the traditional anti-religious bias in parts of the social scientific study of religion. The decades spanning the 1980s through the 2010s have thus witnessed burgeoning research showing religion's positive influences: reducing risky behaviors among adolescents, building social capital, promoting physical healing, facilitating democracy, reducing mortality, advancing positive psychology and happiness, creating deep cultural conditions propitious for the scientific revolution, and a host of other personal and social goods.[119] One signpost of that shifting perspective was this observation made by Rodney Stark and Roger Finke in 2000:

> Unabashed village atheism no longer passes for scholarship. . . . Ironically, the most important factor in creating a truly scientific study of religion was the growing participation in it of persons of faith. . . . Men and women of deep religious commitment, they also had been well trained in research methods, most had attended leading graduate schools, and all were extremely concerned to obtain unbiased results. . . . It now is impossible to do credible work in the social scientific study of religion based on the assumption that religiousness is a sign of stupidity, neurosis, poverty, ignorance, or false consciousness, or represents a flight from modernity.[120]

This pendulum swing has not gone uncriticized; some American scholars view it as rather Pollyannaish.[121] But on the whole, it seems to me that social science in the United States has come to a more balanced view of religion.

But balance does not and must not mean naiveté or favoritism. Although we must set aside personal and academic prejudices that obscure religion's positive (as most people see things) role in human life, we must also study and explain religion's dark side. Religion's ordinary and extraordinary causal powers have been and continue to be put to use for ends that are malevolent

119. Smilde and May. "Causality, Normativity, and Diversity."

120. Stark and Finke. *Acts of Faith*. Pp. 14, 15, 17, 18.

121. For example, David Smilde and Matthew May. 2010. "The Emerging Strong Program in the Sociology of Religion." University of Georgia, Department of Sociology. SSRC Working Paper (February 8). http://blogs.ssrc.org/tif/wp-content/uploads/2010/02/Emerging-Strong-Program-TIF.pdf; see the views of Darren Sherkat in Scott Jaschik. 2010. "Sociologists Get Religion." *Inside Higher Ed*. February 9. https://www.insidehighered.com/news/2010/02/09/soc.

and destructive. Genocide, slavery, economic exploitation, pogroms, human sacrifice, crusades, colonial occupation, the oppression and silencing of women, massacres, book burning, child sexual exploitation, torture, social exclusion, the dehumanization of deviants, forced religious conversions, wars, financial malfeasance, caste oppression, witch hunts, fear mongering, sexual mutilation, discouragement of education, emotional exploitation, empire-building, demagoguery, censorship, exterminations, crushing taxations, forced confessions of guilt, environmental exploitation, resistance to scientific advances, twisted inquisitions, sadism, sanctimony, deceptions, hypocrisy, manipulation, and much more have all recurrently been instigated, justified, and aided by the causal powers of religion. That is of course not the whole story—non-religious ideas, institutions, and movements have also engaged in all of the above—but it is an important fact. By now we should have learned that religion is multifaceted and capable of producing many kinds of effects—impressive, good, neutral, problematic, sinister, and horrific. Not prejudice but empirical facts, in dialogue with normative discussions about human goods, should determine our understanding of religion.

Recent "New Atheist" critics of religion are often sadly ignorant about their object of critique,[122] but their works contain enough kernels of truth to have hit a nerve among many people recently. Scholars of religion today who downplay religion's dark side face the same peril as those who made it the dominant framework of understanding for most of the last century. The goal of science is not to describe the world as we wish it would be, but, critical realism tells us, to ascertain as best as is humanly possible the *truth*

---

122. As Eagleton rightly castigated Richard Dawkins, for example, "Imagine someone holding forth on biology whose only knowledge of the subject is the *Book of British Birds*, and you have a rough idea of what it feels like to read Richard Dawkins on theology. Card-carrying rationalists like Dawkins, who is the nearest thing to a professional atheist we have had since Bertrand Russell, are in one sense the least well-equipped to understand what they castigate, since they don't believe there is anything there to be understood, or at least anything worth understanding. This is why they invariably come up with vulgar caricatures of religious faith that would make a first-year theology student wince. The more they detest religion, the more ill-informed their criticisms of it tend to be. If they were asked to pass judgment on phenomenology or the geopolitics of South Asia, they would no doubt bone up on the question as assiduously as they could. When it comes to theology, however, any shoddy old travesty will pass muster." Terry Eagleton. 2006. "Lunging, Flailing, Mispunching." *London Review of Books*. 28(20): 32–34; David G. Myers. 2008. *A Friendly Letter to Skeptics and Atheists*. San Francisco: Jossey-Bass.

about what is real and how it works. Toward this end, in the academic study of religion, we must be guided by the recognition of complexity, fair case selection, empirical honesty, and balanced, fair-minded judgments, however good or bad religion comes out looking in the end.[123]

This reinforces a point that I made in the previous chapter: that this book's theory just as readily informs critical empirical scholarship of religion as it does more establishment-oriented and (purportedly) objective research. Critical realism tells us to practice science in the service of knowledge of the truth about reality, as best as we can (fallibly) understand it, and not in the service of ideology or narrow self-interests. That basic charge immediately tethers science to a *moral* commitment: to learning and speaking the truth. The modern divorce of fact and value is thus overturned.[124] Furthermore, when good social science shares (its best account of) truthful knowledge in a world full of ideology, (self-)deception, misrepresentation, manipulation, exploitation, and lies, the basic scientific "findings" themselves are inherently critical. Some interested group or ideology says X, for example, but the best social science shows Y, so we have good reason to believe that X is wrong. That is criticism. Again, with critical realism, facts and values are reconnected (though not merged) in interesting and important ways. This is relevant to religion's capacities for social control and to its dark side. Social science in no way intends to undermine, discredit, or destroy religion. But insofar as religion exerts powerful and sometimes deeply problematic forces of social control and does have a dark side, the social sciences are best positioned, through empirical research, to illuminate and explain them (which may turn out to be beneficial to religion in the long run). Thus, while at first glance my theory of religion may seem biased toward religious traditions, prescriptions, and authorities, in fact it is well suited also to inform critical empirical research on power, exploitation, disenfranchisement, malfeasance, alienation, exclusion, oppression, transgression, and dissent.

---

123. Models of this kind of balanced research include R. Scott Appleby. 1999. *The Ambivalence of the Sacred*. Lanham, MD: Rowman and Littlefield; Mary Ellen Konieczny. 2013. *The Spirit's Tether*. New York: Oxford University Press; Atalia Omer. 2013. *When Peace Is Not Enough*. Chicago: University of Chicago Press; Lynn Davidman. 1993. *Tradition in a Rootless World*. Berkeley: University of California Press; Penny Edgell Becker. 1999. *Congregations in Conflict*. Cambridge: Cambridge University Press; Miller and Yamamori. *Global Pentecostalism*; Toft, Philpott, and Shah. *God's Century*; among many others.

124. See Smith. *What Is a Person?* Pp. 384–433.

Conclusion

Religion is about much more than practices to access superhuman powers for blessings and help. But the new institutional facts and causal powers that emerge from the performance of religious practices are secondary, derivative, and dependent. They concern not what religion is but what religion can do. Nonetheless, we cannot understand any particular religion well without comprehending these secondary causal powers. Nor, without accounting for them, can we understand religion's power over its own adherents, in the world, and into the future.

3

How Does Religion Work?

Lord of the trees and mountains, this man now ill has in his ignorance offended thee.

If while cutting down the trees he has offended thee, we put a new tree in place of the destroyed one. . . . We bring to you an offering . . . in money weight, and we ask you to have pity. We worship you and request that the sick man, if he is bound by your silver or gold cords, that you will loosen the cords and let him go free. If he be bound by ornamented cords or by the tail of a horse or elephant, we request you to cut those bonds and release him. You are the lord of the trees and the mountains and I request you not to frighten the sick man; for we worship you—Sha.

—BURMESE SEER'S ANIMISTIC PRAYER FOR SICK FARMERS[1]

When the Lord brought back the captive ones of Zion, we were like those who dream.
Then our mouth was filled with laughter and our tongue with joyful shouting.
Then they said among the nations, "The Lord has done great things for them."
The Lord has done great things for us. We are glad!

—HEBREW SONG OF ASCENT (PSALM 126:1-3)

1. J. H. Telford. 1933. "Burmese Animism, or Animism in Kengtung State, Burma." PhD thesis. University of Edinburgh. P. 52.

Religion consists of complexes of human practices oriented toward super-human powers performed in hopes of realizing human goods and avoiding bads. But to better understand religion, we must explore more deeply how it operates. Different ideas about what makes religion work depend on more basic definitions and understandings of religion. Theories of key religious processes follow accounts of religious ontologies. My view of what religion *is* answers the question of how religion *works* as follows. The most essential dynamic that makes religion work is *the human making of causal attributions to superhuman powers.*[2] On this, all of religious practice and experience depends. Of course, religion depends on a lot of different processes and dynamics, but I think causal attribution is key. Apart from the central process of making attributions, religion would collapse.[3]

Making Causal Attributions

What do I mean by the *making of causal attributions to superhuman powers*? "Attribution" means assigning a specific person, reason, or force as the cause or originator of an outcome, work, or behavior. To attribute is to designate causal responsibility for an effect. In the case of religion, that means explaining certain outcomes by attributing the influences that generated them to the exercise of superhuman powers. When an outcome can be explained as the result of the action or influence of a superhuman power, then the religious practices succeed and religious commitment is strengthened. This is the essential process by which religion works.[4]

2. For an excellent survey of the issues in question here, see Ann Taves. 2009. *Religious Experience Reconsidered.* Princeton: Princeton University Press; Ralph Hood, Peter Hill, and Bernard Spilka have a nice discussion of attribution and religion in their 2009 book, *The Psychology of Religion.* New York: Guilford Press. Pp. 13, 44–52.

3. Notice that such a fact could never be learned by collecting systematic empirical data, since no amount of fielded surveys or lab experiments could produce this as a "finding." Instead, it is concluded through a process of *retroduction*, by running counterfactual mind experiments based on all that we know to determine conceptually the crucial elements of any process or outcome. In this case, I asked myself: Of all the cognitive activities involved in religion, which one, if eliminated, would make doing religion impossible? The answer was clearly the making of causal attributions to superhuman powers.

4. Here I build on a history of psychology-of-religion research on the topic, including Wayne Proudfoot and Phillip Shaver. 1975. "Attribution Theory and the Psychology of Religion." *Journal for the Scientific Study of Religion.* 14: 317–330; Bernard Spilka and Greg Schmidt. 1983. "General Attribution Theory for the Psychology of Religion." *Journal for the Scientific Study of Religion.* 22: 326–339; Bernard Spilka, Phillip Shaver, and Lee Kirkpatrick. 1985. "A General Attribution Theory for the Psychology of Religion." *Journal for the Scientific Study of Religion.* 24: 1–20; Ken Pargament and J. Hahn. 1986. "God and the Just World." *Journal for the Scientific Study of Religion.*

Etymologically, the word "attribution" comes from the Middle French word *attribution*, descended from the Latin word *attributio*, which meant "to bestow" or "assignment of a debt." When a bill was due, someone had to pay, and it was the job of "attribution" to determine whose responsibility that was. In art and literature, to "attribute" a work is to ascribe it to an author—that is, to establish a particular person as its creator. It may also mean regarding a work as produced in a particular time or place, as when one says, "This painting is attributed to seventeenth-century Italy." In social psychology, however, the field most closely related to my meaning here, "attribution" is the process by which individuals explain the causes of events and actions.

What religion ontologically *is* points us to the "first movement" of religion, the one from humans toward superhuman powers through culturally prescribed practices. But religion does not end with that activity. In a "second movement," the people who have sought the blessings and help of superhuman powers observe the apparent consequences of their practices to see how effective they were. Their religious practices were not ends in themselves, or at least not *only* ends in themselves, but rather (perhaps also) means to realize other ends.[5] In religion's second movement, those ends are examined and the success of the practices is evaluated, whether consciously and systematically or not. Religious practitioners gauge whether their

---

25: 193–207; Michael Lupfer, Karla Brock, and Stephen DePaola. 1992. "The Use of Secular and Religious Attributions to Explain Everyday Behavior." *Journal for the Scientific Study of Religion.* 31: 486–503; Michael Lupfer, Donna Tolliver, and Mark Jackson. 1996. "Explaining Life-Altering Occurrences." *Journal for the Scientific Study of Religion.* 35: 379–391; Matthew Weeks and Michael Lupfer. 2000. "Religious Attributions and Proximity of Influence." *Journal for the Scientific Study of Religion.* 39: 348–362; Paul Mallery, Suzanne Mallery, and Richard Gorsuch. 2000. "A Preliminary Taxonomy of Attributions to God." *International Journal for the Psychology of Religion.* 19: 135–156; Ann Taves. 2008. "Ascription, Attribution, and Cognition in the Study of Experience Deemed Religious." *Religion.* 38: 125–140; Larry VandeCreek and Kenneth Mottram. 2011. "The Perceived Roles of God during Suicide Bereavement." *Journal of Psychology and Theology.* 39: 155–162; Jacqueline Woolley, Chelsea Cornelius, and Walter Lacy. 2011. "Developmental Changes in the Use of Supernatural Explanations for Unusual Events." *Journal for Cognition and Culture.* 11: 311–337; Michael Ransom and Marck Alicke. 2012. "It's a Miracle." *Archive for the Psychology of Religion.* 34: 243–275; Ryan Williams. 2014. "Attributions in a Spiritual Healing Context." *Journal for the Scientific Study of Religion.* 53: 90–108; Justin Barber. 2014. "Believing in a Purpose of Events." *Applied Cognitive Psychology.* 28: 432–437; and cites below, among other valuable publications in this literature. For a general review, see Ralph Hood, Peter Hill, and Bernard Spilka. 2009. *The Psychology of Religion.* New York: Guilford Press.

5. In the course of actual religious experience, this analytical distinction between means and ends often becomes unclear, as the reward of performing the means can itself become an inherent end.

supplication of superhuman powers actually "worked." This is where the key process of making causal attributions comes into play. The most specific "location" of this process is in the minds of persons, but the process itself is of course also powerfully socially conditioned through the influences of social networks, institutions, and interactions.[6]

Three Examples

Before developing more theory, I first make this idea concrete by providing three quite different examples taken from the news during the days when I was writing this chapter. They are not the ideal illustrations of the point of this chapter, but their simultaneous presence in the news demonstrates the regularity and diversity of the human making of causal attributions to superhuman powers.

The first concerns the negative consequences of what was seen as a violation of proper practices for treating the sacred Mount Kinabalu in Malaysia.[7] In May 2015, four Western mountain hikers—a Canadian brother and sister, a British woman, and a Dutch man, ages 22 to 24—broke away from their larger group of 10 mountain trekkers, stripped off their clothes, and took nude photographs of each other. They also reportedly insulted a tour guide who tried to stop them. Others in the group of 10 apparently joined the nude hikers by also disrobing and taking photographs. Numerous of these photos quickly found their way onto the Internet. Weeks later, on June 5, a magnitude-6 earthquake struck the same mountain area, killing 18 other climbers. Both residents of the area and some Malaysian government officials attributed the earthquake to the nude hikers' disrespect of the gods of the sacred Mount Kinabalu. "There is almost certainly a connection," reported the deputy chief minister of the mountain's home state of Sabah, Joseph Pairin Kitingan. "We have to take this as a reminder that local beliefs and customs are not to be disrespected." Days later, a highly unusual "blue

6. The shift back and forth between the "emic" and "etic" perspectives mentioned in the introduction is particularly evident in this chapter.

7. The following account comes from Austin Ramzy. 2015. "Malaysia Is Shaken, Some Say Literally, by Nudity at a Peak." *New York Times.* June 11. P. A4; Jon Austin. 2015. "Villagers Fear Earthquake Gods Still Angry after 'Blue lights' appear over Mount Kinabalu." *Sunday Express.* June 18. http://www.express.co.uk/news/weird/585412/Villagers-fear-earthquake-gods-still-angry-after-blue-lights-appear-over-Mount-Kinabalu; Chieu Luu. 2015. "Blamed for Kota Kinabalu Quake, Naked Tourists Arrested by Malaysian Police." *CNN online.* June 12. http://www.cnn.com/2015/06/09/asia/malaysia-kinabalu-quake-arrest/. Some of the details in these news accounts differ regarding the number of hikers and their ages, but that is not important here.

rainbow" or "blue light rays" appeared over the mountain, which local villagers took to be a sign that the gods of the mountain were still angry about the nudity incident. The original four hikers were held in custody for four days so an investigation of what Malaysian officials called their "obscene act" could be conducted. Kitingan engaged in an online debate for days with a climber believed to be among those who disrobed on the mountain, defending the position that the earthquake could be attributed to the Westerners' behavioral insult of the sacred mountain. His debate opponent, Emil Kaminski, derided that idea, asking how someone holding government office did not "know anything about plate tectonics, geology, and seismology." Kaminski, for his part, received thousands of angry comments and some death threats from Malaysians.

Here is a clear example of religious causal attributions. The gods of the sacred Mount Kinabalu are considered by area religious adherents to be superhuman powers with the ability to cause deadly earthquakes. To avoid misfortune, the sacred mountain must be treated with reverence. When the proper standards of treatment are violated, the offended gods respond with chastening consequences, such as deadly earthquakes.

The second example of a human causal attribution to a superhuman power comes from the June 18, 2015 release of the Roman Catholic papal encyclical, *Laudato Si* ("Praise Be to You"), on the global environmental crisis, authored by Pope Francis. Its release was greatly anticipated by many diverse communities, and widely covered in the news.[8] The vast majority of this encyclical assigns causal responsibility for events to humans, not divine powers. However, Pope Francis also makes repeated claims about the active, causal work in the world of the creating and redeeming Trinitarian God, Christianity's superhuman power. Because this encyclical intends to contrast God's good work and humanity's destructive treatment of creation, few of the following quotes concern God's response to human religious practices—although many of those appear in other Catholic documents. Nevertheless, this papal encyclical does illustrate the process of humans explaining this-worldly affairs by referencing the causal actions of God.

In *Laudato Si*, Pope Francis writes, "The Spirit of God has filled the universe with possibilities and therefore, from the very heart of things, something new can always emerge: 'Nature is nothing other than a certain kind of art, namely God's art, impressed upon things, whereby those things

---

8. Pope Francis. 2015. *Praise Be to You—Laudato Si'*. San Francisco: Ignatius Press; the references listed in the following quotes are paragraph numbers, not page numbers.

are moved to a determinate end'" (80); and that "the entire material universe speaks of God's love, his boundless affection for us. Soil, water, mountains: everything is, as it were, a caress of God" (84). "God," Francis adds, "has written a precious book, 'whose letters are the multitude of created things present in the universe.' . . . We can say that 'alongside revelation properly so-called, contained in sacred Scripture, there is a divine manifestation in the blaze of the sun and the fall of night'" (85). He goes on to claim that "Christ has taken unto himself this material world and now, risen, is intimately present to each being, surrounding it with his affection and penetrating it with his light. Then too, there is the recognition that God created the world, writing into it an order and a dynamism that human beings have no right to ignore" (221). "The universe unfolds in God," Francis insists, "who fills it completely. Hence, there is a mystical meaning to be found in a leaf, in a mountain trail, in a dewdrop, in a poor person's face" (233). God also works through simple bread and wine served in communion during Catholic Mass:

> It is in the Eucharist that all that has been created finds its greatest exaltation. . . . The Lord, in the culmination of the mystery of the Incarnation, chose to reach our intimate depths through a fragment of matter. He comes not from above, but from within, he comes that we might find him in this world of ours. . . . Joined to the incarnate Son, present in the Eucharist, the whole cosmos gives thanks to God. (236)

All of creation, Francis writes, is infused by the active power of God the Holy Trinity working in and through it: "The Father is the ultimate source of everything, the loving and self-communicating foundation of all that exists. The Son, his reflection, through whom all things were created, united himself to this earth when he was formed in the womb of Mary. The Spirit, infinite bond of love, is intimately present at the very heart of the universe, inspiring and bringing new pathways" (238). These are not mere ethical teachings. They are attributions to God's power and purposes. They interpret existence, real events, and experiences as results of the intervening powers of God. Secular, naturalistic explanations of what is happening in the world and the cosmos miss some, indeed, the most important, aspects of reality, according to Francis. To truly understand nature and environmental crisis, one must interpret the world as a divine creation, the handiwork of a causally powerful superhuman agent, the Christian God. By promulgating this encyclical, Pope Francis hopes to persuade others to make the same causal attributions.

My third example, quite different from the previous one, comes from a racist hate crime: the shooting murders on June 17, 2015 of nine Christians gathered for Bible study in the Emanuel African Methodist Episcopal Church of Charleston, South Carolina, by the 21-year-old white man Dylann Storm Roof. The massacre elicited much religious language in public commentary, including claims that the redemptive power of God was needed to help the community heal and overcome racism, that Dylann Roof would be judged by God for his acts, that he would burn in hell, and that no evil could overcome the saving love of Jesus Christ. For present purposes, however, most relevant in the religious commentary following the murders was the common claim that the killer, Dylann Roof, was not simply acting as a violent racist bigot, but was an agent of Satan, of the devil, the superhuman personification of evil who stands in absolute opposition to God.[9]

The evening after the shooting, for example, the racially mixed Second Presbyterian Church of Charleston held a vigil honoring the dead that drew hundreds of participants. The Reverend Sidney Davis declared forcefully to the crowd that, "Last night, Satan came again. Satan came to say that whites and blacks cannot praise God." Similarly, a statement of the Ethics and Religious Liberty Commission of the Southern Baptist Convention in response to the shootings said, "There is hardly a more vivid picture of unmasked evil than the murder of those in prayer. . . . This act of bloodshed is wicked and more than wicked. It is literally satanic, as our Lord taught us that the devil is a 'murderer from the beginning'" (John 8:44). Online, Jim Denison, founder of the Denison Forum on Truth and Culture, a nonsectarian "think tank" seeking to engage contemporary issues with "biblical truth," observed, "Wherever God is at work, Satan reacts. His first strategy is 'to steal and kill and destroy' (John 10:10). . . . More people are coming to Christ today than at any time in human history, and Satan is again responding through violence." Many similar interpretations were reported in the news.

In addition, Debbie Dills, the North Carolina woman who spotted the automobile of the fugitive killer, leading to his arrest, credits the interven-

<hr />

9. Nick Corasaniti, Richard Perez-Pena, and Lizette Alvarez. 2015. "Races Unite for Nine Killed by Gunman at Black Church." *New York Times*. June 19. P. A16; Anugram Kumar. 2015. "Christian Leaders Respond to 'Literally Satanic' Shooting at Charleston Church." *Christian Post*. June 20. http://www.christianpost.com/news/christian-leaders-respond-to-literally-satanic -shooting-at-charleston-church-4000-residents-gather-for-vigil-140649/; Jim Denison. 2015. "Charleston Attack: When God is at Work, Satan Reacts." *Charisma News*. June 19. http://www .charismanews.com/opinion/50175-charleston-attack-when-god-is-at-work-satan-reacts.

tion of God for her role in Roof's apprehension. According to a Religion News Service article,

> [Dills] first heard the news of the Charleston, S.C., church shooting after attending services at her small, Southern Baptist church in rural North Carolina. The next day, as the florist was running late for work and praying for the grieving families, she spotted Roof's vehicle and noticed the South Carolina license plate. Once she recognized Roof's haircut, she realized she was following the alleged shooter. Dills called her boss, who called the police, and continued to follow the car until Roof was apprehended at a traffic stop down the road.[10]

In describing her role, Dills called herself a "vessel" and "instrument" in the hands of God. "It was Him [God] from the time I left my house this morning," she told CNN. "It was Him that made me look at that car. It was God who made this happen. God heard the prayers of those people [who were praying for Roof's arrest]." In these and similar statements, what could be explained in the naturalistic terms that many other observers used—the shooting as a simple matter of Southern racial hatred and the easy availability of guns in America, Roof's arrest as the result of the random though high-probability chance that someone eventually would spot him—is instead interpreted in religious terms, which makes sense, given the religious traditions of the speakers.

Complexities of Causal Attribution

Attributing causes can be complicated when purposive agents are involved. For one reason, in many situations, it is possible to explain events either by referring to stable personality dispositions or by naming external situational influences. If someone drives to a concert during a snowstorm and wrecks his car, the accident might be attributed to his stubborn personality (evident in his refusal to heed storm warnings) or to the city's poor job of plowing and salting the roads. Causes can be identified by reference to factors with different proximities to the outcome in question. We might say the car wreck happened because the driver slammed the brakes too hard on a curve in the road (a temporally proximate explanation); or, siding with the stub-

---

10. Trevin Wax. 2015. "God Stepped In, Says Debbie Dills, Who Spotted Alleged S.C. Killer." June 19. http://www.religionnews.com/2015/06/19/god-stepped-in-says-debbie-dills-who-spotted-alleged-s-c-killer-commentary/.

bornness explanation, we might point to the known pig-headed personalities of the driver's parents, commenting, "The apple does not fall far
from the tree" (a temporally distant explanation). For these and other
reasons, most events, experiences, and conditions can be explained in numerous ways.

Because any given happening normally results from many causes operating at different levels and in varying time frames, rarely does a single causal
attribution attempt to provide a comprehensive account eliminating all
other explanations. With the exception of those who have some motivation
to expend large amounts of mental energy on identifying truly good explanations, people in most situations generally operate as "cognitive misers."[11]
That is, people conserve time and mental effort by relying on "quick and
dirty" explanations that are mentally efficient and frequently sufficiently
accurate. One way people do this is to rely on "heuristics," that is, "judgmental shortcuts that generally get us where we need to go—and quickly—
but at the cost of occasionally sending us off course."[12]

Even when people are prepared to act as "cognitive splurgers," however,
sometimes the causes of events, experiences, and conditions are uncertain
or ambiguous. The human epistemological capacity to understand the
causes of many things is limited. Even when some causes are known, different possible causes might plausibly explain the outcome, too. Multiple explanations may be compatible with each other, but at other times, they
provide competing or rival accounts of things. Causal explanations are thus
often "underdetermined" by the evidence. In those cases, there remains
space for diverse interpretations of causal responsibility.

Furthermore, while most humans are good enough at accurately ascrib-
ing the causes of events and actions to get by in everyday life, the process of
human causal attribution is also subject to a number of well-known biases.
Due to the "self-serving bias" when it comes to explaining good outcomes
in their own lives, people tend to overemphasize internal factors (such as
intelligence, hard work, or skills) and discount external, situational factors
(like privileged opportunities, help from others, or luck). For instance,
when someone lands a good job, he is more likely to chalk that up to his
own qualifications and job-hunting persistence than to the facts that, say,

11. Susan Fiske and Shelley Taylor. 1991. *Social Cognition* (2nd ed.). New York:
McGraw-Hill.

12. T. Gilovich and K. Savitsky. 1996. "Like Goes with Like." *Skeptical Inquirer*. Pp. 34–40;
Amos Tversky and Daniel Kahneman. 1974. "Judgment under Uncertainty." *Science*. 185:
1124–1131.

economic shifts had created many new jobs in his occupational category and he had help from a relative working in the company's Human Resources department. People bolster their self-esteem by taking undue credit for their successes, and do so even more strongly when they sense threats to their self-images.[13] Similarly, the "group-serving bias" describes people's tendency to attribute their in-group's successes to internal factors, and their group's setbacks to external causes, while making the opposite forms of attributions about out-groups.[14] When our political party wins an election, it is because we have the best message and policies, but when we lose, it is because of insufficient funding from donors or public dissatisfaction with a bad economy inherited from the previous administration. Many other attribution biases can distort the accuracy with which people assign responsibility for events and experiences. These include the "fundamental attribution error," the "correspondence bias," the "actor-observer bias," the "trait ascription bias," the "defensive attribution bias," the "group attribution error," and the "focus-of-attention" bias—some of which I discuss more below. None of these human tendencies are deterministic, and they can operate more or less powerfully in different cultures and situations.[15] The point of noting that human attributions of causal influences are vulnerable to cognitive distortion is relevant for understanding religion because biasing tendencies can also affect how and when humans attribute causal influences to superhuman powers.

Research on attribution biases highlights the reality that processes of causal attribution depend not only on "the facts" of the cases in question, but human *interpretations* of the facts and of the forces that brought them about. This—together with people's tendency to be cognitive misers—means that human attributions of the causes of events, experiences, and conditions are routinely left open to the acceptance of a variety of explanatory accounts, including those referencing superhuman powers when humans believe in them. The conditions, standards, and processes that would theoretically be needed to determine the very best explanations are seldom operative, whether in religious or non-religious contexts. We should keep

13. W.K.C. Campbell and C. Sedikides. 1999. "Self-threat Magnifies the Self-serving Bias." *Review of General Psychology.* 3: 23–43.

14. D. M. Taylor and J. R. Doria. 1981. "Self-serving and Group-serving Bias in Attribution." *Journal of Social Psychology.* 113: 201–211; John DeLamater, Daniel Myers, and Jessica Collett. 2014. *Social Psychology.* Boulder, CO: Westview Press. Pp. 233–239.

15. Charles Stangor. 2011. "Biases in Attribution." *Principles of Social Psychology.* BC Open Textbooks, http://opentextbc.ca/socialpsychology/chapter/biases-in-attribution/.

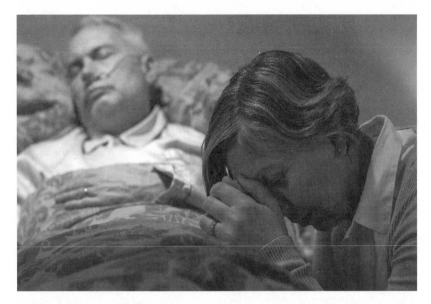

FIGURE 3.1. Seeking and finding answers to prayers depends upon the making of causal attributions to the influence of superhuman powers. People often turn to superhuman powers during times of sickness and disease, not necessarily to ask for miracles but as help accompanying standard medical care and for comfort and assurance. (Copyright: CandyBox Images/ Shutterstock)

this in mind as we examine religious processes of making causal attributions to superhuman powers (figure 3.1).

Excursus: On Miracles and Natural and Supernatural Causes of Earthly Events

Many, especially in the modern West, suppose that the only way a superhuman power could exert causal influences in the world is by a miracle—that is, a positive and astonishing event that cannot be explained by natural or scientific laws. Miracles are believed to happen when a supernatural[16] agent sidesteps or violates the laws of nature by specially intervening in the world's ordinary events to make an outcome different from what natural processes would produce. Nature is normal and predictable; miracles are abnormal and surprising.

16. In this context, the word "supernatural" rather than "superhuman" is most appropriate, in that it directly contrasts with the idea of natural, explicable, law-like processes.

This view, which limits the work of supernatural powers in the world to performing miracles, is misguided. It is the product of a long historical process that unfolded in early modern and modern Europe and North America, and it is constrained by the distinct theological concerns of that world. The full story is too long and complex to recount here, so for present purposes we can simply observe this. Restricting divine action in creation to miracles depends on a specific set of theological assumptions concerning God's transcendence and immanence, which developed in late medieval and early modern Christendom.[17] On the one hand, during this period, God came increasingly to be viewed as disconnected from the intimate workings of nature, something more like the first cause that set in motion a natural order that subsequently perpetuates itself. The Newtonian paradigm of physics shaped this view, which came to full religious expression in various forms of Deism and Unitarianism. On the other hand, paradoxically, people in the same period also increasingly came to view God not as radically transcendent from the created order but as one being among many in the cosmos, who just happened to be the most powerful, knowing, long-lived being in existence.[18] Since God was no longer Totally Other than all things created, knowledge of God shifted from being necessarily negative ("God is not . . .") and "analogical" ("God is only something like . . .") to being potentially "univocal" ("God is like what we know to be . . ."). God could thus be understood through a rational "natural theology" that did not require revelation or an acknowledgment of mystery.

These changes both removed God from the task of making sense of the natural world, on the one hand, and placed God "within" the cosmic order as essentially one powerful causal force among others, on the other hand. Science alone could explain everything by reference to the natural laws that the creator God had established. Meanwhile, apart from setting everything in motion, God's activity was restricted to events that did not seem to conform to natural laws, that is, to miracles. Thus arose the "God of the gaps"

17. The key late medieval influence came from the Franciscan nominalism of Duns Scotus and William of Occam. See William Placher. 1996. *The Domestication of Transcendence*. Lousiville, KY: Westminster John Knox Press; Michael Gillespie. 2009. *The Theological Origins of Modernity*. Chicago: University of Chicago Press; Brad Gregory. 2012. *The Unintended Reformation*. Cambridge, MA: Harvard University Press. Also see Marcel Gauchet. 1999. *The Disenchantment of the World*. Princeton: Princeton University Press.

18. The meaning of other theological terms correspondingly shifted: "eternity," for example, changed from signifying God's being transcendently outside of (yet also encompassing all) temporality to meaning something like "unending time" or "time without end," a very different matter with extensive ramifications.

mentality, in which divine agency fills in for what science could not (yet) explain. God's agency in the world thus suffered a double blow: First, it was hardly needed to understand reality and, second, it had to "compete" against the very natural laws that God ordained.

Eventually, many decided that God was not needed to explain anything at all—hence the tale of the French scientist Pierre-Simon Laplace's reply to Napoleon Bonaparte when the latter asked why he had not mentioned God in his book on astronomy: *"Je n'avais pas besoin de cette hypothèse-là"* ("I had no need of that hypothesis"). Those who still wanted to believe in God and his meaningful actions in the world were forced by the logic of these theological developments to think of God's agency as evident in the unnatural, the irregular, the otherwise inexplicable. And so many today, inheritors of this tradition, assume that the exercise of superhuman causal powers must take the form of a miracle.

This assumption is erroneous, however, for both theological and philosophical reasons. Understanding why opens a more expansive view of how different religious people expect superhuman powers to affect their lives. Returning to Christian thought briefly, the historical theological developments described above were deviations from orthodox Christian beliefs about God. Mainstream Christian orthodoxy had held that God was both absolutely transcendent from the created order and yet simultaneously immanently present to and involved with all of creation. Nothing in creation shares the same kind of being as God, so the qualitative differences between God and creation are absolute. At the same time, God is not removed from creation but continually proximate to every part of it. According to the Christian scriptures, in God all people "live and move and have their being," and by Jesus Christ, "all things were created" so that "He is before all things, and in Him all things hold together" (Acts 17:28; Colossians 1:16–17). God is thus not merely "spatially close" to or morally concerned about nature. God, in orthodox Christian theology, is in fact the enduring source and principle of all being itself, something like the energy and form by which matter and life themselves subsist. God's agency is therefore at work not only in miracles but also in every moment, every aspect of the entire cosmos.

Philosophical reflections on causation, meanwhile, tell us that if superhuman causal powers exist, they do not need to compete in a "zero-sum game" with natural and human causal influences. As we have seen, most events in our world are brought about by the simultaneous operation of multiple types, levels, and proximities of causes. This philosophers call "causal compatibilism." Rather than conflicting with each other, many causes work in parallel, mutually reinforcing, and synergistic ways. In other cases, several causes may represent distinct elements of the same process, only operating at different levels of the same complex, stratified reality (as critical realism defines the term).[19] This means that superhuman powers, if they exist, could very well exert causal influences in any number of ways that are compatible with and potentially indistinguishable from the operation of natural and human causes. Many ordinary religious people seem to understand this.[20] "In many [religious] communities," for example, "requests for miracles supplement rather than replace medical treatments."[21]

For this reason, the Malaysians who believe in the angry spirits of Mount Kinabalu may be more philosophically sophisticated (on the question of multiple sources and levels of causation) than their Western ridiculer Emil Kaminski in supposing that those believed-in mountain spirits could have exerted their causal powers *on and through* "plate tectonics, geology, and seismology" to bring about a deadly earthquake in order to express displeasure with the hikers who offended them. There is no good reason to think the possible agency of sacred spirits and the natural causes of earthquakes are not compatible, if the former do exist; they are only incompatible if one

19. Reality is *differentiated*. It does not consist of one indivisible monad, but of different parts. Those parts that together comprise reality are also *ordered*. They stand in relationship to and interaction with many other parts in ways that are normally stable across space and time. That is in part what makes reality scientifically understandable. Reality is *complex*, not simple. Its many parts are normally related in intricate, interdependent ways, so that a change in any one part usually has consequences for other parts, making most parts causally subject to potential influences by many other parts. Reality is also *stratified*. Subsystems of reality cluster together as if in "layers" operating "above" and "below" other subsections. Particular types of interdependent parts operate together, such as atoms interacting in molecular systems, biological organs operating in body systems, and human persons interacting in social systems. These subsystems are not literally situated at different levels of space, but it is common to use the language of "higher" and "lower" metaphorically. What makes different subsystems of reality "higher" and "lower" are not their different coordinates in three-dimensional space. The different strata instead exist in what we might call "multi-dimensional unified space."

20. C. Mansfield, J. Mitchell, and D. King. 2002. "The Doctor as God's Mechanic?" *Social Science and Medicine.* 54: 77–86l; Chaves. "Rain Dances"; Simon Dein and Kenneth Pargament. 2012. "On Not Praying for the Return of an Amputated Limb." *Bulletin of the Menninger Clinic.* 76: 235–250; Courtney Bender. 2008. "How Does God Answer Back?." *Poetics.* 36: 476–492; Margaret Poloma and George Gallup. 1991. *Varieties of Prayer.* Philadelphia: Trinity Press International.

21. Dein and Pargament. "On Not Praying for the Return." P. 242; also see Wendy Cadge. 2013. *Paging God.* Chicago: University of Chicago Press.

presupposes a priori either that sacred spirits do not exist or that they do not possess the ability to instigate earthquakes in the mountains they inhabit. Pope Francis's theological claims about God and nature in his encyclical *Laudato Si* embrace both the theological orthodoxy I sketched above and the causal compatibilism of philosophy. God does not compete with nature, Francis says, but, while stopping short of pantheism, he teaches that God creates, orders, upholds, sustains, and expresses divinity in nature and all of its features and laws, past, present, and future.

When it comes to the idea of Satan prompting the racist murders of nine Christians in a Charleston church, in a strictly formal sense, if it were the case that Satan exists, then it is in no way impossible that he had some causal influence in the murders. Those of us who do not belong to religious traditions that teach about "spiritual warfare" or angry mountain spirits may not feel comfortable with such claims, but our comfort is not what matters. The issue at present is the logical point that, if we grant for the sake of argument the premise of Satan's existence, the fact that it was Dylann Roof who actually shot the nine Christians does not preclude the possibility of satanic causal influences on the event as well. If, as one pastor said, Satan "still whispers lies into people's hearts," then Satan could have been among many agents and influences that could be said to have caused Roof's actions. Debbie Dills also never claimed that the way God used her to help apprehend Roof was miraculous. She merely described herself as a "vessel" and "instrument" in God's hands. By her account, in response to the prayers of many people, God helped arrange the delay in her work schedule that made it possible for her driving path to cross Roof's, and God made her look at his car when she might not have. But these possibilities need not have involved any suspension of the ordinary laws of nature. The superhumanly powerful God in whom Dills believes could have caused everything she claimed God did without performing one miracle. To think otherwise not only denies philosophy's causal compatibilism, but presupposes theologically that God is normally not at work in ordinary life, a belief that Debbie Dills, at least, does not hold. Whether or not Dill's premises about God are objectively correct, her position is not guilty in principle of being irrational or specious.

My general point here is this: If we grant religious people's premises about superhuman powers that animate their religious practices, we have no good reason to think that the exercise of these powers' influences in the world must be miraculous. Superhuman causal influences can normally operate through ordinary, natural means, and that is how most religious people expect them to operate. This belief, in turn, shapes their religious attributions.

Ordinary "Religious Experiences"

Something similar is true about the vast majority of people's "religious experiences." In everyday speech, that phrase usually connotes an extraordinary encounter, something transcendent, overpowering, or mystical.[22] But few religious people have such experiences frequently. Still, social scientific research has tended to reinforce the idea of "religious experiences" as powerful, direct encounters with the spiritual or supernatural world: Scholars describe them as "peak experiences," "hyperconsciousness," and "not accessible in everyday life," and ask survey questions like "Would you say that you have had a 'religious or mystical experience'—that is, a moment of sudden religious awakening or insight?" and "How often have you . . . felt as though you were very close to a powerful, spiritual force that seemed to lift you up out of yourself?"[23] Such surveys show that many people claim to have had such experiences at least once in their lives. However, the majority of people's "religious experiences," broadly understood, are fairly ordinary, having to do with "lesser, mellower experiences of transcendence," such as "receiving an unexpected check in the mail or finding a job."[24] This is because people often attribute many ordinary events in their lives to the workings of superhuman powers.[25]

As Timothy Nelson observes, "Because it is the attribution that makes one's experiences religious and not the quality of the experience itself . . . *any* experience, no matter how ordinary or mundane it may seem, can be

22. Timothy Nelson. 1997. "He Made a Way Out of No Way." *Review of Religious Research*. 39: 5–26.

23. George Gallup. 1978. *The Gallup Poll, Public Opinion, 1972–1977*. Wilmington, DE: Scholarly Resources; George H. Gallup Jr. 2003. "Religious Awakenings Bolster Americans' Faith." January 14. Princeton: George H. Gallup International Institute. http://www.gallup.com /poll/7582/religious-awakenings-bolster-americans-faith.aspx; Linda Borque. 1969. "Social Correlates of Transcendental Experiences." *Sociological Analysis*. 30: 151–163; Andrew Greeley. 1974. *Ecstasy*. Englewood Cliffs, NJ: Prentice Hall; David Yamane and Megan Polzer. 1994. "Ways of Seeing Ecstasy in Modern Society." *Sociology of Religion*. 55: 1–25; per Nelson. "He Made a Way Out." Pp. 6–7.

24. Peter Berger. 1992. *A Far Glory*. New York: Doubleday. P. 134; Nelson. "He Made a Way Out." P. 24.

25. Ammerman. *Everyday Religion*.

FIGURE 3.2. Religious practices both individual and collective are often evident at sporting events, such as this team's prayer after a high school football championship game in Louisville, Kentucky, in December 2008. Such prayers, which are premised on the belief that God is interested in and can influence the game experience, can build group solidarity and team focus, ritualize leadership, and channel desired emotions in response to different game outcomes. (Copyright: Jonathon Palmer, Palmer Media Group LLC)

religious if the individual attributes some aspect of the event to the operation of spiritual beings or forces."[26] For a religious experience to be a religious experience, however, the connection to superhuman powers must be made explicit: "No matter how unusual the emotional or cognitive states or how intense the physical sensations associated with a particular episode, if individuals do not consciously connect them to the operation of spiritual beings or forces, then they have not had a religious experience."[27] Making this connection requires some reference to the culturally specified beliefs about superhuman powers embedded in a certain religious tradition (figure 3.2). "Because attribution is a cognitive act, it is ultimately based on belief. . . . Theology thus plays a role of fundamental importance in religious experience, for one must believe that spiritual agents exist and are active in human affairs in order to attribute some concrete event or experience to their interventions."[28]

26. Nelson. "He Made a Way Out." P. 8. Italics in original.
27. Ibid.
28. Ibid. P. 13.

This means that a larger institutional context of cultural socialization, however diffuse, is usually necessary to give those having religious experiences the cues and know-how to interpret them as such. In many circumstances, knowing how to make religious attributions is a learned process, requiring socialization into the official and, often more importantly, "folk" knowledge of a religious group. "This socialization not only gives individuals the cognitive tools with which to make spiritual attributions, it also informs them of the types of events and circumstances in which it is appropriate to make these attributions."[29] The making of religious attributions also draws heavily on metaphors, narratives, congregational histories, and other social processes, "most fundamentally because the beliefs upon which attributions rest are collectively produced, maintained, and transmitted."[30] Further, the likelihood of having an experience that one attributes to spiritual, religious, supernatural, or paranormal causes appears to vary by individual mental features.[31] Thus, while religious experiences are usually very personal incidents, they are normally informed by the cognitive and interpretive resources of religious traditions and communities, however distant they may be from the religious experience in question.

The Varieties of Religious Causal Attributions

Let us think more systematically about the various ways that human attributions of superhuman causal influences can work. First, when it comes to *specificity of outcomes*, religious people can hold varying expectations about how closely their religious practices will correspond to possible superhuman responses. On one end of the spectrum, cultural prescriptions may promise that some religious practice produces very specific results. Perform the correct rite, for instance, and one will be able to coerce women into

---

29. Ibid. P. 15; Woolley, Cornelius, and Lacy. "Developmental Changes in the Use of Supernatural Explanations."

30. Nelson. "He Made a Way Out." Pp. 16–19, 24; also see Lupfer, Brock, and DePaola. "The Use of Secular and Religious Attributions"; Micael Lupfer, Stephen DePaola, Karla Brock, and Lu Clement. 1994. "Making Secular and Religious Attributions." *Journal for the Scientific Study of Religion*. 33: 162–171; Mary Jo Neitz and James Spickard. 1990. "Steps toward a Sociology of Religious Experience." *Sociological Analysis*. 51: 15–33; Tuija Hovi. 2004. "Religious Conviction Shaped and Maintained by Narration." *Archive for the Psychology of Religion*. 26: 35–50; Scott Schieman. 2010. "Socioeconomic Status and Beliefs about God's Influence in Everyday Life." *Sociology of Religion*. 71: 25–51; Ammerman. *Everyday Religion*.

31. Kirsten Barnes and Nicholas Gibson. 2013. "Supernatural Agency." *International Journal for the Psychology of Religion*. 23: 42–62.

sexual submission.[32] This Zuni prayer for rain similarly requests quite specific results:

> Cover my earth mother four times with many flowers.
> Let the heavens be covered with the banked-up clouds.
> Let the earth be covered with fog; cover the earth with rains.
> Great waters, rains, cover the earth. Lightning cover the earth.
> Let thunder be heard over the earth; let thunder be heard;
> Let thunder be heard over the six regions of the earth.

On the other end of the spectrum, some religious practices promise extremely general outcomes, such as prosperity, good luck, and happiness. Sometimes, too, the results of practices are ambiguous in their specificity; they could be treated in definite or general terms, depending on the circumstances and hopes of the practitioners.

Religious cultures can likewise vary in expectations about the *timing of outcomes* of religious practices. Religious practices may be anticipated to produce immediate results—as, for example, when a faith healer promises to cure blindness on the spot through exorcism or prayer. On the other side of the continuum, the results of religious practice may be expected to materialize in the distant future. This is the case when the outcome requested from the superhuman power is something like union with Brahman, a peaceful death in old age, or the repose of one's soul in heaven. Again, a range of expectations exists between these extremes.

Religious cultures can prescribe practices that vary in how *empirically verifiable* are the consequences they hope to produce. Some hoped-for outcomes of religious practices are easily verifiable, like a bountiful harvest, success in battle, safe childbirth, or winning the state championship. Others seem, in this life, to be entirely unverifiable by empirical methods, including the effects of karma on one's next life, the rewards of paradise after death, and *moksha* as freedom from *saṃsara*'s cycle of death and rebirth. Some might be verifiable, or at least falsifiable, in principle, yet fail to offer any obvious metrics for determining their validity, as with the requests of this common Zoroastrian prayer:

> For the reward of virtue and the forgiveness of sins, I do deeds of righteousness for the love of my soul. May all virtuousness of all good ones of the earth of seven climes reach the width of the earth, the length of

---

32. Richard Kieckhefer. 1994. "The Specific Rationality of Medieval Magic." *American Historical Review*. 99: 813–818.

the rivers, and the height of the sun in their original form. May there be righteousness and long life. Thus may it come as I wish.[33]

And once again, between these extremes there exists a range of degrees of empirical verifiability of the outcomes people hope to gain from the causal influences of superhuman powers. Consider, for instance, this evening prayer from the Anglican *Book of Common Prayer* (1979):

> Keep watch, dear Lord, with those who work, or watch, or weep this night, and give your angels charge over those who sleep. Tend the sick, Lord Christ; give rest to the weary, bless the dying, soothe the suffering, pity the afflicted, shield the joyous; and all for your love's sake. Amen.

How would one know whether God had heard and answered this prayer? Its requests are quite specific with regard to the differences the Lord's interventions might make: Those working night shifts are kept safe, the weary rest, the suffering feel better, and so on. Then again, most of the verbs—"keep watch," "tend," "bless," "pity," "shield"—make it difficult to determine what exactly an answer to this prayer might look like. Such ambiguity can work in religion's favor, as we will see below.

Involved in the variance of the empirical verifiability of religious practices' outcomes is the question of whether superhuman causal influences will yield positive evidence (something happens) or negative evidence (something does not happen). People who believe that an "evil eye" of a human nemesis can curse them may post a "talisman"—in their homes, hanging from trees, on their vehicles or prows of boats, or worn on jewelry—to ward off that malign spiritual force, bending the wicked gaze back to the sorcerer who delivered it. Is its effectiveness verifiable? If nothing particularly bad happens, presumably so. The power of the talisman is validated by the absence of evidence to the contrary. Anticipated religious outcomes that require positive evidence to validate raise the standard of verification to a higher level. For example, the Catholic rite of demonic exorcism, which only ordained priests are permitted to conduct, might be deemed successful only if all signs of the diabolical spirits previously present subsequently vanish.

Another dimension by which the results of religious practices may vary: Some blessings and averted misfortunes might be *expected* by practitioners before they materialize, others are surprises that are only *recognized after*

---

33. Avesta: Khorda Avesta. Srosh Baj, 5.

the fact as attributable to the exercise of superhuman powers. For example, when Aztec Tlenamacac priests performed human sacrifices to Huitzilo- pochtli, the sun god, who needed constant nourishment in the sacred life force of human blood, the Aztecs fully expected this practice to (among other things) keep the sun moving from east to west across the sky. They recreated divine mythological events through rituals with the intention and expectation of thus sustaining the cosmic order. By contrast, Debbie Dills did not practice her faithful Christian life in order that someday she might help to catch a mass murderer. She simply did what she believed was good and necessary, and being used as God's instrument for good in the world arrived as an unanticipated divine gift. Insofar as many unexpected good things in life can be interpreted as the result of superhuman causal influ- ences, a vast territory of events, experiences, and conditions opens up for the recognition (in the believer's sense) or projection (in the skeptic's sense) of the work of religious powers and their attendant meanings. Some- times people do not profess to recognize some happening in their lives as the work of the superhuman powers they posulate until years or decades later. The attribution, usually grateful, is entirely retrospective.

Attributions of superhuman causal influences also differ according to the degree to which they are understood to work through *ordinary, natural pro- cesses* versus *extraordinary, perhaps miraculous* means. This recalls the dis- cussion of the excursus above. Religious practitioners expect much of what they seek from superhuman powers to be realized through natural means. The priest blesses a peasant's field in the spring to ensure a bountiful har- vest; the sun, rain, and soil do their natural work well; and the peasant and priest thank the gods in the autumn for their blessing. Fundamentalist Prot- estant families gathered at dinner hold hands and "say grace" not only to thank God but also to "bless this food to our bodies," as many say, and then natural biological processes of digestion proceed so that the food provides energy and health to those eating. Members of a Catholic prayer meeting ask God's "healing hand" for a sick friend, knowing full well that the friend is under a doctor's care in the hospital and content with the prospect of medicine and rest bringing their restoration. In these cases, nobody is look- ing for a miracle. They expect superhuman causal influences to operate through the natural mechanisms of sun, rain, soil, proteins, carbohydrates, vitamins, antibiotics, and so on.

However, most religious practitioners at least sometimes seek things from superhuman powers that require more extraordinary means. Clear examples are healings of terminal illnesses when doctors say there is no hope, the saving of one's job when one's employer is going bust, and the raising of the dead back to life.[34] Between these examples and those in the preceding paragraph lie a host of possible requests that rely on some presumed combination of natural and extraordinary causal forces. These might include the end of a drought, the safe return of a son or daughter who is fighting in a foreign war, divine guidance in making a major life decision, or money needed to keep a tenuous religious organization afloat.

We see, then, that the kinds of superhuman causal influences that religious practices seek to animate are myriad and diverse in many respects. Some are specific; others more general. Some requests from practitioners are expected to be answered quickly; others not for ages. Some are empirically verifiable, while others cannot be validated or falsified. Many outcomes of religious practices are quite expected, whereas others are unforeseen. Some are assumed to employ natural means, while others require more extraordinary or supernatural interventions. Exactly which attribution is brought into play depends not only on the outlooks of persons but on the particular social and cultural contexts in which those persons are located.

Case Study: Falwell and Robertson's Fundamentalist Angry God

To put more flesh on these conceptual bones, let us consider in greater depth an infamous case of human attributions of superhuman causal powers. The day after the terrorist attacks of September 11, 2001, the fundamentalist minister Jerry Falwell appeared as a guest on fellow preacher Pat Robertson's *700 Club* TV program and causally attributed the attacks to the retributive anger of God for America's contemporary apostasy and sins.[35] On the positive side, Falwell said, God had protected America "wonderfully these 225 years." But, with 9/11, "since 1812, this is the first time that we've been attacked on our soil and by far [with] the worst results." The terrorist attacks, he said, were caused not only by the motivations and capacities of the terrorists, but by God as a divine retribution and warning:

---

34. On contemporary resurrections of the dead, see Miller and Yamamori. *Global Pentecostalism.*

35. Marc Ambinder. 2001. "Falwell Suggests Gays to Blame for Attacks." ABC News. September 14. http://abcnews.go.com/Politics/story?id=121322; "Falwell Speaks about WTC Disaster." Christian Broadcasting Network. https://home.comcast.net/~joe.grabko/falwell.mp3.

Throwing God out successfully with the help of the federal court system, throwing God out of the public square, out of the schools. The abortionists have got to bear some burden for this because *God will not be mocked.* And when we destroy 40 million little innocent babies, *we make God mad.* I believe that the pagans and the abortionists and the feminists and the gays and the lesbians who are actively trying to make that an alternative lifestyle, the ACLU, People for the American Way, all of them who have tried to secularize America, I point the finger in their face and say, "you helped this happen."[36]

Robertson responded, "Well, I totally concur." Falwell continued: "Yesterday, the Democrats and the Republicans in both houses of Congress . . . went out on the steps and called out to God in prayer and sang 'God Bless America' and said, 'Let the ACLU be hanged.' In other words, when the nation is on its knees, the only normal and natural and spiritual thing to do is what we ought to be doing all the time, calling upon God." To which Robertson replied, "Amen." Robertson then responded with this prayer:

We have sinned against Almighty God, at the highest level of our government, we've stuck our finger in your eye. The Supreme Court has insulted you over and over again, Lord. They've taken your Bible away from the schools. They've forbidden little children to pray. They've taken the knowledge of God as best they can, and organizations have come into court to take the knowledge of God out of the public square of America.

These comments provoked widespread outrage. In a subsequent phone call to CNN, Falwell tried to soften his position, saying that the hijackers and terrorists alone were actually responsible for the attacks, and apologizing to gays, feminists, and lesbians.[37] But in that conversation he also reasserted that, "I do believe, as a theologian, based upon many Scriptures and particularly Proverbs 14:23, which says 'living by God's principles promotes a nation to greatness, violating those principles brings a nation to shame,'" that the ACLU and other organizations "which have attempted to secularize America, have removed our nation from its relationship with Christ on

36. Italics added for emphasis. https://web.archive.org/web/20130401182609/http://archives.cnn.com/2001/US/09/14/Falwell.apology/.

37. "Falwell Apologizes to Gays, Feminists, Lesbians." CNN.com. September 14. https://web.archive.org/web/20130401182609/http://archives.cnn.com/2001/US/09/14/Falwell.apology/.

which it was founded. I therefore believe that that created an environment which possibly has *caused God to lift the veil of protection* which has allowed no one to attack America on our soil since 1812."[38]

These claims by Falwell and Robertson during a time of national trauma caused millions of Americans' jaws to drop in incredulity and raised firestorms of protest from many quarters, including public reprimands from then-President George W. Bush, which helped produce Falwell's lukewarm apology. But our present concern is the nature of Falwell and Robertson's attribution of superhuman influences with regard to the terrorist attacks of September 11.

Reconstructing Falwell and Robertson's reasoning, we can surmise that they believed the following: (1) Because of its former righteousness as a nation, God had afforded the United States special protection against violent attacks on its land. (2) Secular forces in America, however, have recently poked their finger in God's eye, "mocked" God, and made God "mad." (3) As a result, God in his anger lifted his covering of protection over the United States, allowing evil Islamic terrorists to attack the nation. (4) The 9/11 terrorists therefore succeeded in their plans. By implication, there remained one unstated point that provided the central rhetorical significance of their case: (5) If America were to reject the ungodly secularists, repent of its sins, and return to its former righteousness, then God's anger would subside and he would again lower his veil of protection around the United States to shield it from further danger.

Such claims seemed to many Americans then, and may seem to most readers now (as they do to me), to be outrageous, some even said treasonous.[39] However, we might observe for analytical purposes and historical perspective that Falwell and Robertson's claims reflected a central narrative of Israelite nationalism and Hebraic prophetic denunciation that is pervasive in the biblical Old Testament. They also embodied a reiteration, how-

---

38. Italics added for emphasis.

39. The atheist Christopher Hitchens accused Falwell on television of treason against the United States, describing him as "an extremely dangerous demagogue who lived by hatred of others, and prejudice, and who committed treason by saying that the United States deserved the attack upon it and its civil society on September 2001 by other religious nutcases [Islamic extremists] like himself." Hitchens. 2007. "Christopher Hitchens and Ralph Reed Square Off over Late Leader's Influence; the Christian Right." Hannity & Colmes. FOX News. May 17. http://www .foxnews.com/story/2007/05/17/christopher-hitchens-and-ralph-reed-square-off-over-late -leader-influence.html; Eric Powell. 2007. "Hitchens Takes on Fox News on Jerry Falwell." *Atheist Nexus*. May 31. http://www.atheistnexus.org/profiles/blogs/hitchens-takes-on-fox-news-on -jerry-falwell.

ever vulgar, of the time-honored "American Jeremiad," which originated with the settling of British America and runs up to and beyond the activism of Dr. Martin Luther King, Jr.[40]

Numerous analytical points noted in the preceding pages help interpret this case. First, this example of human causal attributions of superhuman influences depends minimally on the "raw facts" of the event and very heavily on a particular interpretation, the imputing of specific meanings, the free assignment of causal relations to elucidate the larger significance of the basic facts. Attribution was thus an active, creative, explanatory process in this case, as it always is.

As an operation of thought, attribution is less about deductive, inductive, or "retroductive" reasoning than about "abductive reasoning"—that is, making an inference by moving from an observation about facts to a hypothesized framework that purports to best explain the observation.[41] Abduction invites inquirers to mentally experiment by fitting the known facts of a case into a particular interpretive framework, and then judging how well the framework explains the facts relative to alternatives. When, for example, a neo-Marxist theorist says, "I can best explain what is really going on in our world economic crisis if you just consider it in light of my theory," she is asking us to engage in an exercise of abductive reasoning. This is also what Falwell and Robertson were doing, only from the viewpoint of right-wing fundamentalism. Two observations about abduction are worth noting.

For one thing, people engage in abductive reasoning all the time in everyday life. It is one of the ways we routinely make inferences about what is going on in the world. For another, abduction is one of the worst methods of seeking the truth, in that in the end it only produces convinced beliefs, not definite knowledge. Deductive reasoning, by contrast, always produces truthful conclusions, when its premises are true. Inductive and retroductive reasoning allow for drawing inferences with reasonable confidence, even if in the end they too can only yield convinced beliefs. Abduction has the particular weakness of convincing inquirers to believe the interpretive

---

40. Sacvan Berkovitch. 2012 [1978]. *The American Jeremiad*. Madison: University of Wisconsin Press; Willie Harrell. 2011. *Origins of the African American Jeremiad*. Jefferson, NC: McFarland; David Howard-Pitney. 2005. *The African American Jeremiad*. Philadelphia: Temple University Press.

41. Berth Danermark, Mats Ekstrom, Liselotte Jakobsen, and Jan Karlsson. 2001. *Explaining Society*. London: Routledge. Pp. 90–108. The logic of abductive inference was first introduced into formal logic by Charles Sanders Peirce.

framework *only if it seems to them* to make best sense of the data. Inescapable subjective and intuitive judgments always operate in abductive reasoning. And, as we know, for reasons discussed earlier, different people presented with the very same evidence often find different interpretive frameworks to be intuitively convincing (although, again, even defining what "the facts" are usually requires selection and interpretation, about which people also often disagree—just ask a neoliberal economist what he thinks of what gets emphasized in the neo-Marxist's interpretive framework).[42] Thus both the active, creative, explanatory process of human narration and the often inconclusive nature of abductive reasoning are inevitably involved when humans make attributions of superhuman causal influences, rendering the central cognitive process that makes religion succeed open, indeterminate, and contestable.

Another notable facet of Falwell and Robertson's remarks is that they did not claim or suggest that God directly caused 9/11 through supernatural or miraculous means, but rather "allowed" it to happen (by "lifting the veil of protection") through the natural agency of the human terrorists—not unlike the way Yahweh is said to have allowed the heathen Assyrians and Babylonians to punish and chastise wayward Israel and Judah. Even such an unrefined causal interpretation of September 11 as theirs did not make the simplistic claim that the divine and human forces that may have been at work were an either/or equation. Some may question Falwell's description of himself as "a theologian," but his and Robertson's account—however objectionable it may be on historical, moral, and theological grounds—was, in formal terms, conceptually more sophisticated (on the specific matter of potential multiple causation) than those who said in reply that because 9/11 was caused by human terrorists, it could not have been caused by God. Again, the reality that a single event results from multiple, complex, stratified, and interactive causes must inform our investigations of how religious practitioners operate and how religion works.

Falwell and Robertson's "angry God" interpretation of 9/11 also illustrates some of the complexities described in the previous section. The consequences of superhuman influences, by their account, were highly *specific*: the terrorist attacks of September 11 in which thousands of people died. The outcome of God's supposed causal intervention was only somewhat *tempo-*

42. This very book is itself an exercise in abductive reasoning, an invitation to re-conceptualize religion in the terms of the theory I am developing in its pages. Nothing I write here can "prove" my theory to be correct, but I hope that by describing how the evidence so well fits the framework, I will persuade readers to adopt my theory.

rally prompt, given that most of the secularizing forces that offended God, according to Falwell and Robertson, only began in earnest in the 1960s and '70s. The *results* of God's believed influence in allowing 9/11 to happen were empirically verifiable. While most of the nation did not expect the terrorist attacks and did not seem to be anticipating a retributive act of God for America's disobedience, Falwell and Robertson could at least say that they predicted such a divine event, since they had been warning people for decades about the awful consequences of the nation's turning away from God.[43] For them, at least, and for some of their followers, the believed divine intervention that took place on 9/11 was, in general terms, expected. Finally, as I noted in the previous paragraph, God's supposed causal intervention to rebuke America was taken to operate through the entirely natural means of the human terrorists who committed the attacks—his "permissive" role was to allow America's enemies to succeed. With al-Qaeda extremists on hand, God did not have to resort to a miracle.

Finally, this case highlights an important observation relevant to all of the social sciences, not merely the study of religion. That is that causes and meaning are interdependent and necessarily work to inform and interpret each other. That is, in religion particularly and human social life generally, it is impossible to specify causal relations that explain outcomes without also delving into the attribution and interpretation of cultural meanings, just as it is badly misguided and insufficient to seek only to understand cultural meanings among communities of people while disavowing the task of identifying the causal forces that produce outcomes of interest. In brief, causal explanation cannot do without cultural interpretation, and the interpretation of meanings cannot defensibly be divorced from the task of causal explanation. Why does this matter? It matters, first of all, because the social sciences have long been divided between those who emphasize causal explanation and others who accentuate the interpretation of meaning. The former think predominantly in positivist, materialist, mechanistic, rationalist, and quantitative terms, while the latter favor hermeneutics, idealism,

43. Robertson, especially, had a history of predicting disaster. In 1976, for example, he predicted the end of the world in October or November 1982. In a May 1980 episode of *The 700 Club* he declared, "I guarantee you by the end of 1982 there is going to be a judgment on the world." Two weeks after Hurricane Katrina killed nearly 2,000 people in 2005, Robertson suggested in another broadcast of *The 700 Club* that the disaster was God's punishment for America's abortion policy. And in May 2006, Robertson announced that bad storms and possibly a tsunami would hit a US coastline, likely in the Pacific Northwest, sometime that year. Another of Robertson's predictions of divine punishment is discussed below.

qualitative analysis, subjectivity, culture, and causal anti-realism.[44] But if my observation is true, then the divide between the two factions dissolves, and we realize that each side presupposes and relies upon the other for its major concern. Causal explanation and the interpretation of meanings fuse into a single, complex approach to the social sciences.[45]

How does this relate to the case of Falwell and Robertson? There exist many levels and threads in their causal reasoning and our causal analyses of their careers and public significance. But let us pull out and examine the one thread examined above, concerning their views of 9/11. In the very same discursive act, Falwell and Robertson were positing a set of *causal relations* (represented in my reconstruction of their assumptions and beliefs) and also interpreting the *meanings* of the events they were causally explaining. In their brief exchange on *The 700 Club*, they would not have been able to attribute the terrorist attacks to superhuman agency as they did without explicitly and implicitly developing and commending particular culturally meaningful significations that make the explanation they proposed plausible. At the same time, the cultural meanings of events that Falwell and Robertson assumed and endorsed were irrelevant apart from their role in the larger narrative of causal explanation that they were constructing. Causation needed meaning, just as significance served the purpose of causal explanation. If this were not so, the linkages between the ACLU, America's special role in the world, God's sense of honor and dignity, and the events of September 11 would be not only implausible (to those who are not Christian fundamentalists) but absurd non sequiturs. Without an *interpretation* of what the elements in their account *mean*, all causal explanation collapses; and without the challenge of *causally* explaining why 9/11 *happened*, the meaning of various elements in their account is trivial.

Who cares whether some Virginia pastor thinks "the ACLU offends God" is a meaningful idea, if that is not connected to a causal account explaining a hugely important event that could also, if popularly accepted, influence the outcome of many other important events? And who thinks we could causally explain anything in the social sciences without reference to the cultural meanings that make life significant to people and help to

44. George Homans, Peter Blau, and Robert Hauser might be considered archetypes of the "causal" party, while Peter Winch and Clifford Geertz are iconic representatives of the "interpretation" faction.

45. Which Max Weber had said all along but in that view was too often endorsed but neglected by subsequent thinkers. Weber. 1978. *Economy and Society*. Berkeley: University of California Press. Pp. 4–62.

motivate their actions? In social science, as in all of human life, causes and meaning are interdependent and necessarily work to inform and interpret each other. Stating this in terms of the "Are Reasons Causes?" debate in the philosophy of social science, my theory—as informed by critical realism and personalist theory—takes this position: In human life, people's reasons are definitely causes, and plausible explanations of causes ultimately always require some account of people's reasons.[46] This means, when it comes to the study of religion, that we always need to be both culturalist *and* causal, to be seeking understanding *and* explanation in all of our scholarly accounts. Only that more complex and integrative approach can produce the kind of insights and understanding that the social sciences ought to deliver.

Interpretive Evaluations of Superhuman Causal Influences

Let us now return to this chapter's theoretical concern with understanding human attributions of superhuman influences on worldly events as the key process by which religion works. Doing so involves not only analyzing the diverse expectations religious people have about the outcomes of their practices, as explicated above. It also requires investigating how religious practitioners evaluate and interpret various kinds of outcomes. Religious practitioners usually live on promises and hopes, not entitlements and guarantees. And not every superhuman power that religious people seek to engage is considered steadfast, benevolent, and trustworthy. As part of the larger process of "doing religion," therefore, most religious people assess the results of their practices in some way for feedback about their success. Are their religious practices producing the expected results? Are the superhuman powers exerting the causal influences promised and hoped for?

Consider, as an illustrative mind experiment, two extreme cases. In the first, a religious practitioner (of any given religion) finds that all of their attempts to access the superhuman powers in which they believe succeed wildly. They ask and it is granted. They perform and it is rewarded. They therefore suffer no ambiguity, no anomalies, no doubt. Their religion works exactly as promised. The second case is precisely the opposite. None of the promises of the prescribed religious practices are realized. No evidence of

46. Roy Bhaskar. 1998. *The Possibility of Naturalism*. London: Routledge. Pp. 80–93; Hilliard Aronovitch. 1978. "Social Explanation and Rational Motivation." *American Philosophical Quarterly*. 15:197–204.

superhuman causal influences in life is detectable. Prayers go unanswered, sacrifices unacknowledged, obedience unrewarded. There is little reason in this case to believe that the religion is worth practicing. The practitioner seriously doubts, or tries to reform, or perhaps just abandons his or her religion. These ideal-type cases suggest the importance of the results of religious practices, both as raw facts and as evaluated by practitioners. What religious practices produce matters a great deal over time. So it is worth investigating in more depth the possible outcomes of religious practices and the alternative ways that religious people interpret their meanings.

I see six possible distinct results of human religious practices. By "results," I mean perceived outcomes of possible superhuman causal influences that the practices were meant to activate. The six are: outright success, success reinterpreted, presumed satisfaction, no response, failure, and rejection. The following pages describe each of these possible outcomes in turn and the various ways that religious people respond to them—that is, from a primarily "emic" perspective. Some of my illustrations come from real-life religious experience, others from well-known sacred texts, mythologies, or traditional histories.

1. *Outright Success*. This outcome is easy to understand. The superhuman powers deliver what the religious practices hoped to achieve; the process of religious entreaty and response is completed. A community prays to change the path of a hurricane and it swerves out to sea. A struggling soul asks God for inner peace during a trying time and soon enjoys tranquility. The high priest implores the gods for protection against the enemy, and presently the adversary's army surrounding the city walls is stricken by an outbreak of infectious disease. In this case, religion "works," and as a result the religiousness of its practitioners is validated and strengthened. In one national survey in the United States, 95 percent of adults who pray reported that their prayers have been answered.[47] Among Christians, such outcomes elicit this kind of speech: "God answers prayer!," "God is good, all the time!," and "Our God is great!"

2. *Success Reinterpreted*. In this more complex case, religious practitioners judge *in the end* that their practices were effective—that their prayers were answered, their rituals were honored, their faithfulness rewarded. But the results of the superhuman causal influences turn out to be different from those hoped for or expected. What religious practitioners originally desired

---

47. George Gallup and Michael Lindsay. 1999. *Surveying the Religious Landscape*. Harrisburg, PA: Morehouse.

does not come to pass. But they come to understand what *did* happen as a *substitute* or *superior alternative* provided by superhuman powers. Religious people can count their practices as successful in this case, but only after reinterpreting the causal effects of the powers they implored. To the two-part process of religious entreaty and response in the "outright success" scenario just described, a third step is added here: Religious practitioners reframe the apparent response of the superhuman powers in a way that meaningfully connects it back to their original entreaty. Ideas such as " 'My thoughts are not your thoughts, neither are your ways my ways,' declares the Lord" (Isaiah 55:8) and "We know that in all things God works for the good of those who love him, who have been called according to his purpose" (Romans 8:28) prove helpful in making sense of such unexpected outcomes.

Success can be reinterpreted in many ways. One involves superhuman powers simply changing the *means* by which a desired end was realized. For example, a pastor might pray privately for more faithful stewardship of his entire congregation, especially so that badly needed repairs on the church roof can be made. Depressingly, the financial giving of his flock actually declines in the months that follow, yet just before the onset of winter, one parishioner gains an unexpected bequest from a recently deceased uncle and decides to use part of it to pay for the roof repair. "The Lord works in mysterious ways!" the pastor muses to himself. His prayers were answered, though through different means than he had wished.

Another version of success reinterpreted involves superhuman powers replacing the *content* of the originally desired outcome with a suitable or better *substitute*. For instance, a young religious believer may pray to the gods to be able to attract the attention of and marry a particular person of interest. However, circumstances preclude the prospect of marrying this person but another, seemingly better, mate comes along and marries the believer. He or she may then conclude that the gods answered his or her prayer in a way better than the original request. A superior answer was substituted.

Still another form of success reinterpreted occurs when the religious practitioner's desired outcome fails to materialize, but a completely differ-ent outcome is received, which the practitioner then "realizes" is in fact the response to their original concern. In this case, superhuman powers do not provide an alternative means to or substitute for the original desire, but "change the subject," so to speak. For instance, a peasant may ask the vener-ated spirits for good health in the coming year. In subsequent months, the peasant ends up suffering ill health, which seems to be a rejection of his requests by the spirits. However, his crops grow magnificently and his live-stock prosper and multiply, creating conditions of prosperity and health in his larger household. The peasant then concludes that the gods indeed had good intentions in mind for him and heard his prayers, but with superior knowledge intended to bless him in different and perhaps more important ways than he asked for.

In a final variation of success reinterpreted, superhuman powers are un-derstood to be intentionally *rejecting* or *defeating* the religious practitioner's original desires in order to prepare them to receive a greater or worthier outcome later. In this case, the interpretation involves coming to realize that something about the original desire was misguided, tainted, or compro-mised, and thus needed to be refined or destroyed, after which a renewed or superior object of desire is provided. Some commentators interpret in just this way Yahweh's command to Abraham to sacrifice his only and ear-nestly desired son, Isaac, and then, at the last moment, staying his hand and providing a ram as a substitute sacrifice (Genesis 22:1–18). Yahweh, it is thought, had to defeat Abraham's personal investment in his promised and only son, in order not only to test his faith but also to purify his heart and trust in God in a way that would make him worthy to become the promised "father of many nations" and more fully appreciate his progeny. Some Christians draw a similar meaning from the gospel text in which Jesus says, "Very truly I tell you, unless a kernel of wheat falls to the ground and dies, it remains only a single seed. But if it dies, it produces many seeds" (John 12:24). This line of reasoning the American evangelical leader Bill Go-thard—the longtime head of an influential para-church ministry, the Insti-tute in Basic Life Principles—generalized as a common pattern of God's dealing with his people, teaching that "God will use the disappointments, drawbacks, and dead ends in life to motivate us to look to Him for His strength and timing for fulfilling a vision. As we wait on Him, God often works in ways that we never would have expected."[48]

In some cases, success reinterpreted may involve feelings of disappoint-ment or resentment among practitioners, as if the superhuman powers

---

48. "How Does God Work Through the Birth, Death, and Fulfillment of a Vision?" Oakbrook, IL: Institute in Basic Life Principles. http://iblp.org/questions/how-does-god-work-through -birth-death-and-fulfillment-vision. Gothard began his ministry in 1961, and his respect and influ-ence in evangelicalism peaked in the 1970s and continued, despite waning, until early 2014. At that time he was accused of sexually harassing and molesting several female employees and was put on administrative leave. He later resigned, which tarnished his reputation and sent his orga-nization into a tailspin.

were only prepared to award them a "consolation prize." "What I really wanted was promotion to division manager, but I guess I should be thankful for the salary raise I got." In other cases, however, religious practitioners are actually happier they received the outcome they did instead of having their original desires fulfilled. Depending on the circumstances, an unexpected answer to prayers or religious practices may be taken to demonstrate that the superhuman powers are not simply doling out minimal responses as if out of obligation, but are paying close enough attention to consider and produce an even better outcome than the practitioner imagined. That shows that the superhuman power is interested in the personal concerns of the human practitioners, and cares that they receive the best response. Frequently accompanying this outlook is a sense that the superhuman powers know better what humans need than the humans themselves. "I desperately wanted God to give me the job in Toledo, but instead he dropped in my lap an even better one in San Diego!" No doubt the lame beggar in the temple felt this way when the Apostle Peter said to him, "Silver and gold have I none, but what I do have I give you; in the name of Jesus Christ of Nazareth, rise up and walk"—which, according to the New Testament story, he did. "He jumped to his feet and began to walk. Then he went with them into the temple courts, walking and jumping, and praising God" (Acts 3:1–10).

3. *Presumed Satisfaction.* This outcome of religious practices is noteworthy for the absence of anything noticeable about it. It especially pertains to practices that are ongoing and routine. In this case, the human religious practitioners have performed their prescribed practices more or less well, and the apparent result is neither success nor failure but not much to speak of. Essentially, nothing notable happens, and that is judged satisfactory. To belong to this category, human religious practitioners need to interpret these results not as "no response" in the sense described next, and definitely not as failure, but as adequate and a sign of the superhuman powers' approval. The practitioner also must not have expected something concrete or immediate from their religious practices—otherwise the lack of change in any situation might appear to be failure. Instead, the basic idea behind this kind of outcome is "No news is good news."

Seemingly, here, the practices are being performed adequately, the superhuman powers in question are satisfied, and everything is okay. The Shinto practitioner has performed his rituals of purification, offerings, and the leaving of amulets for *kami*, the Shinto spirits, and all seems to be well with regard to his health and luck. The Greek Orthodox believer attends church services fairly regularly, observes major feasts and fasts, and feels satisfied with life. The traveler prays for safety in traveling and, upon returning home safely and without incident, assumes her prayers were answered. The implication of this "presumed satisfaction" outcome is simply to continue performing the practices that one has already been performing until further notice, and, most likely, when the need arises for a more definite, concrete result from the superhuman powers, all will be well. Meanwhile, practitioners' attitude is something like, "If it ain't broke, don't fix it." Presume that all is well and keep moving forward. While this is not a particularly interesting or complicated outcome, it may be the most common experience of most religious practitioners most of the time.

4. *No Response.* Sometimes religious practitioners do not observe any response to their practices from superhuman powers. Nothing happens, it appears—no refutation, no answer, just silence. This need not mean that the religious practices failed. Failure is a distinct experience that requires the empirical disconfirmation of expected outcomes. No response is more ambiguous. What sets it apart from the presumed satisfaction just described is that something about it seems problematic or troubling. The religious practitioner was expecting more. The lack of response may be only slightly worrisome or it may be highly disconcerting, but it is at least noted.

Religious people may make sense of these noticeable no-response situations in various ways.[49] They may tell themselves that "God works on his own timetable." They might decide that the superhuman power is trying to teach them patience or endurance, or is testing their faith. They could conclude that something was wrong with the way they were or are performing their religious practices, which they need to correct in order to receive the desired response. They may think that the superhuman powers are distracted or angry or otherwise ill-disposed at the moment. Or they may settle on some other explanation attempting to make sense of the lack of response in a way that is consistent with their religious tradition and practices.[50]

---

49. Shane Sharp. 2013. "When Prayers Go Unanswered." *Journal for the Scientific Study of Religion.* 52: 1–16.

50. In one study of 1,500 white and black elderly Americans, respondents were most likely to give answers between "agree" and "strongly agree" to the two prompts "Learning to wait for God's answer to my prayers is an important part of my faith" and "When I pray, God does not always give me what I ask for because only He knows what is best." (The other two answer options were "disagree" and "strongly disagree.") The average of all responses was 3.31, with a standard deviation of 1.0 on a 4-point scale (only scale scores, not the percentage of respondents choosing each option, were reported). Neal Krause. 2004. "Assessing the Relationship among Prayer Expectancies, Race, and Self-Esteem in Later Life." *Journal for the Scientific Study of Religion.* 43: 395–408.

Religious traditions tell of many adherents who wrestle with this no-response outcome, and they offer counsel on how to respond to it. The primordial figure of Job, whose grueling story of tragedy and divine silence is told in the Hebrew Bible and Christian Old Testament, is an archetypically righteous worshipper of God whose experiences in life are nevertheless those deserved by a wicked man. His demands for explanation and justice from God are ignored for a time, until, at the end of the story, Job's case is not divinely answered but essentially overwhelmed.[51] The ancient Hebrew psalms contain numerous complaints about Yahweh's lack of response to supplications, such as:

> How long, Lord? Will you forget me forever?
> How long will you hide your face from me?
> How long must I wrestle with my thoughts
> and day after day have sorrow in my heart?
> How long will my enemy triumph over me? (Psalms 13:1–2)

Pagan Greeks and Romans commonly expected the gods not to respond to their practices, according to Rodney Stark:

> Most of the Greeks and Romans believed that their gods *could* hear their pleas, but that they mostly didn't listen and didn't care. Aristotle taught that the gods were incapable of real concern for humans—lust, jealousy, and anger, yes, but never affection. Such gods may require propitiation and it may be possible to sometimes bargain with them for favors. But they cannot be counted on. . . . Most of their gods were quite undependable, being capricious and amoral. Sometimes they kept their word, and sometimes they provided humans with very valuable rewards. But sometimes they lied, and they often did humans great harm for very petty reasons.[52]

Many Roman Catholic saints have reported suffering what has come to be called the "dark night of the soul"—after a 1584–85 poem and treatise penned by the Spanish Catholic mystic St. John of the Cross—when, despite their pleas to God, they feel abandoned, alone, and in spiritual gloom. Mother Teresa of Calcutta, for example, despite mystical experiences of Jesus early in life and years devoted to serving God in the destitute, spent most of her adult life wrestling with God's failure to answer her prayers for

---

51. Harold Kushner. 2012. *The Book of Job*. New York: Jewish Encounters.
52. Stark. 2003. *One True God*. Princeton: Princeton University Press. Pp. 21, 22.

spiritual intimacy and vitality. Thus, in a 1961 letter to her spiritual adviser, Mother Teresa wrote, "Darkness is such that I really do not see—neither with my mind nor with my reason—the place of God in my soul is blank—There is no God in me—when the pain of longing is so great—I just long and long for God. . . . The torture and pain I can't explain."[53] Sometimes the non-responses of superhuman powers resonate in historical memory, and questions about them are retrospective. During a 2006 visit to the former Nazi concentration camp of Auschwitz, for example, the distressed German Pope Benedict XVI asked, "Where was God in those days? Why was he silent? How could he permit this endless slaughter, this triumph of evil?"[54]

Ordinary religious people, too, confront and struggle with unanswered prayers and the unresponsiveness of superhuman powers. Christian magazines and the Internet contain countless articles starting with stories that open like this: "Ten years ago, it seemed as though God had packed up, moved far away, and left me no forwarding address. I was unable to sense his promptings and overall presence as I searched for him during trying times. I felt abandoned, confused, and terribly alone."[55] A plethora of contemporary pastoral and popular books, both Catholic and Protestant, also advise believers on how to "get through" their own dark nights of the soul, with such titles:

- Waiting on God: What to Do When God Does Nothing
- How to Pray for Healing: And What to Do If Nothing Happens
- The Surprising Grace of Disappointment: Finding Hope When God Seems to Fail Us
- When God Doesn't Answer Your Prayer: Insights to Keep You Praying with Greater Faith and Deeper Hope
- Praying When Prayer Doesn't Work: Finding a Way Back to the Heart of God
- Seeking God's Hidden Face: When God Seems Absent
- Learning to Pray When Your Heart Is Breaking: How to Pray in Life's Tough Times, When God Seems Silent[56]

53. Mother Teresa and Brian Kolodiejchuk. 2009. *Mother Teresa*. Colorado Springs: Image Books. http://www.christianitytoday.com/ct/2007/augustweb-only/135–43.0.html.

54. Jeff Jacoby. 2013. "The Silence of God." http://www.aish.com/ho/i/48961526.html; http://www.zenit.org/en/articles/pope-s-message-at-auschwitz.

55. Verla Wallace. 2003. "When God Seems Silent." *Today's Christian Woman*. March. http://www.todayschristianwoman.com/articles/2003/march/2.44.html.

56. Wayne Stiles. 2015. *Waiting on God*. Grand Rapids, MI: Baker; Mark Dahle. 2006. *How to Pray for Healing*. La Jolla, CA: Mark Dahle Portfolios; John Koessler and John Ortberg. 2013. *The*

One evangelical prayer manual explains, "One of the great benefits of God's silence is that it makes you appreciate the times when He speaks. . . . God reserves the right to be silent. He reserves the right to delay answers, leave certain issues unaddressed, and become seemingly quiet."[57] And Garth Brooks sings in the country music hit "Unanswered Prayers": "Sometimes I thank God for unanswered prayers; Remember when you're talkin' to the man upstairs that just because he doesn't answer doesn't mean he don't care. Some of God's greatest gifts are unanswered prayers."[58]

Apparently following such advice, elderly Americans who participated in one study found a variety of explanations for the lack of divine answers to prayers. One individual, for instance, explained, "It seems to me that sometimes things that seem to be a temporary denial or a 'no' answer . . . require some effort on your part. . . . I don't want to assume that things are going to be dropped into your lap because I prayed for them." Another said: "I feel sometimes that you have to wait. You know. I want it and I want it now. But that isn't the way. You have to wait. He said, 'Wait on the Lord,' and we have to wait from time to time. . . . Pray for it and ask Him, and then you wait."[59]

5. *Failure.* In the case of failure, superhuman powers do not merely appear to not respond to religious practices, leaving room for uncertainty and hope for later success. Instead, the superhuman powers positively miscarry, disappoint, and fail to produce what practitioners expected. Outright failure depends on desired outcomes that are positive and empirically verifiable. Unlike non-responses, then, practitioners cannot easily explain them away, although, as Maarten Boudry and Johan De Smedt point out,

---

Surprising Grace of Disappointment. Chicago: Moody; Jerry Sittser. 2007. *When God Doesn't Answer Your Prayer.* Grand Rapids, MI: Zondervan; Jack Getz. 2010. *Praying When Prayer Doesn't Work.* Bloomington, IN: iUniverse; Denise George. 2011. *Learning to Pray When Your Heart Is Breaking.* Freemont, CA: Sine Qua Non Publishing; Cecil Murphey. 2001. *Seeking God's Hidden Face.* Downers Grove, IL: InterVarsity Press.

57. Margery Feinberg. 2005. *God Whispers.* Orlando, FL: Relevant Books, quoted in Luhrmann. *When God Talks Back.* P. 282.

58. Lyrics by Pat Alger, Larry Bastian, and Garth Brooks. 1990. *No Fences*—country music arguably representing the actual theology of most American people.

59. Similar explanations focused instead on prayers not being answered because they asked for the wrong things, for instance, "I think that if you prayed for . . . an Oldsmobile 88, I don't think you're going to get it. That isn't the way to go," and "I would never say, 'Gee, I hope Michigan wins the title this year.' I think there are prayers that should not be made." Neal Kraus, Linda Chatters, Tina Meltzer, and David Morgan. 2000. "Using Focus Groups to Explore the Nature of Prayer in Late Life." *Journal of Aging Studies.* 14: 191–212, quotes pp. 199, 200.

"negative evidence rarely threatens religious belief in God."[60] Failure is normally more threatening to religious commitment than the non-response of superhuman powers, for it calls into question the existence and purpose of religion itself. Still, some scholars claim, the cognitive dissonance of failure can sometimes strengthen people's beliefs.[61] Failure is less complicated than success reinterpreted and no response, so it merits less discussion here. But let us consider three examples of failure in religious outcomes, two historical accounts drawn from religious traditions and one involving more contemporary events.

According to traditional accounts of the life of the Buddha, Siddhartha Gautama, before discovering his successful "Middle Way" to awakening and enlightenment, renounced his family and privileges at age 29 and devoted himself to mendicant poverty, yogic meditation, and severe, nearly fatal ascetic self-mortification. All of his striving, however, failed to achieve the results that Siddhartha was pursuing. His disappointment motivated him to seek an alternative approach, which eventually led to his famed enlightenment under the Bodhi tree.[62] Had his ascetic self-denial not failed him, we may never have heard of Buddhism.

Or consider the story of Elijah and the 450 prophets of Baal on Mount Carmel (1Kings 18:16–40). In this contest by fire to see which was the true and powerful divinity, Baal or Yahweh, the prophets of Baal failed miserably, since their god failed to light the fire of their altar:

> They called on the name of Baal from morning till noon. "Baal, answer us!," they shouted. But there was no response; no one answered. And they danced around the altar they had made. At noon Elijah began to taunt them. "Shout louder!," he said. "Surely he is a god! Perhaps he is deep in thought, or busy, or traveling. Maybe he is sleeping and must be awakened." So they shouted louder and slashed themselves with swords and spears, as was their custom, until their blood flowed. Midday passed,

60. Maarten Boudry and Johan De Smedt. 2011. *Religion*. "In Mysterious Ways: On Petitionary Prayer and Subtle Forms of Supernatural Causation." 41. P. 460; A. Village. 2005. "Dimensions of Belief about Miraculous Healing." *Mental Health, Religion, and Culture*. 8: 97–107. However, at some point, as Weber notes, "Should the effort to influence a god prove to be permanently inefficacious . . . he is abandoned." *Economy and Society*. P. 427.

61. Conrad Montell. 2001. "Speculations on a Privileged State of Cognitive Dissonance." *Journal for the Theory of Social Behaviour*. 31: 119–137; Reeve Brenner. 1980. *The Faith and Doubt of Holocaust Survivors*. New York: Free Press.

62. Stephen Laumakis. 2008. *An Introduction to Buddhist Philosophy*. Cambridge; New York: Cambridge University Press; K. Upadhyaya. 1971. *Early Buddhism and the Bhagavadgita*. Delhi, India: Motilal Banarsidass.

and they continued their frantic prophesying until the time for the evening sacrifice. But there was no response, no one answered, no one paid
attention. (vs. 26–30)

By contrast, according to the story, although Elijah had his altar drenched
with 12 large jars of water, Yahweh, whom the prophet Elijah served, came
through with a smashing religious success:

> The prophet Elijah stepped forward and prayed: "Lord, the God of
> Abraham, Isaac and Israel, let it be known today that you are God in
> Israel and that I am your servant and have done all these things at your
> command. Answer me, Lord, answer me, so these people will know that
> you, Lord, are God, and that you are turning their hearts back again."
> Then the fire of the Lord fell and burned up the sacrifice, the wood, the
> stones and the soil, and also licked up the water in the trench. When all
> the people saw this, they fell prostrate and cried, "The Lord—he is God!
> The Lord—he is God!" (vs. 36–39)

The failure of Baal had adverse consequences for his 450 prophets: They
were seized, hauled away, and slaughtered (v. 40).

Another example of the failure of religious practices concerns the death
of children whose parents believe for religious reasons in abstaining from
modern, professional medical care. Some religions, including Christian Science, Jehovah's Witnesses, and small, independent denominations and congregations, teach on grounds of the Bible or philosophy that believers
should avoid mainstream medicine, including blood transfusions. The Jehovah's Witnesses have expelled some members for accepting blood transfusions. The Christian Science faith teaches that physical disease is a lie, that
healing is a metaphysical process, and that sick believers should rely on
prayer, not modern medicine. Many adherents of these religions obey their
teachings, including parents with sick children. Hundreds of cases of children who have died as a result of their parents' decisions have been re-
corded over the decades.[63] When parents believe that following their religion's practices will cause their children to be healed, and their children
instead remain ill or die, their practices have failed.

---

63. Shawn Peters. 2007. *When Prayer Fails*. New York: Oxford University Press; Seth Asser
and Rita Swan. 1998. "Child Fatalities from Religion-motivated Medical Neglect." *Pediatrics.* 101:
625–629. Caroline Fraser. 1995. "Suffering Children and the Christian Science Church." *The Atlantic.* April.

6. *Rejection.* This final category of possible results of human religious practices is worse than failure, from the practitioner's point of view. For religious practices in this case not only fail to bring about the desired outcome, but are actually rebuffed by the powers they sought to access and influence. Rejection happens under one or more of three conditions. First, superhuman powers might by nature be volatile or malicious, so may reject religious entreaties for amusement or out of spite. Many religions around the world tell of "trickster" gods and spirits, who may be counted on to fool and cheat those who seek to work with them.[64] Second, the religious culture prescribing the practices might have lost touch with the true or changing interests and character of the superhuman powers in question, causing the latter to reject the supplications of their practices as wearisome or repellant. Third, the religious cultures and superhuman powers may be sound, but the particular religious practices that drew rejection may have been somehow neglected or performed badly.[65]

One example of rejection comes from the Hebrew Bible. The prophets recount God's rejection of the very temple sacrifices required by divine law, as when God spoke to the leaders and people of Judah—whom he compared to those of Sodom and Gomorrah—through the prophet Isaiah:

> I have more than enough of burnt offerings, of rams and the fat of fattened animals.
>
> I have no pleasure in the blood of bulls and lambs and goats.
>
> When you come to appear before me, who has asked this of you, this trampling of my courts?
>
> Stop bringing meaningless offerings! Your incense is detestable to me.
>
> New Moons, Sabbaths and convocations—I cannot bear your worthless assemblies.
>
> Your New Moon feasts and your appointed festivals I hate with all my being.

64. Richard Erdoes. 1999. *American Indian Trickster Tales.* New York: Penguin; Lewis Hyde. 2010. *Trickster Makes This World.* New York: Farrar, Straus and Giroux; Paul Radin. 1956. *The Trickster.* New York: Schocken; Klaus-Peter Koepping. 1985. "Absurdity and Hidden Truth: Cunning Intelligence and Grotesque Body Images as Manifestations of the Trickster." *History of Religions.* 24: 191–214; Virginia Driving Hawk Sneve. 1999. *The Trickster and the Troll.* Lincoln: University of Nebraska Press; Mike Vasich. 2012. *Loki.* CreateSpace Publishing; Martin Bennett. 1994. *West African Trickster Tales.* New York: Oxford University Press.

65. Weber observes: "Priests may find ways of interpreting failures in such a manner that the responsibility falls, not on the god, but upon the behavior of the god's worshippers." *Economy and Society.* P. 428.

They have become a burden to me; I am weary of bearing them.

When you spread out your hands in prayer, I hide my eyes from you.

Even when you offer many prayers, I am not listening. (1:11–15)

Rejection, indeed. Or consider these words God said to the people of Israel through the prophet Amos:

I hate, I despise your religious festivals; your assemblies are a stench to me.

Even though you bring me burnt offerings and grain offerings, I will not accept them.

Though you bring choice fellowship offerings, I will have no regard for them.

Away with the noise of your songs! I will not listen to the music of your harps.

But let justice roll on like a river, righteousness like a never-failing stream! (5:21–24)

In both cases, the religious sacrifices and temple celebrations that God himself ordained are invalidated by the sins and injustice of these nations, and incited his forceful rejection.

Another example of perceived rejection by a superhuman power is less direct. Rather than centering on religious practices that superhuman powers explicitly repudiated, it involves a catastrophe that humans sought to explain after the fact by pointing to human impiety and sin believed to have angered God. I mean the various frenzies connected with the Black Death pandemic that swept medieval Europe in the fourteenth century, wiping out one-third of the population. The Plague was not only horrific and devastating but, for the people it struck, confusing and unprecedented. Responses to it were many and varied; they included murderous mass attacks on Jews, lepers, friars, and gypsies. Some explanations insisted that the Black Death was clearly punishment from God, who had been angered by a corrupt Church, the sins of Christians, and a divided and warring Christendom. Some people expressed extreme repentance and penance through spontaneously formed self-whipping "flagellant groups," such as the Brothers of the Cross, who roamed from town to town in Germany and the Low Countries in 1347 and after, striking and flogging themselves into bloody messes to prophesy the Lord's anger and call the people to repentance.[66]

66. Barbara Tuchman. 1987. *A Distant Mirror*. New York: Random House; David Nirenberg. 1998. *Communities of Violence*. Princeton: Princeton University Press; Philip Ziegler. 2009. *The*

In summary, religious people encounter many kinds of empirical outcomes and experiences that may seem to validate, leave uncertain, or discredit the causal influence of superhuman powers in response to their religious practices. They always actively participate in the interpretation of those outcomes and experiences, continually evaluating the seemingly larger meanings of the clues and signs they acquire to determine whether and how superhuman powers are responding to their religious practices. The conclusions they reach through their ongoing attributions of causal influences depend on a dynamic interaction of the actual facts and the subjective meanings assigned to them, as well as the social contexts that influence their lives. Other factors internal to religious traditions and organizations—such as the possible controlling interests of religious authorities, the need some feel to maintain boundaries around "orthodoxy" by excluding unacceptable views, and the readiness of some to silence or discredit troublesome and dissenting voices—also play into the process of "correctly" interpreting the influence of superhuman powers. The outcomes of religious practices usually leave room for many plausible religious interpretations.

Figure 3.3 schematically depicts the theory I have described in the previous pages. Analytically, the process of attributing causes to superhuman powers begins with people performing religious practices (a). They then observe outcomes that they expect to be related to their practices (b) and interpret their meaning (c). Depending on the interpretation—especially when the outcomes are different from what was expected—outcomes can be reconsidered and "re-observed" (indicated by the bidirectional arrow for "c"). The specific type of response from the superhuman power or powers is assessed (d). After this, religious people can head in various directions, depending on the type of response attributed. Religious practitioners can continue to engage in the same practices (e) or they can adjust or change their practices somehow (f) as a result of their experiences and attributions (as represented by the dashed line). Also potentially influenced by types of responses from superhuman powers to religious practices are people's premises about the existence and nature of superhuman powers (appropriated from religious traditions and culture) on which the practices are based, which they may revise (x)—for example, when people decide their superhuman power does not answer those kinds of prayers or maybe does not even

---

Black Death. New York: Harper. Pp. 84–109. For a comparative view of a modern flagellant movement, see Michael Carroll. 2002. *The Penitente Brotherhood.* Baltimore: Johns Hopkins University Press.

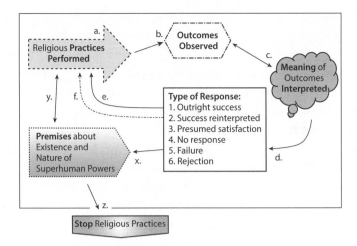

FIGURE 3.3. Schematic representation of the process of causal attributions to superhuman powers

exist. Changing their premises may cause people to revise the religious practices they performed (y). Or it can cause people to stop practicing religion altogether (z).

Capacities for Interpretive Cognitive Flexibility

Readers familiar with religion may easily recognize the kinds of interpretive processes described above. Readers not personally familiar with religion may have greater difficulty understanding how reasonable religious people could engage in this kind of attribution. Some may struggle with "the nonbeliever's puzzle: How can sensible, educated people believe in an invisible being who has a real effect on their lives?"[67] The social scientist's job is to neither defend nor criticize such meaning-making. Our job is to describe, understand, and explain religious attributions. To do that, it is useful to refer back to some of the normal cognitive processes and biases at work when humans try to make sense of the world. In some cases, an outside observer may see some "friction" between the actual circumstances and the religious attributions made concerning them. Common thought processes and biases may provide "lubrication" to reduce that friction—like oil helping internal combustion engines run smoothly. (The rest

67. Luhrmann. *When God Talks Back*. P. 300.

of this chapter makes an obvious shift from a primarily "emic" to a fully "etic" perspective.)

To begin, all attributions of causal explanations operate amid limitations in human conditions of knowing ("epistemology"). By this I mean, first, that any given outcome is the result of a *multiplicity of complex causes* operating at different levels of reality and varying depths of background in time, as I explained above. Neither in religion nor in the rest of life is it possible to explain anything by pointing to just one or two clear causes. The causal multiplicity and complexity always present allow plenty of room for humans who believe in superhuman powers to "work them into" their larger causal explanations. Being religious very rarely requires denying all of the natural causal processes at work that nearly all people use to make sense of life in the world. It simply means including the causal influences of superhuman powers among them. And that, it turns out, is not very hard for many people to do.

The process of attributing conditions and events in one's life to superhuman influences is made easier by the fact that *no one* enjoys the ability to test their causal explanations through "comparative counterfactuals." That is, nobody gets to re-run life exactly as it happened except for changing one "experimental intervention" to see what difference that makes. In perfect experimental conditions, all possible causal variables but one are kept constant, and the one "experimental treatment" whose causal influence is being tested is varied between the experimental group (which gets the treatment) and the "control group" (which does not). To rigorously test whether religious practices make a difference in causal outcomes would require something similar: the running of two identical worlds and lives, embracing religious practice in one and ignoring it in the other. If the two worlds produced identical outcomes, then one might reasonably judge that the religious practice made no difference. However, performing this experiment is impossible. We can only try to make sense of one reality as it moves irreversibly forward in time.[68]

But, note, *even if we could run a counterfactual experiment*, in situations where the superhuman power in question was believed to be personal—to possess something like conscious perceptions, reflections, and purposes—

---

68. However, empirical experimental studies show that counterfactual *thinking*—especially when the counterfactual possibilities involve negative outcomes, where events might have turned out to be worse—tends to increase people's interpretation of events in religious or divine terms. Anneke Buffone, Shira Gabriel, and Michael Poulin. 2016. "There But for the Grace of God." *Social Psychological and Personality Science*. 7: 256–263.

we still might not be able to pin down the superhuman causal influence. That is because it would be possible for the personal superhuman power to *decide* not to respond to someone's religious practice, and so make its causal powers appear not to exist when in fact they do. Precisely because it is a superhuman power, it might opt to outwit the human counterfactual experiment, to play a trick on it by refusing to submit to the test. (Some personal superhuman powers do not take kindly to being made the objects of human experiments, to being tested, pinned down, or measured as one causal force among many.) Therefore, even if counterfactual comparisons in human life *were* possible, there is no guarantee that they would detect the causal influence of superhuman powers. For skeptics, this adds to the conditions that make religion seem entirely unreasonable,[69] but for religious believers, it underlines the seeming reasonableness of making attributions of casual influences of superhuman powers in life.

Some religious people, especially in certain religious traditions and social locations, appear to hold back from making requests of their superhuman powers that seem too demanding—such as miraculous healings from cancer—when failure would be empirically obvious. They do so, it seems, for two reasons. First, they wish to avoid the "cognitive dissonance" that would result from such failure. Second, they wish to preserve their relationship with their superhuman power by avoiding ultimatums that would be hard to back down from.[70] In other words, religious people manage not only the meaning of the (non-)responses of superhuman powers, but also their own initial hopes and requests. This is not true of all religious people: Some are bold enough to make high-stakes requests of superhuman powers.[71] But the ability to limit one's religious petitions does help to lessen the cognitive perils of making religious attributions.

As I noted earlier, religious people who do make clear and strong requests of superhuman powers can still *reinterpret* outcomes that do not

69. See, for instance, Steven Weinberg. 2001. *Facing Up*. Cambridge, MA: Harvard University Press. Pp. 230–242.

70. Justin Barrett. 2001. "How Ordinary Cognition Informs Petitionary Prayers." *Journal of Cognition and Culture*. 1: 259–269; Simon Dein, J. Stygall, and P. Martin. 2006. "The Use and Expectations of Prayer among Women with Breast Cancer." *Healing Ministry*. 13: 23–31; Kenneth Pargament. 1997. *The Psychology of Religion and Coping*. New York: Guilford Press; Chaves. "Rain Dances"; Dein and Pargament. "On Not Praying"; E. Taylor, F. Outlaw, T. Bernado, and A. Roy. 1999. "Spiritual Conflicts Associated with Praying about Cancer." *Psycho-Oncology*. 8: 386–394; also see T. J. Mawson. 2007. "Praying for Unknown Outcomes." *Religious Studies*. 43: 71–87.

71. Maarten Boudry and Johan DeSmeet. 2011. "In Mysterious Ways." *Religion*. 41: 449–469.

fulfill their original hopes in seeking the help of superhuman powers. In few cases are the hopes animating the religious practices so specific and empirically testable that a lack of desired response is fatal to religious believing. Humans demonstrate amazing abilities to engage in "post-hoc rescues" of all kinds of expectations and activity gone awry, and not only in the realm of religion.[72] We know, for instance, that when dramatic prophecies fail, even (or perhaps especially) in obvious and embarrassing ways, humans do not necessarily decide that the prophecies were false. Instead, they frequently do all kinds of mental explanatory work to rescue them.[73] In many less dramatic ways, human beings, including religious people, are easily able to reinterpret conditions and events in ways that do not falsify their beliefs and commitments.

Placebo Power

Understanding how and why religious attributions work may also require appreciating the power of "placebo effects." These are remarkable forms of causal influence in which people's *belief* that they have received some treatment, when they actually have not, produces the same physical and psychological changes as the real treatment. The classic case is when patients in a medical test of, say, a painkiller are, without their knowledge, given dummy pills of inert material instead of the real painkiller, and afterward report a significant reduction in pain. The dummy pill is the placebo and the reduction in pain is its placebo effect. Decades of research have demonstrated an amazing range of placebo effects, where people's perceptions, beliefs, and expectations cause real physical and psychological changes in major areas of health.[74] The main causal mechanism by which placebo effects work is the *self-fulfilling outcomes of "response expectancies,"* that is, people's belief that they will feel different leads them to actually feel different.[75] These ef-

72. Carol Tavris. 2008. *Mistakes Were Made (But Not by Me)*. Boston: Mariner Books; Robert Burton. 2009. *On Being Certain*. New York: St. Martin's; Diana Tumminia. 2005. *When Prophecy Never Fails*. New York: Oxford University Press.

73. Leon Festinger and Henry Riecken. 2012. *When Prophecy Fails*. Eastford, CT: Martino Fine Books; Simon Dein. 2012. *Lubavitcher Messianism*. New York: Bloomsbury; Timothy Jenkins. 2013. *Of Flying Saucers and Social Scientists*. London: Palgrave; Jon Stone. 2000. *Expecting Armageddon*. New York: Routledge.

74. Fabrizio Benedetti. 2014. *Placebo Effects*. New York: Oxford University Press; Anne Harrington. 1999. *The Placebo Effect*. Cambridge, MA: Harvard University Press; Daniel Moerman. 2002. *Meaning, Medicine and the 'Placebo Effect.'* Cambridge: Cambridge University Press.

75. Irving Kirsch. 1985. "Response Expectancy as a Determinant of Experience and Be-

fects are not "all in the head," but actually work at least in part through physical, neurological mechanisms.[76] The sociological analogue of the placebo effect is expressed in the "Thomas theorem," which states, "If [people] define situations as real, they are real in their consequences."[77]

When it comes to religion, placebo effects can help to validate religious attributions by aligning people's lived experiences with the expectations associated with their religious practices.[78] For example, when a religious practitioner who is suffering severe anxiety prays for "peace of mind and heart," their prayers combined with their belief that "prayer changes things" can by themselves actually decrease their anxiety. This is not mere wishful thinking. Real neurological and physiological transformations are triggered by certain beliefs, practices, and expectations. The same dynamic can operate in religious contexts to produce many other desired outcomes, which then increases the credibility of the religious attributions concerning the influence of superhuman powers believed to have caused them. The consequences of religious practices are thus not "competing on a level playing field," so to speak. Whether a religious practice appears effective is not determined by random chance, which would make it difficult over the long run for religious people to sustain their beliefs about superhuman interventions. No, the outcomes of religious practices are often causally influenced in the hoped-for or expected direction by the power of placebo effects. The very fact of expecting some outcome helps to bring that outcome about. So the field is tilted toward results that are more likely to reinforce the credibility of religious attributions than not. The belief that entreating the gods to provide the self-discipline necessary to resist some temptation can *itself* help to generate that self-discipline, and the temptation is better resisted. The belief that the consecrated bread and wine are efficacious channels of God's grace *itself* helps those receiving the Eucharist to experience God's grace. Such placebo effects help to explain the plausibility of religious

---

havior." *American Psychologist*. 40: 1189–1202. Placebos can also operate through classical conditioning.

76. David Scott, Christian Stohler, Christine Egnatuk, Heng Wang, Robert Koeppe, and Jon-Kar Zubieta. 2008. "Placebo and Nocebo Effects Are Defined by Opposite Opioid and Dopaminergic Responses." *Archives of General Psychiatry*. 65: 220–231; Sarah Lidstone and Jon Stoessl. 2007. "Understanding the Placebo Effect." *Molecular Imaging and Biology*. 9: 176–85; Barry Oken. 2008. "Placebo Effects." *Brain*. 131: 2812–2823.

77. W. I. Thomas and D. S. Thomas. 1928. *The Child in America*. New York: Knopf. Pp. 571–572.

78. Matt Rosanno. 2010. "Harnessing the Placebo Effect." In Ulrich Frey (ed.). *The Nature of God*. Marburg: Tectum.

attributions of the causal influences of superhuman powers. More generally, they powerfully enable religious practitioners to imagine, believe, and act within "life worlds" that seem completely real.[79]

Of course, placebos do not have absolute power, since not all causal effects are influenced by the mind, beliefs, and expectations. A placebo cannot raise a dead child back to life or turn fields green that are withered by drought. In medicine, too, placebo effects are usually not as strong as those of active treatments. But many areas of human life, particularly those involving subjective well-being and the body, are subject to significant placebo effects. Their power is sometimes astonishing. Indeed, while placebo effects generally require people to believe they are receiving the active treatment, some research has shown that the effects can materialize even when people *know* they have taken a placebo.[80] It seems that, for humans, simply taking some action to address a problem—whether swallowing a pill or offering sacrifices to the gods—itself can help to ameliorate that problem. In religious contexts, it is even more likely that performing whole *complexes* of interconnected religious practices—prayer, singing, sharing, receiving support, reading scripture, knowing one is being prayed for, lighting candles, meditating, sacrificing, and so on—will have synergistic, multiplying, and mutually reinforcing effects on practitioners, compared to performing only one practice.

To be clear, I am not suggesting that the real power of placebo effects means that religious attributions of the causal interventions of superhuman powers are necessarily invalid. Placebo effects and influences of superhuman powers are by no means incompatible. Real religious effects may have the primary role in some circumstances and placebo effects in others. Superhuman powers' intervention may account for part of an outcome and placebo effects for another part, working additively. Religious effects may conceivably also work *through* the mechanisms of placebo effects, whereby a superhuman power influences outcomes through the self-fulfilling results of response expectancies. In such cases, placebo effects may be very real *and* religious claims entirely valid. Furthermore, to turn the tables on religious skeptics, just to keep this intellectual playing field level, the mechanisms of placebo effects can equally help to produce outcomes that confirm the expectations, interpretations, and attributions of non-religious people.

79. Martin Lindhardt's ethnography of Chilean Pentecostals illustrates this point beautifully. Lindhardt. 2014. *Power in Powerlessness*. Leiden: Brill.

80. Cara Feinberg. 2013. "The Placebo Phenomenon." *Harvard Magazine*. January–February. http://harvardmagazine.com/2013/01/the-placebo-phenomenon.

"If the irreligious define situations as really godless, they are really godless in their consequences." Placebo effects cut both ways, in short, putting the claims of religious skeptics at no less risk than those of believers. In any case, it is not the job of social science to decide the veracity of religious or anti-religious claims. I am only outlining some of the *human* mechanisms by which religious attributions—claims about superhuman powers exerting causal influences in response to religious practices—may prove to rational religious practitioners credible, as a result of the outcomes, both real and interpreted, that those practices produce.

Cognitive Lubricants for Religious Attributions

Studying some common cognitive biases and social psychological effects that shape people's ability to make sense of the world sheds further light on the plausibility of religious attributions. These biases and effects apply to human perceptions and cognitions in all domains of life; however, they especially help account for how and why many people can make and believe religious attributions with little apparent difficulty. The following list, itemized in alphabetical order, illustrates the kinds of "cognitive lubricants" that can help make religious attributions, which at least to some outsiders may seem strained, quite plausible to many religious believers. In each case, I first define the bias or effect, then suggest how it might serve the process of making religious attributions.

- The Bandwagon effect (aka the Groupthink and Herd Mentality effect): the tendency of people to believe and do things because other people believe and do the same.
  - *Possible religious application*: Religious people may more easily embrace particular causal interpretations that are common and encouraged in their religious communities than plausible alternatives that might be unpopular in the same setting.
- The Barnum effect (aka the Forer effect): the tendency of people to evaluate descriptions of their situations or personalities that they believe are tailored specifically to them as accurate, when the descriptions are in fact ambiguous and broad enough to apply to a wide range of conditions and people (for example, Chinese fortune cookie fortunes and horoscopes).
  - *Possible religious application*: Religious people may take vague and general information that they believe may apply to them and

interpret it as a "sign," confirmation, or personal reassurance sent to them by superhuman powers.

- The Clustering illusion: the tendency of people to see patterns where none exist.
  - *Possible religious application*: Religious people may piece together facts and events in ways that create meaningful narratives, purposes, or interventions that are not necessarily accurate or real.
- The Confabulation bias (aka the False Memory effect): Recollecting an event that never actually happened.
  - *Possible religious application*: Religious people may incorporate "facts" from the past that have no basis in reality into meaningful narratives that support religious commitments.
- The Confirmation bias: the tendency to select and interpret information in a way that confirms one's assumptions and preconceived notions.
  - *Possible religious application*: Religious people may focus on those facts that confirm the hopes and expectations of their religious practices and ignore or downplay facts that do not.
- The Congruence bias: the tendency to evaluate a possible explanation by directly testing only that explanation, rather than also considering possible alternative explanations.
  - *Possible religious application*: Religious people may conclude that their religious practices were effective by focusing on evidence that seems to verify superhuman influences without contemplating alternative or competing interpretations of the evidence.
- The Egocentric bias: the self-serving tendency of people to remember their past as better than it actually was.
  - *Possible religious application*: Religious people may create meaningful narratives for themselves and others that support religious commitments by telling their story in a way that paints a rosier picture of the past than actually happened.
- The Exposure-Preference effect: the tendency for people to prefer things merely because they are more familiar.
  - *Possible religious application*: Religious people may privilege religious attributions over others simply because they are more recognizable and common in their discourse and subculture.

- The Focusing effect: the tendency of people to bias their understandings by placing too much emphasis on one aspect of an event rather than all relevant factors.
  - *Possible religious application*: Religious people may sustain their religious attributions and expectations by focusing selectively on the features of relevant events and information that especially seem to validate them.
- The Framing effect: the tendency of people to draw different conclusions from the same information, depending on how that information is presented to them.
  - *Possible religious application*: Religious people may be susceptible to embracing religious attributions of events when they are framed by religious leaders and fellow adherents in ways that make religious attributions most plausible, when other, non-religious framings of the same information may be equally or more plausible.
- The Frequency illusion: the tendency of people who have recently learned about or noticed something to begin to see it everywhere.
  - *Possible religious application*: Religious people may, upon the apparent success of one set of religious practices, start frequently noticing similar evidence that confirms the reliability of religious practices generally.
- The Hindsight bias (aka the "I knew it all along" effect): the tendency of people to see past events as predictable, based on their knowledge of later events.
  - *Possible religious application*: When recalling outcomes of religious practices that happened to fit their hopes, religious people may come to believe that they felt confident about their expected outcomes beforehand.
- The Illusion-of-Control effect: the tendency for humans to believe they can influence or control outcomes that they clearly cannot.
  - *Possible religious application*: Religious people may resort to religious practices to seek the help of superhuman powers in circumstances that are hopeless, and this bias makes them highly motivated to find evidence that their religious appeals made some difference.

- The In-Group bias: the tendency of people to give preferential treatment to those who are members of their own social groups.
  - *Possible religious application*: Religious people may privilege the interpretive views of fellow religious adherents that support their religious attributions and discount those of non-religious outsiders or believers in other religions, whose interpretations may provide equally plausible if not better interpretations.
- The Irrational Escalation bias: the tendency of people to make new irrational decisions based upon previous rational decisions in order to justify their prior commitments or actions.
  - *Possible religious application*: Religious people may make religious attributions that strain credulity in new situations in order to sustain the validity of previous, related religious attributions that seemed to make complete sense at the time.
- The Just-World bias: the tendency of people to believe that the world is just and meritocratic and that therefore people get what they deserve.
  - *Possible religious application*: Religious people who faithfully perform culturally prescribed religious practices may be primed to find evidence of superhuman influences responding to their practices in order to sustain their assumption that proper practices lead to promised results.
- The Loss-Aversion effect (aka the Endowment or Sunk-Costs effect): the tendency of people to require much more persuasion or payment to abandon an idea or object than they would be willing to expend to acquire it in the first place.
  - *Possible religious application*: Religious people may hold on to their religious beliefs and interpretations of life longer and more tenaciously than they "should," based on available evidence, because abandoning them would represent a loss of something into which they have already invested many resources and their personal identity.
- The Observer-Expectancy bias: the tendency of people who expect a given result to unconsciously direct an experiment or misinterpret evidence in order to find what they expect.
  - *Possible religious application*: Religious people who very much want to see superhuman powers respond to their religious practices may unconsciously do what they can to nudge events

and circumstances in a way that helps produce the desired
outcome.

- The Positive Outcome bias (aka Wishful Thinking): a tendency of
  people to overestimate the probability of good things happening to
  them in the future.
  - *Possible religious application*: Religious people may, despite
    evidence to the contrary, continue to engage in religious practices
    in the hope that they will succeed.
- The Post-Purchase Rationalization bias: the tendency to work to
  persuade oneself through rational argument that an acquisition was
  a good value, more so than it actually might have been.
  - *Possible religious application*: Religious people may continue to
    affirm and invest in religious commitments and practices on
    which they have already spent resources in order to maintain
    the belief that those commitments and practices were worth
    making.
- The Self-Fulfilling Prophecy effect: the tendency to act consciously
  or subconsciously in ways that produce results that confirm prior
  expectations and beliefs.
  - *Possible religious application*: Religious people may behave in
    ways that help to realize the expectations that motivated their
    religious practices, perhaps without acknowledging their
    capacities to have done so.
- The Texas Sharpshooter fallacy: the tendency of people to select or
  adjust an idea or explanation after the evidence about it is
  possessed, making it impossible to fairly evaluate the idea or
  explanation.
  - *Possible religious application*: Religious people may reinterpret the
    original hopes and expectations animating their religious
    practices after the outcome is known in order to make the result
    fit the alleged original intention.
- The Von Restorff effect: the tendency of people to remember ideas
  and objects that are highly conspicuous more strongly than they
  remember less remarkable ideas and objects that may be of equal
  importance.
  - *Possible religious application*: Religious people may be more likely
    to recall a few instances when superhuman powers appeared to
    intervene in the world in dramatic ways than the possibly

numerous times when the powers did not seem to respond to religious practices.[81]

To be clear, I am *not* saying that all or most religious beliefs and attributions are distortions, delusions, and lies. Nor am I saying that these kinds of biases are particular to religion. They regularly operate in all spheres of human life, including business, politics, academia, and science.[82] But these cognitive biases and effects are sometimes operative in religious cognitions, and their existence helps explain the plausibility of some religious attributions of causal influence to superhuman powers. What goes on in the minds of religious people when they "do religion" is never objective and infallible—which is also true of everything else we humans do.

In fact, one of my larger points here is that what specific people are doing when they make religious attributions is what all people do all the time and everywhere: assigning the causes of conditions and effects that concern them in order to make sense of their lives and how the world works. And in all cases, these attributions can be affected by the biases and effects described above. The only difference when it comes to making *religious* attributions is that, in addition to all the other culturally acceptable explanations for life's outcomes, religious people include in the mix the influences of superhuman powers. The latter influences almost never displace the former; rather, they are among the many causal factors that help humans understand and explain reality. In this sense, given the way human minds operate, religion is a natural part of the larger fabric of human life.

Conclusion

Religion works because humans attribute the causes of certain life events and experiences to the intervening influence of superhuman powers. That is the essential cognitive and cultural practice process that makes possible

81. Rüdiger Pohl. 2012. *Cognitive Illusions*. New York: Psychology Press; Thomas Gilovich, Dale Griffin, and Daniel Kahneman. 2002. *Heuristics and Biases*. Cambridge: Cambridge University Press; Jonathan Baron. 2007. *Thinking and Deciding*. Cambridge: Cambridge University Press; Daniel Kahneman, Paul Slovic, and Amos Tversky. 1982. *Judgment under Uncertainty*. Cambridge: Cambridge University Press; Howard Ross. 2014. *Everyday Bias*. Lanham, MD: Rowman and Littlefield; J. P. Caverni, J. M. Fabre, and M. Gonzalez. 1990. *Cognitive Biases*. Atlanta: Advances in Psychology; Mahzarin Banaji and Anthony Greenwald. 2013. *Blindspot*. New York: Delacorte; Dan Ariely. 2010. *Predictably Irrational*. New York: Harper; Thomas Gilovich. 1993. *How We Know What Isn't So*. New York: Free Press.

82. Gilovich. *How We Know*; Michael Shermer. 2002. *Why People Believe Weird Things*. New York: Henry Holt; Michael Shermer. 2011. *The Believing Brain*. New York: St. Martin's.

and sustains religion. However, making attributions is not limited to religious doings. Assigning causal forces to results of interest is a fundamental feature of all of human life, demanded by the basic need to understand how life and the world work. It is also rooted in the need to make life meaningful, to have existence make sense. Humans everywhere resist the notion that everything that happens is random, arbitrary, and meaningless. People know that everything that happens is caused by something, and many humans tend to believe that many of the determining causes of their lives are intended, purposive, and meaningful. Building and inhabiting cultural worlds that make sense of life that way are part of what it means to be human. And for many humans, those cultural worlds are also inhabited by superhuman powers with capacities to influence their lives for better or worse.

4

Why Are Humans Religious?

I have breathed into man of My spirit.
—QUR'AN 15.29

Then did I recognize Thee in mind, to be the first and the last,
   O Lord. . . .
As the holy one I recognized thee, O Wise Lord, when he came to
   me as Good Mind;
The Silent Thought taught me the greatest good.

—ZOROASTRIAN AVESTA, YASNA 31.8, 45.15

The single question that provides this chapter's title actually contains within it three distinct inquiries. The first concerns what motivates religious people in a proximate or immediate sense to practice religion. That question is easy to answer; in fact, it was already answered in the previous chapters. The second inquiry concerns which kinds of people in any given social setting tend to be religious. These are matters of religious*ness*, as defined above, not religious ontology (just to keep that key distinction clear). The third related question asks why we human beings appear to be the only species on earth that practices religion. Answering that will take a bit more work. The answers to these three inquiries also raise a fourth significant question, which is rarely addressed: Why aren't all humans religious? Given the force of the answers to the three questions about why people are religious, we need to explain why some humans feel no need or desire to be religious.

What Motivates Religion?

The definition of religion given in chapter 1 of this book and the account of secondary features and capacities that religion produces described in chapter 2 together provide the answer to the first question. Humans are religious because they hope for superhuman powers to help them realize human goods and avoid bads, especially to grant them blessings, prevent misfortunes, and aid them in crises; and because they wish to enjoy the various forms of identity, community, meaning, expression, aesthetics, ecstasy, control, and legitimacy that practicing religions offer. If religion could not promise the help of superhuman powers, then religion would not exist. But it does promise, and so religion does exist and humans do practice it. Religions also generate many secondary capacities and features that people need and want, which further motivates them to practice religion.[1] Altogether, these—taken not as utilitarian choices about costs and benefits, but opportunities for persons to realize their natural human goods—provide more than sufficient motivation for many people to practice religion.

Excursus: What People Seem to Pray About

One focused way to access this matter empirically is to ask what people pray for and about. We cannot identify all of the things that religious people around the world seek from superhuman powers. But one way to learn more about what religious people are looking for in their religious practices is to examine the things for which they pray. Even here, we are limited to narrow samples and sometimes unreliable methods of data collection. But the findings of existing studies converge on the same conclusion and so are, at the very least, highly suggestive.

---

1. According to the findings of the 2010 China General Social Survey, for example, the Chinese people believe that religion helps people find inner peace and happiness (83 percent of religious Chinese agree; 53 percent of non-believers agree), find comfort in sad and difficult times (80 percent of religious Chinese agree; 53 percent of non-religious agree), make friends (58 percent of religious Chinese agree; 40 percent of non-religious agree), and meet the right people (50 percent of religious Chinese agree; 20 percent of non-religious agree)—this in a country whose authoritarian, atheistic, communist government actively repressed all religion for decades. Wang Weidong and Tang Lina. 2016. "Social Survey in Religion in CGSS." Beijing: National Survey Research Center of Renmin University of China; Lina Tang. 2014. *Social Change and Religious Belief—Based on the Positive Analysis of CGSS2010*. PhD dissertation. Renmin University of China; Zhifeng Zhong and Li Lulu. 2016. "Open but Not Tolerant: An Empirical Study of Chinese Social Attitudes toward Religions." *Logos and Pneuma*. 45: 34–56.

TABLE 4.1. Topics Adult Americans Prayed About

Prayer Content	This-worldly	Spiritual
Family	89.4	
Friend or acquaintance	75.3	
Relationship with God		66.2
General world concerns	53.2	
Confession of sin		61.2
Personal health	49	
Praise or adoration of God		49.4
Someone not known	46.8	
Financial security	33	

Source: 2005 Baylor Religion Survey (N=1,465 praying subsample; total N=1,721).

In one survey, for example, a representative sample of 1,721 adult Americans who reported ever praying were given a list of possible topics of prayer and were asked: "The last time you prayed, did you pray about the following?" Table 4.1 displays the percentage who answered "yes" for each item.[2] We see that Americans are most likely to pray for and about their family members and friends (exactly what about them we do not know, but very likely it involves their well-being and relations). Americans also tend to pray a lot about world affairs and personal health, as well as financial security and people they do not know. The more spiritual topics on the list—relationship with God, sin, and worship of God—were of middling popularity. Clearly, American adults pray for both spiritual and worldly concerns, but the latter seem dominant.

Similarly, table 4.2 shows the results of an online survey of 1,137 adult Americans conducted in 2014.[3] The coding of answer categories here is somewhat different, but the overall pattern is comparable to that of table 4.1. Personal relationships and problems dominate, and blessings, worldly concerns, and personal prosperity fall lower on the list. Again, sitting in the middle range of topics of prayer are the more spiritual issues: in this survey, sin, worship, and the faith of other people.

2. From Joseph Baker. 2008. "An Investigation of the Sociological Patterns of Prayer Frequency and Content." *Sociology of Religion.* 69: 169–185, table from p. 178.
3. LifeWay Research. 2014. "American Prayer Practices." Nashville, TN: LifeWay Research. http://www.lifewayresearch.com/files/2014/09/American-Prayer-Practices.pdf and http://www.lifewayresearch.com/2014/10/01/americansprayforfriendsandfamily-2/.

TABLE 4.2. Topics of Prayer among Adult Americans (Percentages)

	This-worldly	Spiritual
Family and friends	82	
Personal problems or difficulties	74	
Good things that occurred recently	54	
Personal sin		42
Victims of natural disasters	38	
God's greatness		37
Future prosperity	36	
People of other faiths or no faith		20
Government leaders	12	
Celebrities and other public figures	5	

Source: American Prayer Practices Survey 2014 (N=1,137).

Table 4.3 focuses specifically on American Catholics. It shows the *first-mentioned* items that praying, non-Hispanic, registered Catholic parishioners reported they prayed about in a 1984 study of Catholic parish life.[4] Their answers indicate not whether they *ever* pray about a given topic—only whether it was the first thing they mentioned when asked what they prayed about. Again, the most frequently reported subjects of prayer are personal well-being and family relationships. Those two alone represent 66 percent of all answers. Nearly one-quarter first mentioned giving thanks to God, and smaller percentages mentioned praying for help in being a good person and for forgiveness. Social concerns, divinity (including prayers to Mary and praying the Rosary), spiritual growth, the afterlife, and the Church were the first-mentioned topics of prayer for a miniscule number, summing altogether to only one-seventh of 1 percent of all answers. Again, worldly issues dominate the prayers of American Catholics, and more "spiritual" concerns—with the exception of giving thanks to God—recede far into the background.

4. The survey question was: "Describe briefly in your own words the content of your prayer or meditation; that is, what do you pray about?" Reported here are the first mentioned answers, with most specific reported items grouped into major categories. Those reporting not praying and whose prayers had no content were removed from the calculations. See David Leege and Michael Welch. 1989. "Religious Roots of Political Orientations." *Journal of Politics*. 51:137–162; Jim Castelli and Joseph Gremillion. 1987. *The Emerging Parish*. San Francisco: Harper & Row.

TABLE 4.3. Content of Prayers of Parish-Registered, Non-Hispanic US Catholics (Percentages)

Content of Prayer	This-Worldly	Ambiguous	Other-Worldly
Well-being: health, emotions, guidance, growth, success, safety, financial security, others' welfare, stillness	48.8		
Family: safety, health, emotions, guidance, thanks, parenting	17.3		
Thanksgiving		23.4	
Be a good person		10.1	
Forgiveness		5.3	
Social concerns: ministry to poor and depressed, national crisis, peace, social justice, peacemaking	0.06		
Divinity: Godhead, Mary, Sacred Heart, Corpus Christi, Rosary			0.03
Spiritual growth of family		.03	
Afterlife: get to heaven, souls in purgatory, repose of the soul			0.01
The Church: help pastor, guidance to serve, vocations, pope or bishops		0.003	

Source: Notre Dame Study of Catholic Parish Life: Parishioners Sample, 1984 (N=2,229).

In 2000, Dutch scholars conducted a nationally representative survey of adults in the Netherlands (N=1,008) on the topic of prayer, including personal prayer outside of church.[5] Eighty-nine percent of the sample participants answered the open-ended survey questions about prayer, which included these queries: "How do you pray?" "When do you feel the need to pray?" "What do you hope to achieve with prayer?" Thirty-nine percent of respondents said they felt a "need" to pray and 48 percent reported desiring an "effect" of their prayers. Table 4.4 shows the topics of felt needs and desired effects that were mentioned most often. Because the Netherlands is a relatively secularized society, the percentages shown here are lower than those found in more religious countries. Our focus here, however, is on the content of the prayers of Dutch adults who do pray. Once again, the reported felt needs revolve around the very practical matters of sickness,

5. Sarah Bänzinger, Jacques Janssen, and Peer Scheepers. 2008. "Praying in a Secularized Society." International Journal for the Psychology of Religion. 18: 256–265, tables from p. 260.

TABLE 4.4. Felt Needs and Desired Effects of Prayers of Dutch Adults (Percentages)

Felt Needs	(% Total Sample)	Desired Effects	(% Total Sample)
Sickness	16	Inner rest	13.4
Death	13.7	Help	9.6
Difficult times	7.8	Insight	6.7
Problems	5.9	Power	6.3
Thank God, happiness	4.3	Support	6.2
For other people	3.5	Turn out to be all right	3.4
Problems in relationships	3.1	Pour out one's heart	2.4
Birth	2	Thanksgiving	2.4
Sadness	1.6	Relationship with God	2.4
School examinations	1.6	Happiness	2.4
		Good health	1.9
		Forgiveness	1.9
		Remission	1.9
		Acceptance	1.9

Source: Religion in Dutch Society 2000. Sarah Bänzinger, Jacques Janssen, and Peer Scheepers. 2008. "Praying in a Secularized Society." *International Journal for the Psychology of Religion*. 18: 256–265, tables from p. 260.

death, difficult times, and personal problems. The most commonly hoped-for results of prayer are inner peace, help, insight, power, and support. A similar study of Dutch youth produced comparable results: Most of the expressed needs in prayer had to do with personal problems, sickness, and happiness; and most of the desired effects involved help, support, a favor, remission, and rest.[6]

What about prayer in less developed, non-Western countries? Perhaps the prayers of people there are more "spiritual" than in the materialist West. Studies of populations in such countries are scarce. But one in particular is instructive. Table 4.5 shows how Christian residents of rural Tanzania, Africa, answered a 2011 survey question about "the primary focus of [their] prayers."[7] They were most likely to name earthly subjects. Topping the list

6. Jacques Janssen, Joep DeHart, and Christine DenDraak. 1990. "A Content Analysis of the Praying Practices of Dutch Youth." *Journal for the Scientific Study of Religion*. 29: 99–107.

7. Freddy Manongi and Peter Balint. 2014. "Prayer Behavior in Rural Kilimanjaro, Tanzania." *Journal for the Scientific Study of Religion*. 53: 760–774, table from p. 769.

TABLE 4.5. Primary Focus of Prayers of Christians in Rural Tanzania, Africa, 2011 (Percentages)

Family and children well-being	31.5
Good health, free from diseases	27.5
A good life	25.4
Food	6.4
Money	3.8
No particular wish	5.5

Source: Manongi and Balint 2014 (N=349). Freddy Manongi and Peter Balint. 2014. "Prayer Behavior in Rural Kiliminjaro, Tanzania." *Journal for the Scientific Study of Religion* 53: 760–774.

is the well-being of family and children, followed by good health and a good life. A minority reported that food and money are the main topics of their prayers. Far from being more occupied by spiritual and otherworldly affairs, Christians in poor, rural Tanzania pray primarily about mundane life issues, like having enough to get by on, staying healthy, and being happy in life.

Other studies of the contents of people's prayers, using a variety of different samples and analytical methods, produce similar results (findings not shown in tables here). One qualitative study of prayer among American Catholic, Protestant, Buddhist, Jewish, and Unitarian congregations in central New Jersey, for instance, showed that among the most common topics of prayer were global unrest, finding romance, family illness, interpersonal conflicts, fear, family troubles, success at work or school, protection from enemies, and loneliness. The only more spiritual topics people mentioned were forgiveness and thanksgiving, and even those could have been oriented toward this-worldly concerns.[8] A time-diary study of college students found that the vast majority of their prayers involved *asking for things* ("petition"), as opposed to offering adoration, thanksgiving, or reparation. These students petitioned God 10.8 times more frequently, for instance, than they offered adoration.[9] "Online" prayers offered on a Church of England prayer website were dominated by requests for God's help with (in

8. Karen Cerulo and Andrea Barra. 2008. "In the Name of . . . : Legitimate Interactions in the Dialogue of Prayer." *Poetics*. 36: 374–388; also see Kevin Ladd and Bernard Spilka. 2002. "Inward, Outward, and Upward: Cognitive Aspects of Prayer." *Journal for the Scientific Study of Religion*. 41: 475–484; Robert Wuthnow. 2008. "Teach Us to Pray." *Poetics*. 36: 493–506.

9. John McKinney and Kathleen McKinney. 1999. "Prayer in the Lives of Late Adolescents." *Journal of Adolescence*. 22: 279–290.

descending order of frequency) illness, relationships, work, and personal growth.[10] Another study of prayers written on prayer cards left in a church in rural England found that 71 percent cited a specific need for which help was requested and, of those, 76 percent involved illness, a death, conflict, or a disaster.[11] A content analysis of prayers written in volumes of prayer books by patients, visitors, and staff of the Johns Hopkins Hospital in Baltimore, Maryland, shows that 28 percent of the prayers contain only petitions to God, and another 27.5 percent contain both petitions and thanks to God. Of the prayers of petition, 43.3 percent concerned family or other people, 40.7 percent asked for an intervention from God in a specific situation, 25.5 percent concerned the petitioner's own life, 25 percent concerned health issues, and 21.2 percent asked for general blessings or divine presence.[12]

What do we learn from these studies? Despite its shortcomings, this body of research suggests that most people who pray do so to *ask a superhuman power for help* and that the majority of topics about which people pray are *this-worldly, practical matters* as opposed to more "spiritual" or otherworldly concerns. Prayer is only one religious practice among many. But, to the extent that it is a central practice for many religions, these findings imply that humans indeed seek to access superhuman powers especially to secure blessings, avoid misfortunes, and solve problems. And, if the Tanzania study is indicative of a broader pattern, that generalization is probably

10. Tania ap Siôn and Owen Edwards. 2012. "Praying 'Online': The Ordinary Theology of Prayer Intentions Posted on the Internet." *Journal of Beliefs and Values*. 33: 95–109.

11. Tania ap Siôn. 2007. "Listening to Prayers: An Analysis of Prayers Left in a Country Church in Rural England." *Archive for the Psychology of Religion*. 29: 199–226. More examples: In 2001, scholars conducted a survey about prayer with a random sample of white and black, Christian and non-religious, elderly residents, age 66 and older, in the United States (N=1,500). Survey questions about the content of respondents' prayers were closed-ended. When asked, "When you are by yourself, how often do you pray for other people?," the sample on average prayed for other people on a nearly daily basis. Respondents also reported praying for God's will, for their own health, and in thanksgiving on average about halfway between "fairly often" and "very often." Praying for material things was reported much less, on average somewhat more than "never" and less than "once in a while." R. David Haywood and Neal Krause. 2013. "Patterns of Change in Prayer Activity, Expectancies, and Contents during Older Adulthood." *Journal for the Scientific Study of Religion*. 52: 17–34, table from pp. 22, 25—only scale scores, not frequency distribution percents, were reported. Also see Helen Black. 1999. "Poverty and Prayer: Spiritual Narratives of Elderly African-American Woman." *Review of Religious Research*. 40: 359–374; Kathrin Hanek, Bradley Olson, and Dan McAdams. 2011. "Political Orientation and the Psychology of Christian Prayer." *International Journal for the Psychology of Religion*. 21: 30–42.

12. Wendy Cadge and M. Daglian. 2008. "Blessings, Strength, and Guidance." *Poetics*. 36: 358–373.

more accurate the more insecure life is. Clearly, more research is needed on this topic.

What Kinds of People Tend to Be Religious?

This second inquiry is an empirical matter to be answered not by theory but through observation of the facts in specific cases. The answers will vary depending on the religious situations in question. The types of people who show the most religious devotion in an Amazonian tribe may differ from those who did in ancient Egypt, which may differ again from those who do in contemporary Beijing, a rural village in Paraguay, or Chicago. Only empirical research can provide the correct answer for a specific context. Nonetheless, my theoretical account in this book suggests some general hypotheses about predispositions to religious practice worth noting. I offer three here with a bit of elaboration.[13]

The Default Religious Laxity Tendency. The first theoretical expectation my account suggests we might call the "Default Religious Laxity" tendency. By this I mean that, in the absence of other causal factors that influence it, *religiousness in human life should tend to default to a "baseline" of a modest level of practice, to an "equilibrium" that maintains future opportunities to increase religiousness but invests only in modest religious practice in the meantime.* Here is my reasoning. Human beings are "naturally" religious in certain ways, as I argue below. But humans are not naturally *highly* religious. Sustaining a degree of religiousness beyond the natural equilibrium requires the activation of particular causal forces. Countervailing forces liable to decrease religiousness are frequently in play in most social contexts. And in general, a certain kind of "entropy" operates in human social life that pushes demanding activities, including religious ones, to weaken and decay. When it comes to practices addressing superhuman powers, this means at least a propensity for expressions of religiousness to regress to more basic, less

13. I do not propose the following as associations between variables, much less anything like general laws. Critical realists, in contrast with positivists, do not believe that what is most important about reality is evident in the form of correlations between variables measuring events on the "surface" of the empirically observable world. Reality is a complex, differentiated, ontologically stratified, and ordered assemblage of myriad natural and constructed entities possessing various causal powers—which they exercise only sometimes, depending on the specific conditions of the "open systems" in which they exist in different spaces and times—which together interact (or not) in complex ways to produce similar, diverse, or no outcomes. The best way to describe basic generalized knowledge about such entities is to speak of the "tendencies" and perhaps, at strongest, "demi-regularities" to be found among them.

sophisticated, or less demanding forms. What Nancy Ammerman has called "Golden Rule Christianity" and I have described as "Moralistic Therapeutic Deism" in American religion may be relevant examples of this dynamic.[14] Religious clergy sometimes seem to expect that their followers will be deeply faithful and committed to practicing religion, and feel disappointed and frustrated when they are not. They are likely just facing the results of this Default Religious Laxity tendency.

This theoretical expectation, however, is not based on assumptions about calculating actors minimizing costs and maximizing rewards, as rational choice theory would propose.[15] That, as I have argued elsewhere, is a problematic model of human actors.[16] I instead assume critical realist personalism's view of humans as constitutionally social animals continually seeking to navigate the realization of multiple, irreducible, and naturally "telic" goods in complex, evolving contexts of sometimes incommensurate values, moral binds, and limited resources.[17] Personalism frames the matter in terms different from those of rational egoism. However, even this perspective implies that, if my account of religion is correct, most people will naturally tend to become moderately lax in their religiousness, unless other causal forces intervene. The causal mechanism at work is people's natural inclination, under the conditions described by personalist theory, to seek to balance the realization of multiple, incommensurate natural human goods toward their *eudaimonic* flourishing, not to maximize pleasure or utility or rewards as typically conceived by rational choice theory. Only under conditions in which greater religiousness appears to promise to help people better realize those goods will human practices of religion tend to strengthen considerably.

The Vulnerable Religious Demand Tendency. A second general propensity that we should expect if my larger theoretical account is valid we might call the "Vulnerable Religious Demand" tendency. It suggests that *humans will typically exhibit greater religiousness in personal and social contexts of greater misfortune and crisis—whether feared, anticipated, or actual—in which the*

14. Nancy Ammerman. 1997. "Golden Rule Christianity." In *Lived Religion in America: Toward a History of Practice*. David D. Hall (ed.). Princeton: Princeton University Press. Pp. 196–216; Christian Smith, with Melinda Lundquist Denton. 2005. *Soul Searching*. New York: Oxford University Press. Pp. 118–170.

15. As represented, for example, by Stark and Finke's "Proposition 17: People will seek to minimize their religious costs" and "Proposition 16: People will seek to delay their payment of religious costs" (*Acts of Faith*. P. 100).

16. Smith. *Moral, Believing Animals.*

17. Smith. *To Flourish or Destruct.*

need for superhuman blessings, protection, deliverance, and abilities to cope are more intensely felt. This expectation extends the logic of my definition of religion by one step, suggesting that humans generally tend to be more religious the more they perceive the need for the help that religion promises. Stated otherwise, in the absence of countervailing influences, demand for religion increases when the problems that religion exists to address are believed to be greater. It is not enough for the problems to be objectively real and pressing. People need to subjectively perceive them as potential or actual problems, to register the troubles cognitively and emotionally, in order for them to influence religiousness.

This "Vulnerable Religious Demand" tendency would help explain empirically observed variance of religiousness among different types of people. For example, it can partially account for religious age effects: the fact that in many social settings, younger adults practice religion less intensely than older adults.[18] The young—who are apt to be healthier, further away from death, less damaged by life so far, and prone toward more hopeful, forward-looking outlooks—generally feel less vulnerable than older adults to the kinds of difficulties for which humans sometimes seek superhuman help. And so younger people tend to practice religion less. Something similar holds true, I suggest, for gender differences in religion. Almost universally, women are somewhat more religious than men. Why that is so has been the subject of much debate.[19] My account suggests that women are more likely than men both to be aware of their vulnerabilities and to be prepared to seek help beyond their own resources, including those of superhuman powers, to address those vulnerabilities. Women's greater awareness is rooted both in the dependencies of the biology of motherhood and in the socially structured vulnerabilities of commonly male-dominated social systems that most women confront. Consequently, as the Vulnerable Religious Demand tendency explicates it, women are predisposed in most settings to be more religious than men.

The Vulnerable Religious Demand tendency also makes sense of many of the empirical findings of cross-national studies, which show religion is practiced more intensely in socioeconomic situations of greater risk and

---

18. E.g., Christian Smith. 2009. *Souls in Transition*. New York: Oxford University Press.

19. See, for starters, Marta Trzebiatowska and Steve Bruce. 2012. *Why Are Women More Religious than Men?* New York: Oxford University Press; Jessica Collett and Omar Lizardo. 2009. "A Power-Control Theory of Gender and Religiosity." *Journal for the Scientific Study of Religion.* 48: 213–231; for greater complexity, see Conrad Hackett. 2016. *The Gender Gap in Religion around the World.* Washington, DC: Pew Research Center.

amid lower levels of material well-being. Pippa Norris and Ronald Inglehart have presented empirical evidence demonstrating this tendency, although their thin theory of religion did not, in my view, adequately explain their results.[20] While I have elsewhere criticized their work,[21] in general I think their descriptive empirical findings should be taken seriously. I believe my theory of religion in this book makes the best sense of the religiousness-vulnerability link Norris and Inglehart document. Humans who face a greater risk of illness and deprivation and who suffer lower levels of material well-being will normally feel the need to rely on the blessings and help of superhuman powers. So they tend to be more religious. When socioeconomic conditions improve and provide greater security and well-being for people, the dynamics of the Default Religious Laxity tendency exert greater causal influence and over time reduce people's religiousness.

It is important to note before moving on that these kinds of transformations do not only have to do with *quantitative* amounts of religiousness measured on standardized scales (e.g., how often they pray or perform other religious practices). *Qualitative* differences in the types and meanings of the religious practices that humans undertake also matter. In some cases, as people become more prosperous and their lives more secure, they might maintain the same levels of religiousness but switch religious groups or denominations, and their associated practices, to "move up" in the socioeconomic status hierarchy of a given society and religious ecology.[22] Clear interventions by superhuman powers are frequently downplayed in or are less central to the new religious contexts. For instance, someone raised in an at-risk household of Pentecostals in the United States might, after obtaining a college degree and securing a professional job, remain religious but become Presbyterian. Alternatively, the same person might retain formal ties to his religion of origin but move into a more moderate congregation or denomination within the tradition and reduce the intensity with which he personally practices religion.

Following the same general point, people who occupy different status positions in the same social context may show similar levels of religiousness, but the qualitative nature of their practices may vary dramatically. For

20. Norris and Inglehart. *Sacred and Secular*. See my discussion of their conceptualization of religion in the appendix of chapter 1.

21. Christian Smith. 2006. "Review of *Sacred and Secular*." *Journal for the Scientific Study of Religion*. 45: 623–624.

22. Christian Smith and Robert Faris. 2005. "Socioeconomic Inequality in the American Religious System." *Journal for the Scientific Study of Religion*. 44: 95–104.

example, the relatively wealthy and secure owners and managers of a business in a "company town" might attend church, pray, tithe, and worship just as frequently and fervently as the poor, insecure, semi-skilled workers they employ, while the quality, nature, and ends of each group's culturally meaningful religious practices could be profoundly different. The religion of the wealthy and secure may focus on God's abundant blessings, the justness and beauty of the world, and God's ability to bring inner peace. The religious practices of the insecure, unskilled workers, by contrast, may emphasize God's special love for the poor, God's condemnation of injustice and oppression, and the heavenly reward waiting after death for those who suffered on earth.[23] A social survey with standard questions measuring how frequently respondents attend church and pray would completely miss these differences. Yet they would be the most important and interesting things to know about religion in that context. As this hypothetical example implies, research on the Vulnerable Religious Demand tendency requires sensitive qualitative as well as quantitative investigation.

The Biological Predisposition Tendency. Here I venture a claim that very few social scientists ever hazard: that *intensities of religiousness will tend to vary across persons according to differences in their biologically grounded genetic and neurological traits.* I make this supposition for three reasons. First, accumulating scientific evidence indicates it is likely true. Second, it makes sense within the critical realist view of reality as differentiated, complex, and stratified. And third, the claim fits my theoretical account of religion well. All things social are linked to and interact with the natural world—biology, chemistry, and human brains. We can only improve our understanding of religion in a realist mode if we investigate those connections. I am in no way proposing genetic determinism. There is no "religion gene" that determines anyone's personal religiousness.[24] Reality is far more complex than that, and downward causal powers of the personal, the social, and environmental factors can shape lower-level genetic and biochemical processes. Still, in seeking to comprehend religion, we should seek to understand any possible biological elements affecting religious practice.[25]

23. For a classic text in this vein, see Liston Pope. 1965. *Millhands and Preachers.* New Haven, CT: Yale University Press.

24. Even former advocates—such as geneticist Dean Hamer, author of *The God Gene* (2004. New York: Doubleday)—have conceded the error of this approach (Hood, Hill, and Spilka. *Psychology of Religion.* P. 61).

25. See Patrick McNamara and P. Monroe Butler. 2013. "The Neuropsychology of Religious Experience." In Raymond F. Paloutzian and Crystal L. Park. *Handbook of the Psychology of Reli-*

Toward that end, research on identical and fraternal twins raised in shared and unshared environments, for example, suggests that genetic factors (as opposed to social influences) explain between 19 and 65 percent of the variation in personal religiousness, depending on the specific religious feature in question.[26] Many other studies have shown that differences in people's basic personality traits, which are genetically and neurologically grounded—such as the "Big Five" traits of extraversion, agreeableness, conscientiousness, neuroticism, and openness to experience—are significantly associated with varying levels of personal religiousness.[27] And, in addition

---

gion and Spirituality. New York: Guilford Press. Pp. 215–233; Hood, Hill, and Spilka. Psychology of Religion. Pp. 54–75; Andrew Newberg, Eugene D'Aquili, and Vince Rause. 2002. Why God Won't Go Away. New York: Ballentine; Patrick McNamara. 2014. The Neuroscience of Religious Experience. Cambridge: Cambridge University Press; Patrick McNamara. 2006. Where God and Science Meet. Westport, CT: Praeger; Fred Previc. 2005. "The Role of Extrapersonal Brain Systems in Religious Activity." Consciousness and Cognition. 15: 500–539; Niall McCrae and Rob Whitley. 2014. "Exaltation in Temporal Lobe Epilepsy." Journal of Medical Humanities. 35: 241–255; Brick Johnson, Angela Bodling, Dan Cohen, Shawn Christ, and Andrew Wegrzyn. 2012. "Right Parietal Lobe-Related 'Selflessness' as the Neuropsychological Basis of Spiritual Transcendence." International Journal for the Psychology of Religion. 22: 267–284; Osamu Muramoto. 2004. "The Role of the Medial Prefrontal Cortex in Human Religious Activity." Medical Hypotheses. 62: 479–485.

26. Matt Bradshaw and Christopher Ellison. 2008. "Do Genetic Factors Influence Religious Life?" Journal for the Scientific Study of Religion. 47: 529–544; N. Waller, B. Kojetin, T. Bouchard, D. Lykken, and A. Tellegen. 1990. "Genetic and Environmental Influences on Religious Interests, Attitudes, and Values." Psychological Science. 1: 138–142. See Brian D'Onofrio, Lindon Eaves, Lenn Murrelle, Hermine Maes, and Bernard Spilka. 1999. "Understanding Biological and Social Influences on Religious Affiliation, Attitudes, and Behavior." Journal of Personality. 67: 953–984; Tanya Button, Michael Stallings, Soo Hyun Rhee, Robin Corley, and John Hewitt. 2011. "The Etiology of Stability and Change in Religious Values and Religious Attendance." Behavioral Genetics. 41: 201–210; Lindon Eaves, A. Heath, N. Martin, Hermine Maes, M. Neale, and K. Kendler. 1999. "Comparing the Biological and Cultural Inheritances of Personality and Social Attitudes." Twin Research. 2: 62–80.

27. For example, Jude Henningsgaard and Randolph Arnau. 2008. "Relationships between Religiosity, Spirituality, and Personality." Personality and Individual Differences. 45: 703–708; H.-F. Unterrainer, H. Ladenhauf, M. Moazedi, S. Wallner-Liebmann, and A. Fink. 2010. "Dimensions of Religious/Spiritual Well-being and their Relation to Personality and Psychological Well-being." Personality and Individual Differences. 49: 192–197; P. Hills, L. Francis, M. Argyle, and C. Jackson. 2004. "Primary Personality Trait Correlates of Religious Practice and Orientation." Personality and Individual Differences. 36: 61–73; V. Saroglou. 2002. "Religion and the Five Factors of Personality." Personality and Individual Differences. 32:15–25; Paul Wink, Lucia Ciciolla, Michele Dillon, and Allison Tracy. 2007. "Religiousness, Spiritual Seeking, and Personality: Findings from a Longitudinal Study." Journal of Personality. 75: 1051–1070; Michael McCollough, Jo-Ann Tsand, and Sharon Brion. 2003. "Personality Traits in Adolescence as Predictors of Religiousness in Early Adulthood." Personality and Social Psychology Bulletin. 29: 980–991; Joseph Ciarrochi and Patrick Heaven. 2012. "Religious Values and the Development of Trait Hope and

to working to identify the neurological substrate regions of religious activity, neurologists are beginning to show that alterations in people's neurological functioning bring with them changes in their personal religiousness.[28] Much more research in all of these areas is needed before we may be confident in the reliability and generalizability of such findings. But already there are good reasons to believe that differences in people's religiousness are shaped in part by genetic, biochemical, and neurological factors.

I could continue to advance ideas about dynamics that tend to increase or decrease people's religiousness. Many—related to differences in family and parental socialization, social networks, types of religious traditions, education level, and other factors—are already well known. I am developing a general theory of religion, and for that purpose the three tendencies I have already suggested suffice. Readers interested in detailed empirical data about individuals' propensities to be religious can consult the extensive, relevant literatures.

Why Are Humans Religious?

With this third inquiry, we shift our attention to a deeper level of theoretical concern. The question here is this: What is it about human beings as a species that explains why we are the only animal on earth that practices religion?[29] Answering it requires the mode of thinking that comes naturally to a critical realist and personalist—that is, focusing first on natural human causal *capacities* and *limitations*, on their interactions and confrontations, and on the kinds of activities and institutions that emerge as a result. Human

---

Self-Esteem in Adolescence." *Journal for the Scientific Study of Religion.* 51: 676–688. Pp. 677–679.

28. For example, Paul Butler, Patrick McNamara, and Raymond Durson. 2011. "Side of Onset in Parkinson's Disease and Alterations in Religiosity." *Behavioral Neurology.* 24: 133–141; O. Devinsky and G. Lai. 2008. "Spirituality and Religion in Epilepsy." *Epilepsy and Behavior.* 12: 636–643; Osamu Muramoto. 2004. "The Role of Medial Prefrontal Cortex in Human Religious Activity." *Medical Hypotheses.* 62: 479–485; Brick Johnstone, Angela Bodling, Dan Cohen, Shawn Christ, and Andrew Wegrzyn. 2012. "Right Parietal Lobe-Related 'Selflessness' as the Neuropsychological Basis of Spiritual Transcendence." *International Journal for the Psychology of Religion.* 22: 267–284; Niall McCrae and Rob Whitley. 2014. "Exaltation in Temporal Lobe Epilepsy." *Journal of Medical Humanities.* 35: 241–255; Fred Previc. 2006. "The Role of the Extrapersonal Brain Systems in Religious Activity." *Consciousness and Cognition.* 15: 500–539; Hood, Hill, and Spilka. *Psychology of Religion.* P. 62.

29. My approach is rooted in assumptions about the evolved nature of human animals, though one need not rely strongly on arguments about the exact processes of natural selection to answer the question well.

social life, including religious life, is like the magma that builds up and erupts, so to speak, at the deep, underlying fault lines where natural human *capacities* meet and grind against natural human *limitations*. What do I mean?

To begin, we must affirm that the primary agents of causal influence in human social life are human persons.[30] We need to launch our theoretical explanations of social events and conditions by accounting for the ends, interests, motivations, and actions of persons, since their activities are what give rise through emergence to social and institutional facts that also lie at the origins of religion.[31] All of people's motivations, my account suggests, derive from their objective interest in realizing six natural, "basic goods" of human personhood toward realizing their proper natural end (*telos*) of *eudaimonia* (happy flourishing): (1) bodily survival, security, and pleasure; (2) knowledge of reality; (3) identity coherence and affirmation; (4) exercising purposive agency; (5) moral affirmation; and (6) social belonging and love.[32] Human life consists of sets of practices oriented toward accomplishing a reasonable balance of these six goods—given the relatively limited resources and opportunities people face in their lives—toward the ultimate end of flourishing as human persons. The more persons are able to realize those basic goods, the more they flourish; failure or serious compromise in realizing them leads to stagnation and destruction. Human persons thus live with a built-in orientation toward certain natural ends and motivational energy to realize them. The *means* by which they may do so are highly variable across persons, cultures, and social classes. But the underlying orientation is the same for all.

Human persons normally explore and employ a variety of means to achieve as best as seems possible the six basic human goods named above. Frequently, in seeking to do so, people are severely limited by the available material resources, technologies, conceivable ideas, institutional opportunities, and culturally acceptable practices. But human persons are also creative, and so they often devise new ideas, technologies, practices, institutions, and methods for pursuing their ends. This is where religion comes in. Human beings practice religion (when they do) ultimately because they believe that it will help them in their larger life quests to better realize their natural human ends. Practicing religion, in short, appears to many people to be in their basic interest.

---

30. Smith. *What Is a Person?*
31. Smith. *To Flourish or Destruct.*
32. Ibid. Pp. 159–200.

Although human persons are endowed with immense causal powers to make and remake themselves, their relationships, their cultures, and the material world, all these powers operate within the confines of natural limits on human bodies, consciousness, and action.[33] The meeting of human powers and limitations produces a dynamic tension that fuels the making of human social life and institutions. Human existence is, in this way, a naturally unstable compound, an ever-reactive mix of elements, out of which human practices and institutions solidify. Social meanings, interactions, institutions, and structures—including religious ones—are constructed and transformed by real persons facing the tensions of existential contradictions. The development of society and history is thus rooted in the natural capacities and incapacities of human persons. To understand things social, therefore, including religion, we need to attend to the grinding together of natural human powers and human finitude.[34]

Human bodies, always the starting point of critical realist personalism, entail both astoundingly powerful capacities and strikingly severe limitations. The normal human body is capable of mind-boggling powers, both voluntary and involuntary, yet it is constantly vulnerable to accidents, disease, and death. Human development and socialization are long, complicated processes in which much can go wrong, yet they also require and display remarkable human abilities. Human perceptions and mental life—including memory, belief formation, and judgment—similarly involve a paradoxical combination of amazing capabilities and serious limitations. Human communication through language, emotional life, and moral existence likewise entail remarkable power and clear susceptibility to compromise and breakdown. In fact, in every aspect of human physical and mental life, we find complex interactions of striking natural powers and grave limitations.

Critical realist personalism says that all human persons engage in activities to realize natural human goods, their teleological ends.[35] Engaged in these activities, people quickly reach their many natural limitations, how-

---

33. Alasdair MacIntyre. 1999. *Dependent, Rational Animals*. Chicago: Open Court.

34. My argument here may bring to mind that of Peter Berger's *The Sacred Canopy* (1990. New York: Anchor) (relying on the philosophical anthropology of Arnold Gehlen—in, for example, 1988. *Man, His Nature and Place in the World*. New York: Columbia University Press—to which Riesebrodt also subscribes. *Promise of Salvation*. P. 171), in which Berger claims that the instinct-deficient nature of human beings requires that they overcome their instinctual limitations through the invention of culture. My critical realist, neo-Aristotelian, personalist account, however, places less emphasis on instincts and focuses instead on natural goods, ends, and capacities with regard to human limitations.

35. Smith. *To Flourish or Destruct*.

ever, running up against the many facts of our natural finitude and weaknesses. We confront our inescapable bodily indivisibility, dependence on physical sustenance, realities of biological reproduction, vulnerability to injury and disease, need for protracted socialization, limitations of perceptions and learning and memory, emotional vulnerabilities, reliance on language and interpretation, and need for cultural narratives, moralities, and worldviews. In order to continue living as the kind of creatures that we are—that is, as *persons*—humans respond to their limitations by developing various tools, practices, and systems that advance their natural capacities. Some of these are material, others are cognitive and affective, and yet others are relational. Primary among them are social structures and social institutions.[36] A central accomplishment of human existence is the overcoming of diverse forms of loss, instability, and disruption, which tend to obstruct the realization of robust personhood. The establishment of continuity and security in life is central to the achievement of what is most human about us: our personhood.

How does religion emerge in a way that fits this pattern? The answer implied by the theory developed in previous chapters should be clear. Human persons seek their natural goods (enumerated above), and, in so doing, they run up against their many limitations that threaten the realization of these goods. As naturally imaginative animals, however, humans develop various means to try to overcome or mitigate the hindrances of their incapacities. For a variety of reasons, more of which we will examine below, among those creative means are religious beliefs and practices seeking to access the blessings and help of superhuman powers. With the aid of such superhuman powers, humans hope to surpass some of their natural limitations in order to better achieve their natural teleological ends. Religion thus emerges as one human institution among others developed to extend human powers beyond their natural bounds—through, in the case of religion, belief in and practices accessing superhuman powers.

Why Are *Only* Humans Religious?

We still need to determine why humans, among all creatures on earth, are *uniquely* religious. Human beings are certainly not the only animal that faces tensions between their natural capacities and limitations. All animals do, in various ways. So why are humans the only animals that address those

36. See Smith. *What Is a Person?* Pp. 317–383.

tensions through religion? To answer this question, we need to explore human capacities even more thoroughly. To practice religion requires the possession of a particular combination of capacities that, of all animals, only we humans have.

Let us proceed by thinking retroductively. What must be the case about a creature if it is to be religious? Specifically, what capacities must it possess to be able to practice religion? Conducting this retroductive exercise suggests that doing religion depends on enjoying at least the following ten capacities (all of which and more I have theorized in depth elsewhere[37]):

1. *Mental representation*: the ability to conceive mental images of objects or states of affairs in the world other than oneself, depictions that have an "about-ness" of something to them or are directed at something.

2. *Volition*: the ability to will, to desire, to aspire to, to set purposeful goals.

3. *Assigning causal attributions*: the ability to perceive, intuit, or analyze the relations among events and the causal powers of entities in order to understand the operations of specific causes and effects.

4. *Episodic and long-term memory*: the ability to store and retrieve images, associations, knowledge, reminiscences, and other memory contents providing cognitive links to the past.

5. *Interest formation*: the ability to identify and rank those states, conditions, and experiences believed to serve one's well-being and that of others one values, which one then desires to attain.

6. *Anticipating the future*: the ability to project outcomes of different events and courses of action that have not yet happened.

7. *Inter-subjective understanding*: the ability to understand, at least somewhat correctly, the subjective beliefs, thoughts, emotions, desires, intentions, goals, interests, moods, and meanings of other members of one's species.

8. *Abstract reasoning*: the ability to exercise cognitive powers to reflect, calculate, and analyze abstractly and deliberatively in ways that inform one's understanding and decision-making.

9. *Creative imagination*: the ability to visualize, dream, invent, connect, and conceive ideas, possibilities, and images that do not yet exist in reality.

37. Ibid. Pp. 42–59.

10. *Symbolization*: the ability to use certain ideas or objects to represent other ideas or objects and their attributes, meanings, and emotional associations.

All ten of these capacities—and more basic ones upon which they depend—are required to practice religion. Eliminate any one of them and the practice of religion would not be possible.[38]

Returning to our question of the uniqueness of religion among humans, then, we can say the following. First, many animals possess at least elementary and sometimes fairly sophisticated versions of many of these capacities. So, if, say, the first seven of these capacities were all that were required to engage in the practice of religion, then other primates, such as bonobos and chimpanzees, might be religious, too. However, all ten are necessary to do religion. Without the capacity for significant abstract reasoning, for example, it would not be possible to conceptualize some of the elementary aspects of religious ontology—the ideas of particular superhuman powers, meaningful practices, causally produced blessings and deliverances—necessary to even the simplest of religions. The same is true of creativity and symbolization.

Humans are uniquely religious, therefore, because only human beings possess the capacities for abstract reasoning, creative imagination, and symbolization (and arguably certain other capacities) at levels of sophistication sufficient to generate and sustain the practice of religion. We may even concede to primatologists who insist on the many similarities between humans and other primates, such as Franz de Waal, that bonobos and chimps

38. If there are other non-trivial capacities not listed here that are also necessary to be religious, I cannot think of them. *Conscious awareness* (the ability to exist in a state that is sentient, wakeful, alert, aware, attentive) and *understanding the categories of time, space, quantity, and quality* (the ability to grasp the basic ordering and representational categories for understanding crucial features of the external environment about which perception provides information), for example, are also essential for doing religion, but seem too basic to name in the list above, even though not all animals (e.g., slugs, as far as we know) appear to possess them. However, I remain uncertain whether *language use* is a distinct capacity that is absolutely necessary to practice religion. Language seems to always be employed in the practice of religion, but in principle I can imagine a small group of "primitive" people lacking language use (the capacity for complex, constructed systems of vocabulary, grammar, and syntax expressed in speech and texts that communicate ideas, questions, commands, exclamations, and other types of speech acts to other language users) but nevertheless practicing a rudimentary religion, so I am not considering language necessary for religion. If that is wrong, however, nothing in my basic argument here changes. The same might be observed about the capacities for *emotional experience*, the *creation of meanings, identity formation*, etc.

may not be completely deprived of some of the last capacities on the list.[39] But even so, to whatever degree our ape relatives may have those abilities, it is not advanced enough for them to be capable of understanding and practicing religion. And so, lo and behold, they do not. Thus we see why religion is unique to humans: They and only they possess the set of capacities required to be religious.[40]

But merely possessing a capacity does not itself explain why it is actualized in some way, why, in this case, humans actually *do* practice religion. To shed light on that, we have to return to the argument above. Humans, according to critical realist personalism, possess natural basic goods proper to their being, the realization of which fosters their telic end of flourishing. The same humans also find themselves in possession of powers to employ in pursuit of those goods, yet simultaneously confront their inescapable limitations. Religion emerges and is practiced as a natural human response to this condition by those who can believe in superhuman powers who can and will help them deal with their finitude. In this I agree with Riesebrodt:

> Religious institutions . . . uphold the ability to act in situations where people feel powerless and incapable of action. . . . In this existential sense, religion is a way of coping with contingency. . . . [It] maintains people's ability to act in situations in which they run up against their own limits. . . . Religion allows humans to continue to act even when overtaxed. Religious practices offer humans a structure in situations in which they might otherwise oscillate between panic and despair.[41]

Some theories of religion consider its grounds to be ignorance, superstition, and fear. Aspects of these can indeed be found in religions, sometimes in abundance. But they are not the roots of religion. Religion is instead grounded in human persons pursuing their natural goods amid challenging circumstances, exercising their amazing personal capacities to address their weaknesses, and responding creatively to try to overcome objective limitations and threats. Religion, in this sense, is natural to, in being grounded in, the human constitution and condition.

---

39. Franz de Waal. 2005. *Our Inner Ape.* New York: Riverhead Books.

40. Thomas Tweed makes a similar argument; however, he discusses fewer capacities and focuses particularly on the importance of the human capacity of working with "figurative tools." Tweed. Forthcoming. *Heavenly Habitats: A History of Religion in the Lands that became the United States (working title).* New Haven, CT: Yale University Press. Chapter 1.

41. Riesebrodt. *Promise of Salvation.* Pp. 172, 173.

On the Naturalness of Religion

This last claim about religion is unusual when viewed in the longer history of theories of religion. Much of Western social thought, cultural criticism, and social science in recent centuries have portrayed religion instead as unnatural, irrational, and abnormal. Religious beliefs and practices have very often been described as foolish and absurd superstitions based on ignorance, fear, repression, and oppression. Religion is a kind of proto-science indulged by primitives and savages who do not understand how the world really works, says one version of this general approach. Or religion is a fanciful reaction against the fear of death. Or it is the groaning sigh, the palliative opiate of economically oppressed and emotionally resigned people. Religion is the tool of power-hungry authorities who wish to impose order. Or an illusion driven by an infantile need for a powerful father figure. Or the institutionalized resentment of weak or self-hating masses who think more like slaves than masters. Or the psychologically pathological expressions of insecure or authoritarian minds. Or some other groundless, contrived, or aberrant malformation.

The energy motivating these theoretical accounts of religion as unnatural, irrational, and abnormal has had two related but distinct sources. The first was the broad but fitful movement in early modern Europe to overthrow the power of Christendom in both its Catholic and Protestant forms, especially Christian churches' political authority and social privileges. This movement was driven by anticlerical thinking during the Renaissance and by leaders of the secular and skeptical "Enlightenment," such as Bonaventure des Périers, Baron d'Holbach, David Hume, Denis Diderot, and Voltaire. To achieve their political, social, and cultural aims, they advanced polemics and analyses that cast religion as baseless, delusional, and deviant. By implication, and sometimes explicit argument, "natural man"—reasonable humans unsullied by the dreads, ignorance, and fantasies of religion— would (and should) be secular.

The other impetus behind this general negative approach to religion arose once the secular Enlightenment vision had prevailed among intellectuals and scholars, who then felt the need to explain the persistence and power of religion. The basic template for this project was established by the German philosopher and anthropologist Ludwig Feuerbach in his 1841 work, *The Essence of Christianity*.[42] There he asserted a "projection

---

42. *Das Wesen des Christenthums*; Marian Evans (trans.). 1854. *The Essence of Christianity*. Oxford: St. Mary's.

theory" of religion: the idea that religion is nothing but a human projection into the cosmos of concerns and ideas that have purely human origins—whether psychological, social, economic, political, or otherwise.[43] People do not believe and worship God because God is really "out there," in other words, but because some worldly force motivates them to invent the illusion of God and project it into the cosmos. Thinkers like Karl Marx, Friedrich Nietzsche, Mikhail Bakunin, Sigmund Freud, Emile Durkheim, and many others took Feuerbach's idea and adapted it to elaborate their own particular theoretical vision. They were not so much activists for the idea that "God is dead" as theorists who simply presumed that to be true and sought to explain religion in non-theistic terms. Common among many of them (Durkheim being one exception) was the belief that religion is not ultimately natural to humanity, something that readily springs from human nature and the experience of life; rather, religion is an artificial fabrication imposed on humanity by misunderstood forces or subjugating agents.[44]

43. Like a movie projected onto a screen, the action in the film seems real, but it is actually only so many rays of light produced and projected by a movie-maker. Likewise, God may seem real, but is only the production of humans projected onto the cosmos. From this perspective, humans try to "speak of God simply by speaking of man in a loud voice," in the words of the Swiss Christian theologian Karl Barth (1957. *The Word of God and the Word of Man*. New York: Harper Torchbooks. P. 14). After recognizing that God is an illusion humans themselves created, Feuerbach thought, humans can get on with the business of dealing directly with real human needs, desires, and nature for what they are.

44. The eminent sociologist of religion Peter Berger attempted both to agree with Feuerbach and to relativize him by suggesting that, even if religion, viewed sociologically, is nothing but a human projection, perhaps humans project God into the cosmos because something inside tells them that some gods or God or divine principle truly does exist "out there." Intuitive recognition of this fact compels them to imagine and project their images of God into the universe. Religions, in this case, are human projections, but ones that may actually *respond to* and *correspond with* something real. "If a religious view of the world is posited, the anthropological ground of these projections may itself be a reality that includes both world and man, so that man's ejaculations of meaning into the universe ultimately point to an all-embracing meaning in which he himself is grounded. . . . This would imply that man projects ultimate meanings into reality because that reality is, indeed, ultimately meaningful, and because his own being contains and intends these same ultimate meanings" (Berger. 1990. *The Sacred Canopy*. New York: Anchor. P. 180). Thus, to sustain our earlier metaphor, the film that is projected onto the screen, which seems realistic but is not, *is actually based on a true story*, and so is a piece of human narrative art that responds to, represents, and retells something real and true. This account is eminently plausible; however, from a critical realist viewpoint, it is still problematic, because of the post-Kantian and ultimately Humean philosophical problems informing it, such as, for example, the unbridgeable chasm between the *phenomenal* world of sense perceptions and the *noumenal* sphere of "things in themselves" that leaves us with a Kantian transcendental idealism. Critical realism critiques and replaces this form of idealism with its own "transcendental realism" (see Roy Bhaskar. *Possibility of*

In the last two decades, a surge of new scientific research on religion has called into question this older view and proposed precisely the opposite: that religion is *natural* to how human perception, cognition, and explanation ordinarily work. The point of this research is not to defend the existence of God. It is all compatible with atheism, even if it does not require it. This recent body of scientific scholarship on religion merely observes—in contrast to the long history in the modern West of theorizing religion as unnatural—that religion is best understood as a normal and predictable result of the ways humans are "wired" and of their experiences in their natural and social environments. As one of these scholars writes, "Belief in God or gods is not some artificial intrusion into the natural state of human affairs. Rather, belief in gods generally and God particularly arises through the natural, ordinary operation of human minds in natural ordinary environments."[45] Arguments such as this represent a major change in scholarly attitudes toward religion.

First, a bit of philosophical background. As I have argued elsewhere, the inescapable human epistemic position of being *"believing* animals" creates a continuity between the religious believing in which some humans engage, on the one hand, and all of the other believing that all of us do to live, think, and get on with every part of our lives, on the other hand. The very possibility of getting anything going in human life—whether science or religion or anything else—requires believing, trusting, having faith in the truth of some things that one cannot validate through experience or observation.

Naturalism; Roy Bhaskar, Margaret Archer, Andrew Collier, Tony Lawson, Alan Norrie (eds.). 1998. *Critical Realism*. London: Routledge. Pp. 1–184).

My account in this book might seem on first look to be a "projection theory" of religion, per Feuerbach. But it is not. I have not endorsed the truth claims of any religion, but neither have I denied them. Instead, I have maintained a position of "methodological agnosticism" that is proper to social science—in contrast to Berger's "methodological atheism" (*Sacred Canopy*. P. 180; see Porpora. "Methodological Atheism"). Both Feuerbach and I claim to have described the "true" essence of Christianity/religion, but Feuerbach means that religion is *only* (metaphysically) what his account claims, whereas my account more modestly suggests that religion is (ontologically), from a sociological perspective, *at least* what I claim, but may be more than that (see note 8 in the introduction). Feuerbach generally presumed a narrow set of epistemological and metaphysical commitments, which a priori denied the possible truth of religious claims, whereas my approach remains open and pluralistic. So, rather than being a "debunking" theory of religion, mine is a "compatibilist" theory that should be not inconsistent with a variety of religious accounts (see note 32 in the introduction), although they may prefer to formulate their practices in other terms. This book's theory is thus less Feuerbachian than it might appear, though it also does not deny the possibility of atheism and metaphysical naturalism.

45. Justin Barrett. 2004. *Why Would Anyone Believe in God?* Lanham, MD: Alta Mira Press. P. 124.

We simply take them as reasonable givens. And while the contents of human beliefs are diverse, the underlying fact that humans believe many things to be true without certainty about them is the same everywhere.[46] This implies that trusting in religious beliefs that one cannot verify is as a cognitive move no less natural than trusting in many other human beliefs. I also argued from a culturalist point of view that the moral orders, normative directions, and meanings that religions provide humans as "moral, believing animals"—as opposed to the rational, acquisitive, exchanging animals of utilitarianism and rational choice theory—also make it natural that human beings would practice religion. They do so, in part, as a way to find meaning, order, and morality in traditions rooted in something believed to transcend the self, life, history, and the world. Furthermore, I have suggested, human self-consciousness and self-transcendence naturally tend to drive people beyond the confines of the immanent here and now—of "history"—in search of interpretive frameworks that make better sense of the self, life, and the world from "beyond history."[47]

In recent decades, many philosophers of religion and epistemology have argued that at least some religious beliefs are entirely reasonable, no less warranted than many other beliefs that humans commonly hold. I need not summarize here the complex arguments of these philosophers. Suffice it to say that, in addition to the work of the psychologists and cognitive science scholars discussed next, some of the best philosophical arguments in recent years have also made clear that—contrary to older notions of religion's inherent irrationality and epistemic inferiority—many common religious beliefs are as rationally warranted and justifiable as many other ideas and thoughts that people regularly espouse and rely upon.[48]

46. Smith. *Moral, Believing Animals*. Pp. 45–94.

47. Ibid. Pp. 118–123. Also see Barrett. *Why Would Anyone Believe in God?* Pp. 47–49. Arguably somewhat related is Peter Berger's approach in his 1969 book, *A Rumor of Angels* (New York: Doubleday), which argued that many features of human experience that seem impossible to eliminate from life—order, play, hope, the justice of damnation, and humor—seem to make no sense in a naturalistic universe lacking some transcendent purpose, and so represent what he called "signals of transcendence."

48. See, for example, William Alston. 1992. *Faith, Reason, and Skepticism*. Philadelphia: Temple University Press; William Alston. 1991. *Perceiving God*. Ithaca: Cornell University Press; George Mavrodes. 1986. "Religion and the Queerness of Morality." In William Wainwright and Robert Audi (eds.). *Rationality, Religious Belief, and Moral Commitment*. Ithaca: Cornell University Press. Pp. 213–226; Alvin Plantinga. 1993. *Warrant and Proper Function*. Oxford: Oxford University Press; Alvin Plantinga. 1993. *Warrant: The Current Debate*. Oxford: Oxford University Press; Alvin Plantinga and Nicholas Wolterstorff (eds.). 1983. *Faith and Rationality*. Notre Dame: University of Notre Dame Press; Nicholas Wolterstorff. 1992. "What Reformed Epistemology Is

But how and why exactly is religion thought to be "natural" for human beings? In the sense in which many researchers use the term, religion is "natural" for us because it arises from the abilities and habits of the human brain. For instance, anthropologist Stewart Guthrie has argued in his book *Faces in the Clouds: A New Theory of Religion* that human beings have strong, inherent tendencies to interpret ambiguous evidence—of which the world is full—as caused by an agent or being an agent itself, something like "anthropomorphizing" or making the cosmos into the image of people and perhaps other animals.[49] In *Why Would Anyone Believe in God?*, psychologist Justin Barrett calls this mental tool humanity's "hypersensitive agent detection device," or HADD.[50] This mental tendency, Guthrie and Barrett argue, is inherited through evolutionary natural selection. In a hunt-and-be-hunted world in which one may easily become another animal's next meal, to suspect that unusual objects and movements in one's environment may be an agent (e.g., a big, predatory cat or a poisonous snake) is a cautious strategy that enhances one's survival prospects, even when most unusual indicators are not agents. "Better safe than sorry" is the strategy of the most reproductively fit, a "survival enhancing disposition" in a dangerous world. The habit of suspecting agency builds upon humanity's natural causal and teleological reasoning, that is, the ability of humans to understand things happen for reasons, and that some important events and conditions are indeed traces of the activities of active, purposive agents. When humans possess the concepts of spirits and gods—as our species appears to have held them from its earliest days—it becomes easy and natural for them to

Not." *Perspectives.* 7, no. 9: 14–16; Nicholas Wolterstorff. 1976. *Reason Within the Bounds of Religion.* Grand Rapids, MI: Eerdmans; Joseph Runzo and Craig Ihara (eds.). 1986. *Religious Experience and Religious Belief.* Lanham, MD: University Press of America. Also see Thomas Morris. 1996. *God and the Philosophers.* New York: Oxford University Press; Kelly Clark. 1997. *Philosophers Who Believe.* Downer's Grove: IVP. Even the atheist philosopher Richard Rorty conceded these arguments: "I do not think that Christian theism is irrational. I entirely agree . . . that it is no more irrational than atheism. . . . Plantinga's *God and Other Minds* is quite convincing on many points, and I admire Wolterstorff's *Reason Within the Bounds of Religion.* . . . I admire them both as remarkable philosophers . . . [who] show why we atheists should stop praising ourselves for being more 'rational' than theists. On this point they seem to me quite right" (quoted in Stephen Louthan. 1996. "On Religion—A Discussion with Richard Rorty, Alvin Plantinga and Nicholas Wolterstorff." *Christian Scholar's Review.* 27: 178, 179).

49. Stewart Guthrie. 1993. *Faces in the Clouds.* New York: Oxford University Press.

50. Barrett. *Why Would Anyone Believe in God?* Pp. 34–40. Also see Barrett. 2000. "Exploring the Natural Foundations of Religion." *Trends in Cognitive Sciences.* 4: 29–34; Barrett. 2013. "Exploring Religion's Basement: the Cognitive Science of Religion." In Paloutzian and Park. *Handbook of Psychology of Religion.* Pp. 234–255.

attribute ambiguous evidence to the agency of such superhuman powers.[51] The origins of religion thus derive from the mental tendencies that became widespread due to evolutionary forces.

The kinds of minds that humans have also naturally dispose them toward belief in superhuman powers, Barrett also argues. The awareness of death and the strong human proclivities to hyper-sociality, belief in the existence of other minds, paying particular attention to others who know the most about us, interest in understanding the explanations for unexpected benefits and misfortunes, holding justifications for moral intuitions, and maintaining fair social exchanges all strongly dispose humans to consider credible the existence of superhuman powers.[52] "The sorts of minds we have require little particular inputs from the environment in order to rapidly move us toward belief in gods and full-blown religion," in Barrett's words.[53] The same neuro-cognitive factors also explain why a minority of humans are atheistic.[54] The sociobiologist and Johns Hopkins University neuroscientist David Linden agrees:

> Our brains have become particularly adapted to creating coherent, gap-free stories and . . . this propensity for narrative creation is part of what predisposes humans to religious thought. . . . Our shared human evolutionary heritage, as reflected in the structure and function of our brains, predispose us as a species for religious thought in much the same way that it predisposes us for other human cultural universals such as long-term pair bonding, language, and music. . . . All of us are hard-wired, or at least are strongly predisposed, to believe things we cannot prove. That essential act of faith is central to human mental functioning. . . . Our brains have evolved to make us believers.[55]

The sociobiologist Edward O. Wilson writes similarly that "The [human] brain was made for religion and religion for the human brain. In every second of the believer's conscious life religious belief plays multiple, mostly nurturing roles."[56] For believers, religious practices then further reinforce through various mechanisms the plausibility of religious premises.[57] Barrett

---

51. Barrett. *Why Would Anyone Believe in God?* Pp. 21–44.

52. Ibid. Pp. 45–59, 95–105.

53. Ibid. P. 59.

54. Ibid. Pp. 207–218.

55. Linden. 2007. *The Accidental Mind.* Cambridge, MA: Harvard University Press. Pp. 225, 232, 234.

56. Wilson. 2014. *The Meaning of Human Existence.* New York: Liveright. P. 149.

57. Barrett. *Why Would Anyone Believe in God?* Pp. 61–73.

further argues in his book *Born Believers: The Science of Children's Religious Beliefs* that a great deal of research in developmental psychology demonstrates that the human ability and tendency to believe in (what Riesebrodt and I call) superhuman powers is not imposed on older minds through external socialization. Instead, they develop naturally in the minds of toddlers and children in the normal operations of human cognitive development. "Human minds are [not] like empty containers simply waiting to be filled," he writes, but "are specialized to handle some types of information and problems more readily than others."[58]

Adding to this chorus of voices is that of Robert McCauley, professor of philosophy, psychology, religion, and anthropology at Emory University, whose 2011 book, *Why Religion is Natural and Science is Not*, explains that "religion is cognitively natural," because "religions have evolved to cue a variety of maturationally natural dispositions that develop in human minds on the basis of very different conditions."[59] By "maturationally natural cognitions," McCauley means those about which people have "(similar) immediate, intuitive views that pop into the mind in domains where they may have had little or no experience and no instruction."[60] Popular religions entail cognitions, he suggests, that "involve only *modestly* counterintuitive representations, *at most*, that are mainly the results of *normal* variations in the operation of garden-variety, domain-specific, maturationally natural, cognitive equipment." Science, by contrast, requires highly unnatural types of human cognitions, such as entertaining radically counterintuitive theories and using methods that involve great difficulty to acquire and master. McCauley concludes—perhaps counterintuitively—that, while "science's continued existence is fragile," "traditional comparisons of science and religion are cognitively misbegotten" and "science poses no threat to the persistence of religion."

The scholar of collective memory Pascal Boyer develops a sophisticated argument that parallels but goes into greater depth than that of Barrett in his book *Religion Explained: The Evolutionary Origins of Religious Thought.*[61]

58. Justin Barrett. 2012. *Born Believers*. New York: Free Press. P. 8 for the quote.

59. McCauley. 2011. *Why Religion is Natural and Science is Not*. New York: Oxford University Press. Quotes from pp. 5, 8, 9; italics in the original.

60. Distinct from "practiced naturalness" of cognitions, which "come from having extensive experience in dealing with some domain" of life (p. 5).

61. Pascal Boyer. 2001. *Religion Explained*. New York: Basic Books. Also see Pascal Boyer. 1994. *The Naturalness of Religious Ideas*. Berkeley: University of California Press; Boyer. 2003. "Religious Thought and Behavior as By-products of Brain Function." *Trends in Cognitive Science.* 7: 119–124.

According to Boyer, humans commonly believe and practice religion be-cause that is how our minds were prepared by evolutionary natural selec-tion to operate. In his exposition, Boyer shows how complex systems of the brain process information from natural and social environments, make sense of objects and causes, generate myriad thoughts not only about what is but what might or could be, select those ideas and explanations that best fit the constraints of mind and context, and pass them on selectively accord-ing to their relative advantages and disadvantages in cognitive transmission. Religious ideas and beliefs, Boyer argues, far from being aberrant imposi-tions of irrational provenance, are among those that come most naturally to human minds and are most readily transmitted across persons and time. Todd Tremlin agrees based on his research at Central Michigan University on the cognitive foundations of religion: He contends that mental endow-ments inherited from our ancient human past allow many to easily ponder religious ideas, such that biology and cognitive processes serve as the basis for belief in gods and the social practices of religion that are common to all of humanity.[62]

Yet another recent case for the naturalness of religion for human beings focuses not on cognitive evolution but on the evolution of healing. This ap-proach makes a connection between humanity's perpetual and pervasive need for healing from illness, disease, and injuries; the relative therapeutic success among our human ancestors of induced trances, hallucinations, and other altered states of consciousness; and the ready cognitive association between such "hypnotic" states and other recurring anomalous experi-ences, such as apparitions, extrasensory perception, and out-of-body expe-riences. All of this together gives rise to belief in souls, spirits, life after death, and the power of magic, thus providing the groundwork for shaman-ism, the first form of religion humanity practiced.

The sociologist James McClenon develops just such a "ritual healing theory" in his book *Wondrous Healings: Shamanism, Human Evolution, and the Origins of Religion*, which he grounds in evolutionary neurophysiology.[63] He proposes that belief in superhuman powers comes to be fairly effortless neurologically to humanity through natural selection, in part because in the distant past, sick humans who were more susceptible to the hypnotic states that increased the likelihood of their recovery were more likely to pass on their genes than those who were less susceptible. Thus, eons of evolutionary

62. Tremlin. 2006. *Minds and Gods*. New York: Oxford University Press.
63. James McClenon. 2002. *Wondrous Healings*. Dekalb: Northern Illinois University Press.

development—operating through the influence of proto-religious healing practices on rates of recovery from illness and injury—have produced among *homo sapiens* ideas about superhuman powers, human brains readily disposed to believe in them, and shamans as specialized healing practitioners skilled in both inducing altered states of consciousness and, relatedly, communicating with the spirit world and other superhuman powers. That natural process and condition, McClenon argues, laid the foundation for all subsequent forms of human religiousness.[64]

I generally find the arguments of these scholars, who suggest that religion comes naturally to ordinary human beings, and that religion is not uniquely irrational or epistemologically unjustifiable, to be persuasive.[65] I feel no need to tie this book's theory directly to their specific arguments. However, the theory of religion advanced here contributes to the larger development in religion scholarship on the naturalness of religion for humans, and that is worth noting.

More on Secondary Reinforcements of Religion

I said above that the fundamental "cause" of religion is the motivation of human persons, in the course of their quest to realize their natural goods, to channel the blessings and assistance of superhuman powers. That, to use language from chapter 1, is the core principle, the heart and soul, of religion. However, as we saw in chapter 2, religion also generates through emergence a variety of derivative properties, features, and powers. These represent not what religion essentially *is* (ontology) but rather what religion can *do* (capacities). My argument in the previous pages of this chapter has centered on the former, on religion's ontology. But we can fill out our explanation of why humans are religious by bringing in as complementary factors the 18 secondary products of religion discussed in chapter 2.

In other words, on top of practicing religion to access the aid of superhuman powers, humans are also often religious because they enjoy and desire the many other goods flowing from religion. For example, people

64. For related arguments, see Eugene d'Aquili and Andrew Newberg. 1993. "Religious and Mystical States." *Zygon.* 28: 177–199; Eugene d'Aquili and Andrew Newberg. 1998. "The Neuropsychological Basis of Religion, or Why God Won't Go Away." *Zygon.* 33: 187–201; Michael Winkelman. 2000. *Shamanism.* Westport, CT: Bergin and Garvey. A popularized version of some of this approach is found in Shermer. *The Believing Brain.*

65. In my 2003 book, I fairly severely criticized Guthrie and McClenon, but have since come to be persuaded that their accounts make helpful contributions.

universally desire the security and belonging of personal, social, and collective identities. When religion provides meaningful identities to people, that is one more motive for them—in the absence of more powerful counteracting influences—to practice religion. Religion, by my account, did not arise in order to provide such identities; that is not its primary source. But after developing for other, more basic reasons, religion's provision of personal, social, and collective identities became another, reinforcing cause of people's ongoing religious practice.[66]

The same is true about religion's other secondary products. No religious practitioner or community is motivated to continue practicing religion because of *all* the goods it offers. The products of religion attracting practitioners in a given context vary in number and combination depending on the particular religious tradition, historical and social circumstances, and people involved. In principle, none of religion's derivative effects are required to generate and sustain religious practice. But in reality, numerous of these contribute to explaining why people are religious in concrete circumstances. Questions of power, authority, influence, continuity, voice, inclusion, exclusion, alienation, critique, transgression, and dissent also relate to this matter. At least some people become invested in religious communities because there they find opportunities for the enjoyment of power, status, control, superiority, and perhaps access to material resources, opportunities that they might not have in other spheres of society. This often comes at the cost of subordinating and silencing others who wish to practice religion, too. Discovering how these dynamics play out in real-world religious settings is one important task for empirical social science.

A bit of reflection can tie into this section's theme a body of existing literature on the matter of religion's origins. Throughout the history of the academic study of religion, various scholars have proposed theories purporting to reveal its roots. Most are well known: Tylor, Müller, Frazer, Lévy-Bruhl, Marx, Durkheim, Freud, James, Douglas, Otto, Eliade, Geertz, Berger, Stark, and others. Their accounts offer widely varying claims. Some propose belief in spiritual beings developed out of the human desire to explain natural phenomena in the absence of modern science. Religion resulted from primitive people observing, personifying, and then worshipping impressive or frightening features of nature, such as the sun, the moon,

---

66. Slavica Jakelic's *Collectivistic Religions: Religion, Choice, and Identity in Late Modernity* (2010. New York: Routledge) provides an important counterweight to the assumption that modernity routinely individualizes religion.

and storms. Religion arose from the belief of primitive people that they could at once be themselves and participate in the spirit of their totemic animal, giving rise to animism. Religion was born in the "collective effervescence" of gathered communities, as a way to revere some representation of the highest ideals that a group of people holds about itself.

Such proposals continue to multiply. Religion is said to be an ideology by which the haves of society keep the have-nots in subjugation and by which the have-nots reduce the intensity of their suffering. Religion springs from unconscious longings rooted in childhood anxieties for a dominant father figure, about whom deeply ambivalent emotions and desires are felt. Religion is the human response to individual phenomenological encounters with the "numinous," the *mysterium tremendum*, or "hierophanies." Religion is a cultural system of symbols formulating conceptions of a general order of existence, capable of shaping people's motivations and moods. Religion is a "sacred cosmos" that brings transcendent order and meaning to life and the world. Religion is the invented source of "compensators": benefits not available in ordinary life in this world. And so on. In these and other accounts of religion's origins, we can discern certain recurrent themes. One way or another, these accounts say religion has come into being because at bottom it exemplified or offered desirable explanations, meaning, identity, solidarity, control, representations, or rewards.

My theoretical approach suggests the following response. Religions do frequently offer these things. But none of them finally explains the origins of religion. Most of these accounts concern not what religion is but rather what religion does or can do, what effects it can produce. In my view, that means that they do not so much explain the original sources of religion as help to explain the secondary factors that reinforce the practice of religion, showing why, in concrete circumstances, many people are religious. These products of religion—explanation, meaning, identity, solidarity, control, representations, and rewards—partially map onto the 18 features of religion examined in chapter 2 and discussed just above. If this rendering of these ideas works, then many well-known academic theories of religion's origins can be reconceived as partial contributions to our understanding of the many forces that sustain and reinforce religious practices. That is, instead of confronting a Tylor versus Müller versus Otto question of which theorist *really* explains religion, for example, we can take from all three elements that seem relevant to why specific religious people and groups have believed and continue to believe and practice their traditions. Thus, we might understand these theories, or at least their basic themes, not as adequate accounts of religion's origins but rather as partial explanations for religion's appeal and endurance. And that enables us to avoid a mutually exclusive view of historically rival theories of religion competing for adherents.

We might term this a "multiple, overlapping patchwork" approach to explaining human religious practice. In various times, places, and circumstances, different groups of people may practice religion not only to obtain the help of superhuman powers, but also for various combinations of other reasons, possibly involving different kinds of explanations, meaning, identity, solidarity, control, representations of certain kinds of experiences, and instrumental rewards. The idea of a "multiple, overlapping patchwork" suggests that most religious people practice their religion for more than one reason; they piece together combinations of motives, purposes, and explanations. It may be that for many people, no one reason would be enough to justify practicing religion, but a patched-together set of overlapping interests, reasons, and aims suffices to sustain their ongoing participation. Such differences and multiplicities may entail some weaknesses and incoherence. But they may also have the advantages of providing redundancies. If one piece of the patchwork of motives, purposes, and explanations falls away, that person's religious beliefs and practices need not fall apart, for the remaining patches can still hold them together.

For instance, if particular religious explanations of how the world works as it does become increasingly doubtful to a believer, they will not necessarily cease their religious practices, since the same religion may also provide for them other meanings, an identity, social solidarity, self-control, representations of experiences, social status, authority over others, and other rewards. As a parallel analogy, an overlapping patchwork of causes sustaining religious practice may have similar properties of resilience as mixed-planting agricultural methods do against the threat of plant diseases, compared to mono-agriculture uniformity. The diversity, multiplicity, and overlap of the factors involved in a typical person's religious practice provide a resistance to adversity that a single justifying element would not.

Emotional Energy

Another reason humans engage in religious practices is that it often feeds them positive emotional energy. Emotions are hugely important in religious practice, more so than the scant attention I have thus far given them would suggest. Much more can be said about emotions and religion than is possible here, and the subject deserves new empirical research as well.[67] For present purposes, I wish to focus on one aspect of emotions in religion that ties into this chapter's overarching question. That is the way that "interaction rituals" generate the "positive emotional energy" that humans are highly motivated to seek. I rely here on the theory of the sociologist Randall Collins, who describes positive emotional energy as:

> a feeling of confidence, courage to take action, boldness in taking initiative. It is a morally suffused energy; it makes the individual feel not only good, but exalted, with the sense of doing what is the most important and most valuable. . . . Emotional energy has a powerfully motivating effect upon the individual; whoever has experienced this kind of moment wants to repeat it.[68]

According to Collins, "human beings are emotional energy seekers."[69] Emotional energy, he says (operating in an etic mode), is one of the most prized goods in human life, "the central payoff that persons are seeking." People need not be consciously aware of this desire (from an emic perspective), but they are nonetheless irresistibly drawn to interaction situations that promise to generate positive emotional energy in their lives.[70] Even people's mental lives are governed by this impulse, as "thinking flows into those internal conversations that generate the most EE [emotional energy] in the unfolding mental situation."

Crucially, humans cannot create emotional energy by themselves. Emotional energy is always *socially* generated, not individually produced, the product of what Collins calls "interaction rituals." These, he explains, involve four necessary elements: "1. Two or more people are physically

---

67. Riis and Woodhead. *A Sociology of Religious Emotion*; Davies. *Emotion, Identity, and Religion*; Smith. "Why Christianity Works." Also see Donovan Schaefer. 2015. *Religious Affects*. Durham, NC: Duke University Press.

68. Collins. 2004. *Interaction Ritual Chains*. Princeton: Princeton University Press. Quotes in this paragraph come, in order, from Pp. 39, 49, 121, 134, 105–109, 108. Collins's theory of emotional energy can be detached from his view of human persons, which I reject (see Smith. *To Flourish or Destruct*. Pp. 91–158).

69. Quotes in this and the next paragraph come, in order, from Collins. *Interaction Ritual Chains*. Pp. 373, 172, 183, 48, 118.

70. "This is not ordinarily a process of conscious calculation, of the actor thinking, 'I will get a good feeling of power or status if I interact with so-and-so.' Instead, certain symbols come to mind, or appear in the external environment, and spark off propensities (positive or negative) for social action. The 'expectation' may work on a subconscious level." Ibid. P. 119.

assembled in the same place, so that they affect each other by their bodily presence. . . . 2. There are boundaries to outsiders so that participants have a sense of who is taking part and who is excluded. 3. People focus their attention upon a common object or activity and . . . become mutually aware of each other's focus of activity. 4. They share a common mood or emotional experience." Depending on the character of the specific interaction ritual, participants can either gain or lose emotional energy: Some interactions are energy charging, others are draining. Emotional energy is thus like "affective money" accumulated in and spent from internal cognitive-neurological-emotional-motivational "body banks." Furthermore, interaction rituals are rarely one-shot events. They usually "chain" together, with subsequent ones picking up in mood and intensity where the previous one left off. Between these chained interactions, people live on the stocks of emotional energy they have accumulated, and are particularly influenced by the results of the last interaction ritual. When their interaction rituals have been positive, people are up; when negative, they are down.

Since "emotional energy is what individuals seek," "situations are attractive or unattractive to them to the extent that the interaction ritual is successful in providing emotional energy."[71] This motivation shapes not only individual decisions but also the larger contours of people's ongoing lives (figure 4.1). "People move through chains of encounters that make up their daily lives on an up-and-down flow of EE [emotional energy]. They are more attracted to certain situations than others, and sometimes feel disinterest or repulsion. . . . The end result is motivation to repeating those sorts of encounters with particular persons [who generate positive emotional energy] and to avoid them with others."[72]

How does this matter for religion? Humans can draw emotional energy from all kinds of social interactions, including mundane and secular ones, but religious communities and practices entail particularly favorable conditions for the generation of high emotional energy. When that is so, people are inclined to continue practicing religion. Most group religious practices are performed in settings that exactly match the four necessary elements of an interaction ritual (described above). Through routines and repetitions of gatherings and calendric and seasonal practices, religious interaction rituals are chained together in ways that can build long-lasting emotional energy. Many of the affective modes expressed in religious practices are inherently

71. Ibid. P. 44.
72. Ibid. Pp. 118–119.

FIGURE 4.1. Religious practices have the capacity to generate great emotional energy, often positive but sometimes negative. Religious people often practice their religions in part because of the positive emotional energy that they experience in doing so.

positive: celebration, praise, thanksgiving, wonder, gratitude, adoration, ecstasy, and so on. Practices that entail elements with an initially negative edge—confession, humiliation, prostration, repentance, penance, reparations, etc.—usually unfold in ways that are cathartic and often finally affirming. Rarely are even "self-judging" religious practices designed to leave people feeling terrible. The highly participatory and interactive nature of so many religious rituals also makes them very well suited to engender high emotional energy deriving from the solidarity of shared focus, beliefs, and interactions. Simply performing them together in community can produce powerfully positive affective experiences. Add to those conditions the particular atmospheres pervading many religious practices—mystery, liminality, transcendence, enchantment, gnosis, magic, solemnity, holiness, effervescence, charisma, sacredness, depending on the particular tradition and practice—and religion's capacity to generate powerful charges of emotional energy can be multiplied many times. On top of these qualities of religious practices, most of the 18 secondary products of religious practice (chapter 2) also readily generate positive emotional energy—derived from a sense of shared identity, social support, moral affirmation, collective aesthetic expression, and transcendent experience, for example. Even when religions confront darkness in life (suffering, evil, death, atrocity, injustice), in the end, whether through theodicies or helping people cope with difficulties, they typically turn religious practitioners toward some desired sense of meaning, hope, support, or the promise of a coming day of vindication and justice. Again, I know of no religious practices designed to leave dedicated participants feeling despair, futility, or rage. Religion is not about those emotions but deliverance and blessings.

In such ways, religions often serve as wellsprings of positive emotional energy for their practitioners. In addition to whatever other help they may receive from their superhuman powers, religious people commonly derive high emotional energy from participating in the communities that are together seeking to access superhuman powers.[73] This does not need to take the form of highly charged "religious experiences," since generally feeling "blessed" or "happy" as a result of practicing religion is a common and valid experience of emotional energy.[74] Viewed from this perspective, one of the main tasks of religious specialists—priests, pastors, rabbis, imams, shamans, ministers, elders—is to maintain conditions that sustain the kind of interaction rituals that generate positive emotional energy. Failure in this realm brings discontent, conflict, and declining participation in the community. More generally, religions can of course generate negative or low emotional energy. Those religious communities are the ones that struggle with low morale, schism, and the loss of practitioners—a downward spiral of self-destruction that continues until either the group fails or someone or something alters the dynamic of emotional energy production. But in most cases, religions seem to generate much more positive than negative emotional energy. That religions often possess—arguably uniquely so—the ingredients necessary to generate intense positive emotional energy helps to explain why so many humans (on the demand side) want to practice religion.

Careers and Profits for Religious Specialists and Professionals

A final factor helping to explain (on the supply side) why so many humans are religious is that some *people make money from religion*—or if not money, then sacrificial offerings or other forms of payment, barter, or compensation. Those who benefit materially from religion develop personal interests

---

73. See, for example, Robert Wuthnow. 2001. *I Come Away Stronger*. Grand Rapids, MI: Eerdmans; Timothy Nelson. 2004. *Every Time I Feel the Spirit*. New York: NYU Press.

74. See, for example, Smith. *Soul Searching*. Pp. 118–171.

in the ongoing thriving of religion, for obvious reasons; they face significant incentives to promote the continued practice of religion by those they serve. Exactly who benefits materially in what ways depends on the particular religious tradition, its norms or teachings about the remuneration of its religious specialists, and the economic conditions of the time and place in history that the religion is being practiced. But religion, like every other human practice, takes institutionalized forms. And all social institutions, however basic, require material resources to function. So all religions require some system by which to collect or extract material resources from its practitioners (or inspire an immense amount of volunteering, which is nearly impossible to sustain over time).

All religions involve some people who specialize in the proper conduct of religious practices and in the maintenance of the cultural traditions about superhuman powers on the basis of which those practices are prescribed. That might involve learning specialized knowledge, teaching, conducting rituals, organizing religious communities, or any number of other related activities. These people might be tribal shaman, rabbis in synagogues, part-time storefront church preachers, Hindu sages, imams at local mosques, or ordained priests or bishops. Depending on the situation, they might also include scripture and theology professors, denominational administrators, keepers of shrines and temples, religious musicians, missionaries, and pastoral counselors. People are also frequently paid to write and produce religious books, magazines, and educational curricula; to paint icons and make stained glass and carve statues; to produce incense and colored beads; to teach Arabic, Hebrew, or other languages used in religious practices; to supply animals for sacrifice; to design and sew robes and vestments; to plan and construct religious buildings; to consult on religious fund-raising campaigns; to maintain religious pilgrimage destination sites; to organize or speak at religious conferences; and to perform innumerable other religious tasks and support services. Religion is always a *production*, and producing always requires knowledgeable *personnel*, and personnel always require *material resources* to keep them at work. This is just as true of religion as it is in business and the media.[75]

Once the political economies of a religious community or organization are functioning, however primitive or sophisticated they may be, there come to exist, as noted above, at least some specialists who depend on religion to make at least part of their living. When the religions they serve

75. Robert Wuthnow. 1994. *Producing the Sacred*. Champaign: University of Illinois Press.

thrive, so do they. And if and when the religions they serve decline, so do their incomes. This creates a number of people, often a large number, who have hard, material reasons to want their religion to thrive (on top of any spiritual, theological, and moral reasons they care about). And we know that for even the best and most sincere of people, material incentives can be powerfully motivating. There is nothing unusual or morally suspect about that.

All of this creates labor forces of people who have strong personal incentives to promote religion. This is especially true of religious economies in open markets, as opposed to state-regulated religious monopolies. The job of the workers financially dependent on religion is to make religious practice and belief meaningful, plausible, and rewarding. Their interest is to keep religious practitioners practicing, believers believing, sacrificers sacrificing, and givers giving. This means, to incorporate this book's approach, that religious specialists need to do their best to help religious practitioners experience their practices as effective in helping them to realize goods and avoid bads, especially to avoid misfortune, obtain blessings, and be delivered from crises. That is a complicated but usually practicable task, and can be achieved in various ways (see chapters 1 and 2). Paid religious specialists also need to provide a satisfying mix of the secondary religious products that are well suited to their particular religious groups—namely, personal, group, and social identity; community belonging, social solidarity, and social support; moral order, cosmic and life meaning, and theodicies; artistic creations, opportunities for aesthetic expression, and transcendent experiences; self-control, interpersonal controls, and formal social controls; and institutional legitimations, political legitimacy, and the legitimation of dissent.[76] Especially when religious economies allow religious practitioners to sort themselves into relatively homogeneous niches with shared demands,[77] most paid religious specialists prove adequately if not impressively successful in making religious practices and beliefs meaningful, plausible, and rewarding for those who support them materially.

To be clear, I am not saying that the material remuneration that religious specialists receive for their services is the only or even the main reason that

76. No religious community will maximize all of these secondary religious products and capacities, for most humans feel ambivalent about social controls and self-control, and religious communities that tend to be attracted to political legitimacy will not likely also desire the legitimation of dissent, but most religious communities will want many of them, especially the first nine on the list.

77. Stark and Finke. *Acts of Faith*. Pp. 196–199.

they care to see religion flourish. The vast majority of them, we must assume, are sincerely religious themselves, which is why they were attracted to specialized religious work in the first place. Most religious specialists view money as the means enabling them to focus on ends of a very different nature. But it would be naïve to think that the material incentives embedded in the political economies of religious organizations play no role in generating forces that work to sustain and promote religion. They clearly do, in ways that are neither mysterious nor dubious. Huge numbers of people around the world today would lose the value of the human capital invested in their education, training, and job experience; their occupations and businesses; indeed, their entire material livelihoods, if the human interest in practicing religion was to disappear or dramatically decline. Knowing that, in addition to their "higher" motivations and interests, those people do what they can to prevent that from happening. And their incentivized efforts to promote religion are one reason so many people are religious.[78]

Try evaluating this follow-the-money explanation by contemplating a negative counterfactual. Imagine religion and society exactly as they are today with just one difference: Nobody earns a living from religion. Imagine a world, in other words, in which all personnel contributing to religious productions are volunteers, and in which nobody profits from selling religious products and services. All priests, rabbis, imams, pastors, bishops, apostles, patriarchs, ministers, jathedars, shamans, monks, nuns, lamas, sensei, readers, cantors, gurus, swamis, elders, superintendents, deacons, and other clergy and religious specialists support themselves through "secular" work. All who sell religious books, amulets, music, pilgrimages, and other religious products do so at cost, making no profit. What, if anything, will happen to overall levels of religious practice over time in this scenario? I believe the answer is that they would *decline*. That is because—whatever everyone's spiritual, theological, and moral commitments to religious practice might be—nobody would have the financial incentive to promote religion, to make sure religion was done well, to see to it that religious practitioners were satisfied with their experiences of superhuman help. Religion would not disappear, because most people do not practice religion only because other people, who make money from it, promote it. But religious practice would still decline, because nobody's life investments, careers, or

---

78. My argument here partly resonates with the "supply side," religious economies or religious ecologies paradigm, advocated most forcefully by Rodney Stark, Roger Finke, and other rational choice theorists.

livelihoods would be motivating them to do everything in their power to keep religion meaningful, plausible, and rewarding. The fact that a lot of people in our world do make livings as religious specialists does help to explain why so many people today continue to practice religion.

Why Aren't All Humans Religious?

If this chapter's arguments have been persuasive, one final question arises: Why aren't all people religious? If religion is so natural a response to the human condition, so easy and appealing to our evolved brains, so available to animals with exactly the combination of capacities that humans possess, then why don't all humans practice religion? True, religion is found in every known human society in history and as far back as we can see into the mists of pre-history, according to the scant evidence we have. And at least some modern people seem to engage in what Justin Farrell calls "religious muting," that is, the "conscious and unconscious dampening, obscuring, and sometimes outright rejection of claims and commitments" that people are actually "actively believing in, and acting on."[79] Nonetheless, it appears that all societies, even those in which practicing religion is highly normative, also have their share of skeptics, unbelievers, and religious nonconformists. If religion is as natural and compelling as this chapter has argued, then how do we explain nonreligious people?

The answer to this question is not too complicated, though it involves accounting for various factors operating at different levels. At the most general level, according to critical realist personalism, nothing involving humans is deterministic, in the sense of being causally determined by psychological or social forces. Causation in a critical realist world has to do with *tendencies* grounded in "deep" causal powers, not deterministic relations among "surface" events represented as (quasi-) causal laws.[80] Given humanity's natural ends, goods, capacities, and limitations, and given the kinds of cognitive functioning that humans have developed, it is understandable

79. Farrell. *The Battle for Yellowstone*. Pp. 161–167.

80. Douglas Porpora. 2008. "Recovering Causality." In A. Maccarini, E. Morandi, R. Prandini (eds.). *Realismo Sociologico*. Genova-Milano: Marietti; Douglas Porpora. 1993. "Cultural Rules and Material Relations." *Sociological Theory*. 11: 212–229; Douglas Porpora. 2007. "Sociology's Causal Confusion." In Ruth Groff (ed.). *Revitalizing Causality*. New York: Routledge; Bert Danermark et al. 2002. *Explaining Society*. New York: Routledge. Pp. 52–53, 56, 59, 74; Andrew Sayer. 1992. *Method in Social Science*. New York: Routledge; Ruth Groff and John Greco (eds.). 2013. *Powers and Capacities in Philosophy*. New York: Routledge; Robert Koons. 2000. *Realism Regained*. New York: Oxford University Press.

FIGURE 4.2. Many people do not accept the cultural premises that make sense of religious practices, and in some parts of the world, they are increasingly voicing their skepticism in public—as with this prominent billboard near Riverside, California, seeking to increase atheist group awareness. The billboard was sponsored by the Inland Empire Coalition of Reason. (Copyright: Inland Empire Coalition of Reason)

why many humans practice religion. But it is never inevitable that they will do so. Human beings live in causally "open systems" in which myriad forces exert different influences with and against each other in complex combinations.[81] In addition to the various forces that tend to encourage the human practice of religion, causal forces that tend to undermine its practice are often in play (see the following chapter).

Moreover, even in a single social environment, complex constellations of causal forces have divergent effects on different persons. These depend on their even more complicated interactions with each person's unique brain chemistry, genetic makeup, socialization experience, personality type, family life, social networks, and other factors, perhaps including even body type and birth order. It also depends on the cultures, relational networks, and social institutions that define people's social contexts (figure 4.2). The operation of so many causal forces in various combinations and at different levels impinging upon each individual in a given environment is one reason why some people are religious and others are not—even in the very same family.

Particular biographical details that give people a neutral to negative impression of religion may also contribute to humans' varying levels of religious practice. For various reasons, people who might, in a counterfactual

81. Andrew Collier. 1994. *Critical Realism*. London: Verso. Pp. 33–63.

situation, practice religion faithfully may find religion unappealing if not repulsive in their actual context. The list of possible reasons is long and wide-ranging, from experiencing weak attachments to parents to having been abused by a member of the clergy; from growing up in a boring religious congregation to having suffered an inexplicable personal tragedy, such as the shocking death of a loved one; from being "turned off" by perceived religious hypocrisy, to being influenced by an admired anti-religious teacher; from witnessing a horrible calamity or atrocity, such as a devastating earthquake or a man-made event, such as the Holocaust, to feeling oneself silenced as a woman by the dominant male voices who control one's religious tradition; from learning from religious authorities that being gay or lesbian is not morally acceptable to God, to simply not having been raised in a religious family and so deprived of (or spared?) religious socialization. Stated more generally, sustained experiences of negative emotional energy associated with religion strongly undercut the belief and interest in religion that people might otherwise have. All it takes is some serious reason to doubt the existence of superhuman powers, the causal attributes ascribed to them, the effectiveness of the practices prescribed for accessing them, or one's value or welcome in a religious community of practitioners, and religion can easily stop being plausible or appealing. Many people encounter such doubts and turn-offs.[82] (I keep this section brief here because I pick up the topic again in the next chapter.)

Conclusion

Human beings are religious for good reasons—meaning, not that it is good that humans are religious, necessarily, but that the prevalence of religious practice is explicable in light of what we know about human persons, the human condition, human cognition, and innate human ends, needs, and desires. It makes sense to say that religion is natural for humans, given the kind of animals we are. People naturally and frequently seek aid from available sources of help to solve problems and improve our conditions. They normally seek health, happiness, safe travels, fertility, good marriages, and the safety of their children. For people who believe in the existence of superhuman powers and the possibility of gaining their help, efforts to access

---

82. Callum Brown. 2017. *Becoming Atheist*. London: Bloomsbury; Henri Gooren. 2010. *Religious Conversion and Disaffiliation*. London: Palgrave MacMillan; Phil Zuckerman. 2015. *Faith No More*. New York: Oxford University Press.

them through religious practices in hopes of receiving blessings and deliverance from troubles are reasonable. And, when people believe in them, it is also comprehensible that they would seek eternal salvation over hell, or moksha or nirvana over the continued sorrows of *samsaric* reincarnation. Beyond that, most religious practitioners reap many goods from the secondary capacities that religions generate: identities, community, and so forth. Why then not be religious? Indeed, when viewed from this perspective, it may actually be religious unbelievers and secularists who need more sociological explaining than religious practitioners.[83]

83. This observation has nothing to do with religious apologetics, with which this book has no interest. The theory of religion here is at least as compatible with atheism as with the premises of most religious traditions. If anything, its fundamentally naturalistic, sociological outlook will likely make some religious readers uncomfortable. Nonetheless, for reasons of scholarly evenhandedness, relativizing the secularist outlook that is taken for granted in much of academia is a worthwhile endeavor in a social scientific book about religion. It not only fits the wave of recent work on the naturalness of religion, mentioned above, but also builds upon another body of recent scholarship making secularism, too, an object of explanatory study. (For example, Michael Warner and Jonathan VanAntwerpen. 2013. *Varieties of Secularism in a Secular Age*. Cambridge, MA: Harvard University Press; Craig Calhoun, Mark Juergensmeyer, and Jonathan VanAntwerpen. 2001. *Rethinking Secularism*. New York: Oxford University Press; Talal Asad. 2003. *Formations of the Secular*. Stanford: Stanford University Press; Ann Pellegrini and Janet Jakobsen. 2008. *Secularisms*. Durham, NC: Duke University Press; Linell Cady and Elizabeth Hurd. 2010. *Comparative Secularisms in a Global Age*. New York: Palgrave; Joseph Baker and Buster Smith. 2015. *American Secularism*. New York: NYU Press.) It can also encourage us to think harder about many of our academic verities concerning religion and secularity, which may prompt greater critical thinking about the complex world we live in and seek to understand.

5

What Is Religion's Future?

There is a thing inherent and natural, which existed before heaven and earth.
Motionless and fathomless, it stands alone and never changes.
It pervades everywhere and never becomes exhausted.
It may be regarded as the Mother of the Universe. I do not know its name.
If I am forced to give it a name, I call it Tao, and I name it as supreme.

—LAOZI, TAO TE CHING (1904. CH'U TA-KAO, TRANS., CHAPTER 25)

When the Son of Man comes, will he find faith on the earth?
—JESUS OF NAZARETH (LUKE 18:8)

What will be the fate of religion in the future? Will the resurgence of religions that we witnessed in the last quarter of the twentieth century continue? Will secular culture ultimately overcome religion with skepticism, rationalism, and naturalistic science? Or will religions survive but mutate dramatically under the pressures of technological change, globalization, and cultural evolution?

Confident Expectations

Predicting the future of human events is nearly impossible. Attempts to do so are routinely invalidated by the uncertainties of fate and vicissitudes of history. Forecasting the more short-term future is less risky, but challenging nonetheless. So none of us really knows what the future holds for religion. Even so, the long history of humanity suggests some principles I think we can confidently rely on. I will venture four fairly conservative expectations for the future here. The first is that *some if not many humans will continue to want to practice religion.* For some, the demand for religion will be for low-intensity religiousness, per the "default religious laxity tendency" described above. For others, the demand will likely be for more intense, demanding forms of religion. Why this continued demand? All the reasons described in the first two chapters will be relevant. Many humans experience enough challenges in life that they feel they cannot independently overcome, yet which they hope some superhuman power can help them address or endure, that they desire to access those superhuman powers for blessings and deliverance. Many people also seek the various secondary products of religion: identity, community, meaning, expression, aesthetics, ecstasy, control, and legitimacy of various kinds. Religion, I have said, is natural to the human condition, not an alien imposition. It is an easy move for humans, given our capacities, minds, and experiences. Of course not everybody is religious; indeed, some are positively anti-religious. And there will certainly always be causal forces at work in human social life that counteract religious tendencies. But a purely secular existence is not the human default: Particular causal forces are necessary to produce and explain it. For such reasons, I think we can be confident that some—and in some contexts, many—humans will practice religion into the foreseeable future.

A second trend that I think we can anticipate is that *humans will continue to generate new religions.* This may not be obvious in our everyday experience, but people all around the world are constantly inventing variations of existing religious traditions and new religions whole cloth, that is, new religious movements.[1] Humanity is not limited to the small set of better-known "world religions" that dominate the planet today. People across history have recurrently generated new religious ideas, movements, experiences, and practices. Charismatic religious leaders are usually crucial in promulgating new religions. Most new religious movements fail to survive in the face of forces that mitigate against their endurance. A process of "social and institutional natural selection" weeds out the majority, so almost

1. Elisabeth Arweck. 2007. "Globalization and New Religious Movements." In Peter Beyer and Lori Beaman (eds.). *Religion, Globalization, and Culture.* Leiden: Brill. Pp. 253–280; Christopher Partridge (ed.). 2004. *New Religions.* New York: Oxford University Press; Lorne Dawson. 2006. *Comprehending Cults.* New York: Oxford University Press.

nobody ever even hears about them.[2] But a few new religions may survive and, under the right conditions, enjoy the prospect of spreading broadly and attracting more adherents. Over the long run, a few may rise to become another "great world religion." The process of religious innovation, selection, failure, and success has been repetitively at work over the long course of human history and will likely persist in the future.

We can also be confident that *all living religions will be internally, qualitatively transformed over time*. Some religions make claims to unchanging orthodoxy. They would like to believe that they have never changed, never moved from their primordial, pristine truth. Some do change more slowly and less perceptibly than others. But all religions—like all human societies and cultures—have changed, do change, and will change. Nothing humanly social, including religion, is static. Whether or not the possible truths that religions represent are eternal, the human, social, institutional expressions of those religions are temporal and changeable. Sometimes religions change because of external environmental transformations to which they must adapt or perish. Other times they are modified because of internal dissent and pressure. Often those two go hand in hand. In any case, people sometimes view change—the alteration of something previously thought to be enduring—as a sign of religious decline or loss. But religions' capacity to adjust to ever-evolving historical, social, and cultural conditions can be a measure of resilience, creativity, and strength.[3] Religions often assert that they express eternal truths, and they are usually embedded in long-standing traditions. But religion is also based in the human capacity to anticipate the future, to understand causal dynamics, to exercise capacities for creativity, and to try to exert control over unpredictable and disorderly forces in life. So we can expect that religions—especially the most dynamic and successful ones—will continue to change qualitatively over time. Whether or not such change represents a negative loss or fruitful adaptation can only be judged by the internal standards and expectations of each religion itself—though the answer will frequently be ambiguous and contested (figure 5.1).

The fourth expectation about religion about which we can be confident is that in the future, *some religions will grow in size, strength, and significance, while others will decline*. As human societies and cultures change, not all

---

2. Robert Wuthnow. 1989. *Communities of Discourse*. Cambridge, MA: Harvard University Press. Pp. 10–11, 118–129, 548–554.

3. Smith et al. 1998. *American Evangelicalism: Embattled and Thriving*. Chicago: University of Chicago Press. Pp. 97–102.

FIGURE 5.1. "Professor Sysiphus," the overseer of a Los Angeles storefront shrine for *La Santa Muerte*, reads the prayer requests of followers venerating the female Mexican folk saint *Nuestra Señora de la Santa Muerte*, Spanish for Our Lady of Sacred or Holy Death. *Santa Muerte* is a new, rapidly growing religious movement in Mexico and the Southwestern United States that combines an ancient Aztec Mesoamerican reverence toward death with a Catholic veneration of saints. Devotees associate this folk saint's personification of death with protection, healing, and safe passage to the afterlife, which are highly relevant for people living amid bloody drug cartel violence and undertaking dangerous journeys across the Mexican-US border. (Copyright: Shaul Schwarz/Getty Images Reportage)

religions fare equally well in adapting and appealing to practitioners. Some religions ride waves of growth and social importance, whereas others contract and become less relevant. Pentecostalism and charismatic evangelicalism in the global south are an example of the former today, whereas mainline Protestantism in the United States and Anglicanism in the UK arguably are examples of the latter.[4] Religion may not be going extinct, but in certain contexts secularization is indeed a powerful dynamic. Population dynamics and fertility rates also help to determine such outcomes, since some religions grow more through reproduction and socialization than proselytizing and conversions.[5] Having been an important religion in the past guarantees nothing for the future.

4. See, for example, Philip Jenkins. 2008. *The New Faces of Christianity*. New York: Oxford University Press; Jason Lantzer. 2012. *Mainline Christianity*. New York: New York University Press; Callum Brown. 2009. *The Death of Christian Britain*. New York: Routledge.

5. Darren Skerkat. 2014. *Changing Faith*. New York: NYU Press.

Viewed in the long run, the continual transformation of societies and religions means that in at least some periods of time, certain religious traditions turn out to be "winners," when it comes to number of adherents and other indicators of religious strength, and others prove to be losers.[6] Then things can change again. The dominant religions of powerful ancient empires—Egypt, Assyria, Babylon, the Incas, the Aztecs—are now essentially dead. And one of the largest and fastest-growing religions in the world today, Islam, is a relatively recent upstart, when viewed in the long perspective of human history. So, although we have little reason to expect religion to disappear anytime soon, we should not expect religious stability over time. Religions are dynamic institutions and will likely change at accelerated paces in coming decades.

A Brief Illustration: Wicca's Modern Paganism

Wicca is a new pagan religion, invented in mid-twentieth-century England, but drawing on elements of millennia-old paganism and on early anthropological accounts of tribal magic around the world.[7] Wicca was founded by the British author and amateur folklorist and anthropologist Gerald Gardner ("the Father of Wicca"), who established the clandestine Bricket Wood coven of witches in Hertfordshire, England, in the 1940s.[8] Gardner then published three books—*High Magic's Aid* (1949), *Witchcraft Today* (1954), and *The Meaning of Witchcraft* (1959)—that publicly launched Wicca. Gardner (who went by the magical "craft" name Scire), initiated many women

6. Roger Finke and Rodney Stark. 2005. *The Churching of America, 1776–2005*. New Brunswick, NJ: Rutgers University Press.

7. The following description is based on Ethan Doyle White. 2016. *Wicca*. Brighton: Sussex Academic Press; Helen Berger. 2013. *A Community of Witches*. Columbia: University of South Carolina Press; Margot Adler. 1979. *Drawing Down the Moon*. Boston: Beacon Press; Vivianne Crowley. 1989. *Wicca*. London: Aquarian; Joanne Pearson, Richard Roberts, and Geoffrey Samuel. 1998. *Nature Religion Today*. Edinburgh: Edinburgh University Press; Joanne Pearson. 2005. "Wicca." In Lindsay Jones (ed.). *Encyclopedia of Religion*. Detroit: Macmillan. P. 9730; Ronald Hutton. 1999. *The Triumph of the Moon*. London: Oxford University Press; Kaatryn MacMorgan-Douglas. 2007. *All One Wicca*. Buffalo: Covenstead; Doreen Valiente. 1989. *The Rebirth of Witchcraft*. London: Robert Hale; Janet Farrar and Steward Farrar. 1981. *A Witches' Bible*. London: Phoenix; Michael Howard. 2010. *Modern Wicca*. Woodbury, MN: Llewellyn Publications; Jonathan Tapsell. 2013. *Ameth*. London: Avalonia.

8. Gardner's coven superseded an earlier New Forest coven on the same site, which was probably established in 1924 by a Rosamund Sabine, an esoteric who believed she was a reincarnated witch. Philip Heselton. 2003. *Gerald Gardner and the Cauldron of Inspiration*. Milverton: Capall Bann.

into his Wiccan coven. Among them was Doreen Valiente (craft name Ameth), a high priestess in the 1950s who helped produce important Wiccan liturgical texts and secret oral and written teachings. Other notable early Wiccan leaders were Patricia Crowther (craft name Thelema), Eleanor Bone (Artemis), and Lois Bourne (Tanith).

Gardner and Valiente viewed themselves not as inventing a new faith but as reviving an ancient pagan witchcraft religion. They were not concerned with rediscovering and preserving an authentic pagan "orthodoxy," however; they intentionally borrowed for their syncretistic religion diverse practices and ideas from the occult, witchcraft, magic, esotericism, metaphysics, spiritism, the paranormal, mystery faiths, nudism, and nature worship. Wicca was from its founding decentralized, eclectic, and adaptive in its practices, beliefs, and organization. The original Gardnerian movement branched out over time into a variety of Wiccan traditions and sects, each teaching its own version of Wicca's basic principles and practices. In the last 50 years, Wicca has spread to many countries around the world.[9] It is a religion led and practiced mostly by women—65 percent of Helen Berger's sample of neo-pagans were female.[10] Today, its adherents are estimated to number about 800,000 and the religion continues to grow—although its "membership" is notoriously difficult to tally, in part because many practice Wicca in secret.[11]

The superhuman powers of Wicca are primeval, pre-Christian divinities. Wiccan practitioners believe a vast array of ideas about gods, including polytheism, monotheism, pantheism, duotheism, animism, agnosticism, and atheism. The closest thing to an "official" Wiccan theology is the duotheistic (two gods) belief in a Mother Goddess of fertility and a Horned God—about whom (it is believed) knowledge has been secretly passed down by initiates since Stone-Age times to the present. The Mother Goddess is linked to fertility, life, springtime, and femininity; the Horned God is associated with nature, animals, the afterlife, and masculinity. Many Wiccans view these two as the faces of the unified force of life that animates nature. Many also see them as representing the diverse facets of divinity or as divine archetypes, or perhaps embodying different deities of various

9. Helen A. Berger, Evan Leach, and Leigh Shaffer. 2003. *Voices from the Pagan Census*. Columbia: University of South Carolina Press; Gary Jensen and Ashley Thompson. 2008. "Out of the Broom Closet." *Journal for the Scientific Study of Religion*. 47: 753–766.

10. Berger, Leach, and Shaffer. *Voices of the Pagan Census*. P. 27.

11. http://www.adherents.com/Na/Na_666.html#4222; http://abcnews.go.com/WN/real-witches-practice-samhain-wicca-rise-us/story?id=8957950; Doyle White. *Wicca*.

pagan pantheons. Some Wiccans also believe in other feminine and masculine goddesses and gods, spirits, powers, deities, leaders, angels, kings, and lords. And some believe that one Supreme Deity created many "under-gods" who express different facets of the Supreme Cosmic Power. Different versions of Wicca view the divine power as personal, while others believe divinity is ultimately an impersonal cosmic force or principle.

Wiccan practices, usually performed by covens in private, are intended to alter their practitioners' consciousness, focus them on the true significance of present existence, call down divine powers, perform magical enchantments, and unite members of the coven with the energy and beauty of the cosmos. Most Wiccan celebrations follow the cycles of the moon, which is associated with the Mother Goddess, and the cycles of the sun, associated with the Horned God. Wiccans celebrate eight "Sabbats," seasonal festivals of the year, which together comprise the "Wheel of the Year." These include Halloween, Yuletide, Candlemas, May Day, and Litha. Wiccans also celebrate initiation rituals to induct new members into covens, "Handfasting" festivals to celebrate weddings, and sometimes rituals of "Wiccaning" to present children to the Goddess and God in order to ask for their protection.[12] Many Wiccan rituals are performed within ritually cast or purified magic circles, into which divinities and magical energies are called. Practitioners may wear ordinary clothes, but sometimes they wear ritual robes with cords for belts, and sometimes even practice naked. On occasion they enact ritualized and sometimes actual sexual intercourse in rites in which the God and Goddess are invoked to possess the priest and high priestess. Emphasized in most Wiccan ritual practices—in performing "the Craft"—are music, myth, playfulness, dreams, song, drums, dance, drama, visions, pageantry, wine, cakes, games, and artistic enjoyment. Wiccan tools of ceremonial practice include ritual candles, knives, wands, broomsticks, chalices, incense, cauldrons, altars, statues of gods, and recited liturgical texts. Wiccans have no official scripture, but most rely heavily on *The Book of Shadows*, a collection of texts compiled by Gardner and Valiente, which contains instructions for performing religious rituals and spells, poetry, chants, prayers, and other liturgical texts.[13]

12. Ronald Hutton. 2008. "Modern Pagan Festivals." *Folklore*. 119: 251–273; Raymond Buckland. 2002. *Buckland's Complete Book of Witchcraft*. Woodbury, MN: Llewellyn Press; Ann-Marie Gallagher. 2005. *The Wicca Bible*. New York: Sterling Publishing; Doreen Valiente. 1973. *An ABC of Witchcraft Past and Present*. Robert Hale Publishing.

13. Gerald Gardner. 2015. *The Gardnerian Book of Shadows*. Rochester, NY: Scholar's Choice. See Valiente. *Rebirth of Witchcraft*.

What blessings are Wiccan practices intended to produce, and what misfortunes do they seek to avert? Wicca generally seeks to align practitioners with the fundamental forces and truths of the cosmos, which are believed to be consistent with modern science and expressed in harmony with nature. Wiccans say that their religion engenders mirth, reverence, honor, humility, strength, beauty, power, and compassion, which lead to wellness and happiness. Specific magic spells that cause physical changes in the world are myriad; they include invocations for fertility, protection, healing, and the banishment of harmful influences. Some Wiccans also believe that mediums are able to communicate with the spirits of the dead. Wicca does not emphasize life after death. Wiccans hold different views of the afterlife, including the survival of spirits after death, reincarnation, and no afterlife at all. How to live in the present is the primary focus of Wiccan ethics, which are fairly rudimentary. Most practitioners subscribe to a code known as the "Rede" (meaning "advice" or "counsel"), which says, "An it harm none, do what ye will"—meaning, essentially, "Do what you want so long as it doesn't harm others."[14] Some Wiccans also believe in the "Law of Threefold Return," which teaches that whatever benevolent or malevolent actions a person performs will return to them with three times the force. Overall, Wicca commends positive living, kindness, peace, and the performance of practices, rituals, and spells that help achieve good and happy lives.[15]

Wicca thus illustrates all four expectations about religion offered above. It demonstrates that *many people will continue to want to practice religion* and that *humans will continue to generate new religions*. Wicca began and grew in an archetypically modern country, England, and was invented by a man raised in an upper-middle-class family who traveled and lived extensively in South and Southeast Asia. Even as the mainstream Church of England was on the cusp of a catastrophic decline in adherents, Gardner and his collaborators were inventing a new religion out of disparate parts of paganism, witchcraft, spiritism, nudism, and other esoteric and cultic traditions. Despite being in its early years (and to some extent still) a highly deviant religion and much disparaged by outsiders, Wicca attracted many followers, has spread globally, and continues to grow in numbers. From the last

---

14. Mark Ventimiglia. 2003. *Harm None*. Kensington: Citadel Press. Pp. 186–187; John Coughlin. 2002. "The Wiccan Rede." http://www.waningmoon.com/ethics/rede3.shtml; Judy Harrow. 1985. "Exegesis on the Rede." *Harvest*. 5: 3; http://web.archive.org/web/20050508 032805/http://www.witchvox.com/va/dt_va.html?a=usca&c=words&id=3801.

15. See, for example, S. Zohreh Kermani. 2013. *Pagan Family Values*. New York: NYU Press.

centuries until the 1960s, the idea that hundreds of thousands of ordinary people in twenty-first-century Europe, America, and beyond would be practicing pre-Christian paganism would have been thought preposterous. Yet here we are.

Wicca also illustrates the third expectation named above, that *all living religions will be internally, qualitatively transformed over time*. Wicca was an innovation that has not ossified, but has adapted in various ways to survive and grow. Consider its very name, Wicca. Originally this religion called itself Witchcraft. But by the 1960s, the latter was replaced by Wicca (which comes from the Old English *wicce* and *wicca*, Anglo-Saxon English terms for female witch and male sorcerer, respectively) in order to be more socially palatable than the highly controversial original self-designation, which many associated with black magic and Satanism.[16] Further, when (what were supposed to be) the secret divine names of the Mother Goddess and the Horned God were revealed in 1964 as Aradia and Cernunnos, Wiccan leaders changed their names to make them secret again, thus protecting the mystery and "gnostic" knowledge that help make Wicca exciting to practice. More broadly, the early leaders of Wicca wisely did not impose a rigid orthodoxy or organizational structure on the movement. Instead, they built in a flexibility that appealed to the kinds of followers Wicca attracted and attracts, and that could enable it to adapt to changing times and social conditions. The Wicca of today is not the same religion as in the 1950s, and will likely look different again in another 50 years.

Finally, Wicca reflects the fourth expectation offered above, namely, that over time *some religions will grow in size, strength, and significance, while others will decline*. During the course of Wicca's existence, many religious groups have suffered major losses in membership, social status, and cultural authority. Yet others, including Wicca and Pentecostal Christianity, have spread and grown at impressive rates. In any religious ecology, religions are either growing or shrinking; long-term stability is not the norm. Even in the modern world, religious decline among some groups has always been accompanied by religious advances among others. The fascinating pattern is that in the modern era most of the religions that grow do not conform to modern assumptions and values, but selectively resist and push back against modernity, offering alternative life-worlds that (un-

---

16. Ethan Doyle White. 2010. "The Meaning of 'Wicca.'" *The Pomegranate*. 12: 185–207; "Wicca." William Morris (ed.). 1969. *The American Heritage Dictionary of the English Language*. New York: American Heritage Publishing. P. 1548.

like, say, Amish practices) can still be fitted within largely ordinary modern lives. Consider Wicca and Pentecostalism. As different as they are theologically, sociologically they share numerous commonalities. Both audaciously profess to offer direct contact with divine powers. Both subvert a rationalized, demystified cosmos and open up newly enchanted life-worlds.[17] Both prescribe practices that induce spontaneous, emotionally powerful, ecstatic experiences.[18] Both offer the constructive refurbishment of one's past self and identity.[19] Both situate their practitioners in relatively small, tight-knit religious communities. Both appear to have a special appeal to women, who time out of mind have been relegated to second-class status in most religions.[20] And both offer (and appear often enough to deliver) practical help for navigating life's challenges, attaining blessings, averting misfortunes, and overcoming crises. Although Wicca and Pentecostalism may seem anachronistic today, given what we know about the human condition—and in light of what many experience as emptiness and alienation in a secular, rationalized, bureaucratized, manufactured, out-of-control, modern world—is it surprising that religions like them are growing?

What By This Account Should "Secularization" Mean?

In reflecting on the future of religion, it is impossible to avoid thinking about "secularization," even if the secularization paradigm is increasingly doubted.[21] But just as scholars have disagreed about how best to define

17. Lynne Hume and Kathleen McPhillips (eds.). 2006. *Popular Spiritualities*. New York: Routledge.

18. Helen Berger. 1995. "The Routinization of Spontaneity." *Sociology of Religion*. 56: 49–61.

19. Helen Berger and Douglas Ezzy. 2007. *Teenage Witches*. New Brunswick, NJ: Rutgers University Press; Helen Berger. 2006. *Witchcraft and Magic*. Philadelphia: University of Pennsylvania Press.

20. See Laura Vance. 2015. *Women in New Religions*. New York: NYU Press. Chapter 4; Kathryn Rountree. 1997. "The New Witch of the West: Feminists Reclaim the Crone." *Journal of Popular Culture*. 30: 211–230; Kristy Coleman. 2010. *Re-riting Woman: Dianic Wicca and the Feminine Divine*. Lanham, MD: Alta Mira Press; Constance Wise. 2008. *Hidden Circles in the Web: Feminist Wicca, Occult Knowledge, and Process Thought*. Lanham, MD: Alta Mira Press; Jone Salomonsen. 2002. *Enchanted Feminism*. New York: Routledge; Janet Farrar and Stewart Farrar. 1987. *The Witches' Goddess*. London: Robert Hale Publishing; Laurie Cabot. 1997. *The Witch in Every Woman*. New York: Delta; Mary Jo Neitz. 2000. "Queering the Dragonfest: Changing Sexualities in a Post-Patriarchal Religion." *Sociology of Religion*. 61: 369–391.

21. Historians have made their own contributions to chipping away at secularization theory, as summarized, for example, by J.C.D. Clark. 2012. "Historiographical Reviews: Secularization and Modernization: The Failure of a 'Grand Narrative.'" *Historical Journal*. 55: 161–194.

"religion," so too they have debated how to define secularization. The two are connected: How people think about secularization is strongly shaped by how they conceive of religion. Secularization is not uniform or inevitable, but it is real in many social contexts, so it needs to be understood well. I do not believe that there is one right way to define secularization. Religious changes that seem like secularization take many expressions and various forms at different levels of religion and society. So the one term "secularization" seems like it can validly mean many things. As long as we clarify our meanings and uses in specific analyses, we should be prepared to work with different meanings of the one term.[22]

Nonetheless, for present purposes and consistency in theoretical development, it should be useful to specify what secularization means in light of the definition of religion proposed in chapter 1. There I defined religion as *a complex of culturally prescribed practices, based on premises about the existence and nature of superhuman powers, whether personal or impersonal, which seek to help practitioners gain access to and communicate or align themselves with these powers, in hopes of realizing human goods and avoiding things bad—especially to avoid misfortune, obtain blessings, and receive deliverance from crises.* If that is what religion is and if by secularization we usually mean something like the decline, weakening, or loss of importance or authority of religion, then what is the meaning of the term "secularization"? Secularization denotes *some reduction in the performance of the culturally prescribed practices* that seek to access, communicate with, or align people with superhuman powers. That may sound simple, but it is not. Those prescribed practices are culturally and historically particular—and myriad, complex, interconnected, and situationally variable for all religions. That means that theories about secularization will have to be specific to a certain religion, time period, and geographical context, and to rely on intimate familiarity with the substantive content of the practices prescribed by particular religious traditions. Claims about secularization will need to be based on narrative analyses of change over significant periods of time. And such analyses will be difficult to make comparatively across religious traditions. That should make us suspicious of studies that rely on only one or a few measures of secularization to compare trends across different religious

22. Previous helpful mappings of various meanings of the term include Karel Dobbelaere. 2002. *Secularization*. Bern, Switzerland: Peter Lang; and Casanova. 1994. *Public Religions in the Modern World*; also see Mark Chaves. 1994. "Secularization as Declining Religious Authority." *Social Forces*. 72: 749–774.

traditions in many countries.[23] Instead, it should push us in more historical, cultural, and qualitative directions of case-study research.

What, then, would *cause* secularization, a reduction in the culturally prescribed religious practices intended to access superhuman powers? One cause could be a decrease in *belief or trust in the ideas of the culture that explain and justify those practices*.[24] If a pagan Roman started seriously doubting that the gods exist or respond to sacrifices, she would likely be less inclined to perform her religious practices to access the help of her gods. If a Bangkok businessman stops believing in the reality of samsara, karma, moksha, and nirvana, then he will probably reduce or eliminate his practice of Buddhist meditations, mindfulness, and prayers.

A second possible cause of secularization might be people coming to *feel less vulnerable to life's misfortunes and crises and less in need of blessings* that they hope their superhuman powers can deliver them from and offer. In this case, religious people do not believe less in their religious cultures that prescribe religious practices; they simply feel less need to employ those practices for their desired ends. That change of feeling could result from many factors, including, for instance, a significant enhancement of physical security and well-being accompanying newly attained material prosperity; or a long period in which everything in life goes really well; or a dramatic lowering of expectations and aspirations, perhaps due to clinical depression. A third possible cause of secularization as defined here could be a *new reliance on means other than the help of superhuman powers to address life's misfortunes and desired blessings*, even when the threats of crisis, hopes for blessings, and vulnerability to loss continue to be felt just as intensely. Reasons for this change could again be many. An expansion of government welfare benefits or a major increase in one's financial means, for example, would both provide new resources with which to cope with life's inevitable problems and (as a result) reduce the felt need to rely so much on superhuman powers. Those, I suggest, are the three logical causes of secularization, as defined by this book's view of religion.

23. Such as, for example, Norris and Inglehart. *Sacred and Secular.*

24. That could involve either a decrease in the absolute number of people believing and trusting, or decreases in the levels of confidence of the belief and trust among a constant number of people. In the former case, religious people believe as intensely as before, but there are fewer of them, as new unbelievers cease religious practice; in the latter case, the number of religious people remains the same, but their internal assurance about their religious cultures weakens, affecting their levels of religious practice.

Secularization, however, could also arguably mean *a significant reduction in the capacity of religion to generate its secondary, dependent, and derivative products, features, and capacities* described in chapter 2. Religion commonly produces community belonging, social solidarity, and social support; moral order, cosmic and life meaning, and theodicies; artistic creations, opportunities for aesthetic expression, and transcendent experiences; self-control, interpersonal controls, and formal social controls; and institutional legitimations, political legitimacy, and the legitimation of dissent. Religions that produce these features in abundance we would justly consider to be vibrant and healthy. But is the opposite true? Here the analysis becomes more complicated.

Religious traditions and communities routinely change over time in complex ways that alter their interests in and capacities to produce these secondary outcomes. A decline in religion's production of some of them need not be an indicator of secularization. Sometimes adaptive changes in religions involve other alterations, both expected and otherwise, that do not clearly qualify as religious loss or decline. For instance, when a religious community grows in size—normally considered a sign of increasing organizational strength—that typically results in a decrease among adherents in the experience of religious community solidarity, arguably an indicator of weakening religion. Changes involving secondary religious products, in other words, often entail incommensurate trade-offs. A mainline Protestant church, to take another example, might grow more powerful in its ability to mobilize faith-based political protests, yet along with that shift may suffer some loss in its capacity to provide religious aesthetic expression and transcendent experiences. Does that count as secularization or merely interesting religious change?

The best way to sort out these issues, I think, is to continue working with the logic of the distinction between religious ontology (chapter 1) and religion's causal capacities to generate secondary products (chapter 2). Remember the metaphor of the tree roots, trunk, branches, and leaves (chapter 2). Culturally prescribed practices seeking the help of superhuman powers are the "roots and trunk" of religion, its ontological being. The 18 secondary outcomes that religion can give rise to are its "branches and leaves," which grow out of and in turn give life and energy back to religion's core. Recall, too, that a tree cannot survive when its roots and trunk are damaged or severed, although it can when many of its branches and leaves are shorn, diseased, or wither (figure 5.2). We should count secularization as occurring when we observe over a period of time *a significant reduction*

FIGURE 5.2. While some religions thrive in modernity, others decline. This church building was constructed in 1886 and housed the Friendship Baptist Church of Washington, DC. Listed on the National Register of Historic Places, it has also been used by other congregations, including the Miracle Temple of Faith, Redeemed Temple of Jesus Christ, and the Virginia Avenue Baptist Church. More recently, it was put up for sale. (Copyright: AgnosticPreachersKid/ Creative Commons)

in religious practitioners performing their culturally prescribed practices that seek to access, communicate with, or align them with superhuman powers. Exactly what that reduction involves will always be defined by the relevant religious tradition's culture and the practices it prescribes. We should thus treat decreases (or increases) in the strength, frequency, or intensity of the 18 secondary capacities produced by religion as, at most, only possible *indicators* of secularization (or religious strengthening) at work. Observed declines in the 18 products of religion may, but need not, signify secularization underway. They may simply express some kind of religious change involving no loss or decline.

Imagine a religious congregation or organization that, as a result of religious vitality in prior years, had managed to build for itself strong group identity, solidarity, social support, moral order, life meaning, artistic expression, and so on. Now imagine that for some reason members of this group stop believing in superhuman powers and the need to perform practices to access them, yet as a community still continue to enjoy strong group identity, solidarity, social support, moral order, life meaning, and artistic expressions. I think we would be justified in saying that this group *did* undergo a process of secularization—it lost its religious core—despite that, on its face, it continues to exhibit many of the secondary products originally developed in the past. Imagine next, by contrast, a religious congregation that performs culturally prescribed practices seeking to access superhuman powers, and, as a result of its religious investments, also comes to enjoy strong group identity, solidarity, social support, moral order, life meaning, and artistic expressions. But then, for some reason, the members of this group begin to worry that these secondary aspects of their religious lives have become distractions from their central religious interests, and decide to start concentrating nearly all of their energies on intensifying their faithful performance of practices intended to access superhuman powers. As a result, their formerly strong group identity, solidarity, social support, moral order, life meaning, and artistic expression weaken. Would we be justified in claiming that this group underwent a process of secularization? I think not. If anything, even if important secondary aspects of its community life were lessened, arguably this group experienced something like the opposite of secularization. If so, that tells us that *secularization ought to reference changes related to religion's core being, its ontology*, rather than secondary properties often associated with religious communities.

Three observations complicate matters even further. First, what will count as secularization in one religious tradition may not count in another. Unitarian Universalists are not Southern Baptists are not Hindus are not Rastifarians. Each tradition and sub-tradition will have to be analyzed on its own terms. And that requires substantive familiarity with the histories, cultures, beliefs, and practices of every religion in question.

Also, *within the same religious tradition*, what might count as secularization at one time might *not* count as such at another time. Religious traditions themselves change in ways that *redefine* which prescribed practices are necessary, distinctive, important, and allowable. And that affects what counts as secularization. For example, we might plausibly argue that Mormonism's official abandonment of and ban on its once distinctive and fiercely defended practice of "plural marriage" (polygamy) in 1890 was a clear instance of secularization in that tradition—since that seemed a capitulation to the external pressures of national anti-polygamy laws and US Supreme Court rulings, motivated in part by a growing Mormon desire for greater mainstream cultural acceptance. But we could *not* count the fact that *today's* Mormons do not practice plural marriage as secularization, since now the LDS Church forbids polygamy. In fact, Mormons practicing plural marriage today would demonstrate a breakdown of deference to Mormon church authority, or a weakening of religion.[25]

Said theoretically, like religion, *secularization is itself culturally and historically relative and specific*, so that exactly what qualifies as secularization in one context may not in other situations, even for the same religious tradition. That means that, once some secularizing change has occurred and becomes the new norm in a religious group or tradition, *the standard is reset* for what counts as orthodox, and so what could count as secularization is now relative to the new norm. Secularization, in other words, is a *moving target*, because the changing subject on which it is focused (religion) is not a static entity, but a social, cultural, and historically variable human construction. Thus, for another example, in the early Christian church, new converts were typically baptized stark naked, as a sign of their having stripped away and discarded their former pagan lives.[26] But that fact does not mean that Christians today are "secularized" simply because they remain clothed when baptized—the standards for what is necessary for an "authentic" baptism simply changed over time, and so what could count as loss must change, too. The possible secularization of a religious group *at any time* must therefore be judged relative to that group's own formal or normative expectations *during that time*.

Finally, to really complicate matters, the relativism necessitated by religion's own internal changeability over time is not absolutely limitless. Some losses in religiousness must be judged to be secularization, regardless of what a religious group may say about the change. Logically, a religious community might claim that they have come, over the decades (i.e., as a temporal change), to expect and prescribe almost no practices oriented toward superhuman powers to be performed by their members, and so the fact that few of their members actually engage in any religious practices anymore does not mean the group has been secularized. Logically, that may be so, but substantively probably not. When a religious group progressively lowers its standards to expect less and less of itself, eventually that change per se embodies secularization, regardless of what the religious group says about it. At some point, the analyst has to shift from using the word of a religious group as the standard by which to differentiate mere religious change from secularization, to actually seeing the religious group's own

---

25. Embodied in defiant, schismatic, fundamentalist Mormon sectarian groups. Jon Krakauer. 2004. *Under the Banner of Heaven*. New York: Anchor.

26. Everett Ferguson. 2013. *Baptism in the Early Church*. Grand Rapids, MI: Eerdmans. Pp. 31, 33, 124, 125, 286, 330, 525, 537, 541.

word about itself as evidence of secularization. In other words, we ought, as a default, to treat the stated norms of religions as baselines for assessing whether secularization has occurred in their communities, but those same norms may themselves become empirical data for discerning secularization, under conditions that seem to warrant that move. Which conditions are those? I am afraid there are no solid guidelines about that. Analysts of religion will have to make their best judgments, explain them to their community of peers and students, and be open to their judgments in turn.[27]

Will Modern Secularization Bring Religious Decline?

What, then, should we think about the long-standing expectation in the social sciences that modernity weakens and perhaps even destroys religion? Or is secularization theory wrong, as many have more recently argued?[28] These are important questions. Whether we believe that modern society is inherently secularizing affects how we interpret our empirical observations of religions today. Re-thinking secularization theory also provides a good opportunity to reconsider our deep assumptions about causation and theory-building in the social sciences.

Here, I think, is the correct answer. Religion will be a significant part of human life and societies as long as the human condition is like what it is now. Exactly how significant religion proves to be will vary by social and cultural context and path-dependent contingencies. In some situations, religion will be powerful, in others probably minimal. And those will change over time as well. But unless an epoch of radical biotechnology transforms human nature, I think that some if not many humans will continue to seek the blessings and deliverance of superhuman powers, as our species always has. No matter how modern or post-modern or whatever else human societies become, religion will not wither and expire. In this I agree with Martin Riesebrodt: "Although religion is not a necessary component of human culture and existence, its disappearance is extremely unlikely."[29]

---

27. That is the way of historical, cultural, qualitative, and even most quantitative scholarship: Rules of method only take us so far, and beyond that point we must depend more heavily than often acknowledged on personal and collective judgment, argumentation, and persuasion, all of which are fallible.

28. For a reconsideration of theory to make sense of his recanting of secularization theory as argued in his book *Sacred Canopy*, see Peter Berger. 2014. *The Many Altars of Modernity*. Boston: de Gruyter.

29. Riesebrodt. *Promise of Salvation*. P. 170.

We can expect changes in religions over time, however, some of them involving major declines in religion. New religions will be born. Most of them will die; some may survive. Established religions will mutate in various ways in response to social and cultural changes. Some will grow in numbers and influence, some will hold steady for periods of time, and some will weaken and decline. Again, secularization is real and powerful in some social contexts. Religions will change in their internal cultures, too—in the character of their styles, ideas, appeals, and practices—not only in membership numbers and public status. Established religions may migrate geographically, shifting their centers of gravity, as they have often done in the past. Virtually extinct religions, such as pre-Christian paganism in Europe, may be revived, as well, enjoying some rehabilitation among modern practitioners.[30]

Religions' relationships with other social institutions will also change over time in different ways. No single direction is inevitable or likely; divergent outcomes will be influenced by a variety of baseline conditions and unpredictable contingencies. Different religions may grow more or less militant, for example, promoting violent conflict in some cases but peace and reconciliation in others.[31] Some religions will strengthen their ties to political regimes, while others will distance themselves. Certain religious traditions in particular places will play important roles in educational systems, while elsewhere religions will be excluded from education.[32] Religious and secular actors and institutions may conflict, but that is not inevitable, either.[33] All of these developments will be influenced by (and influence) major technological, economic, military, political, and ideological changes. In short, again, while all things religious will be shaped by identifiable causal powers, all of those powers operate in "open systems," making prediction difficult if not impossible, and forcing social scientists to explain trends only retrospectively, as they ought to.

By implication, discussions about secularization *need to shift paradigms* away from the established view that one or another dominant trend,

---

30. Kaarina Aitamurto and Scott Simpson. 2014. *Modern Pagan and Native Faith Movements in Central and Eastern Europe*. London: Routledge; Robert Anderson. 2005. *The Ghosts of Iceland*. Belmont, CA: Thomson Wadsorth; Graham Harvey. 1997. *Paganism Today*. London: Thornsons.

31. Toft, Philpott, and Shah. 2011. *God's Century*; Appleby. 1999. *The Ambivalence of the Sacred*.

32. Stephen Monsma and Christopher Soper. 2008. *The Challenge of Pluralism*. Lanham, MD: Rowman and Littlefield.

33. Slavica Jakelic. Forthcoming. *The Practice of Religious and Secular Humanism*.

association, or force will determine the fate of religion in modernity. Instead, we need a framework that offers more complexity, openness, and contingency. We need a framework more focused on understanding the influences of multiple causal mechanisms operating below direct observation than on finding correlations between observed variables.[34] Critical realism provides this alternative. Instead of fighting over, for example, whether social or religious pluralism corrodes the plausibility and membership of religions (as traditional secularization theory claimed) or instead mobilizes and strengthens religion (as the rational choice "religious economies" theory maintained), we need to step back and change the framework of the debate. Most importantly, we need to stop expecting one dominant movement, correlation, or causal influence to reflect *the* "correct" theory, whose hypotheses are validated by statistical evidence. That mentality results from the latent influence of positivism. The way the real world works, however, tells us we need to stop thinking like positivists and start thinking like critical realists.[35]

---

34. Smith. *What Is a Person?* Pp. 277–314.

35. Recall the actual history of the sociology of religion. For much of the modern period, most sociologists believed with secularization theory that modernity would undermine the plausibility and influence of religion. Secularization theory predicted that more modernity—as represented by science, rationality, individual freedom, institutional differentiation, market competition, and cultural pluralism—would mean less religion. That view, however, fell into some doubt by the 1980s and was forcefully attacked in the 1990s by advocates of the religious economies theory, especially Rodney Stark and Roger Finke. Their alternative approach argued, among other things, that religious pluralism spurs entrepreneurial religious organizations to mobilize resources and that religious competition increases the share of populations that are religiously affiliated. In short, the more modernity, the more religion. A massive amount of research in the 1990s was devoted to attempting to verify or falsify these two theories, which hypothesized opposing expectations that, in principle, should have been straightforwardly testable with empirical data. It all presupposed positivist assumptions: It searched for regular associations between variables measuring observable facts and events to identify law-like generalizations about modernity and religion that would hold across populations and cases. The assumption was that one theory or another would be vindicated by the empirical evidence and that this theory would hold in whatever context was studied. The debates were heated and protracted. But when all was said and done, a funny thing happened: The sum total of evidence produced by the studies proved inconclusive. A 2001 *Annual Review of Sociology* chapter that analyzed 193 of the most important pieces of empirical scholarship in the debate concluded definitively that no definitive conclusion could be drawn (Mark Chaves and Philip Gorski. 2001. "Religious Pluralism and Religious Participation." *Annual Review of Sociology.* 27: 261–281). Some of the studies showed one thing, some another, and some were simply unclear. After that, the debate lost its energy. So the search for a law-like generalization about modernity and religion ended in failure. Nobody, however, stopped to question the deeper assumptions that led to that failure. The search failed not because modernity does not exert knowable causal influences on religion, but because scholars' presuppositions about how those influences would work was framed by the flawed positivist philosophy operating

An Alternative Analytical Approach

In general terms, thinking like a critical realist means identifying and becoming familiar with the operations of the many important causal mechanisms existing in modern social structures and practices that influence the strength and character of religion. Forget trying to discover some generalizable "covering law" predicting the fate of religion in modernity. That is misguided. Rather than paradigms bashing each other with empirical evidence purporting to validate one rival theory or the other, critical realism directs us instead to identify all of the plausible causal mechanisms suggested by all the relevant theories; to begin to contemplate the varying social conditions by and within which different mechanisms are activated; and to empirically explore the characteristic outcomes produced by different combinations of operative mechanisms at work in different social contexts. That task is much more difficult than searching for two variables that always significantly correlate, which then supposedly proves the correctness of one theory. But it is the scholarly task best matched to reality.

Consider some existing theories that have purported to explain general trends for religion in modernity. But let us instead transform them into valuable partial contributions to a more complex understanding of religion in modernity. We can do this by shifting our attention away from theories' broader claims about modernity and secularization, and onto the *underlying causal mechanisms* that they suggest justify those claims. In almost all cases, the proposed causal mechanisms are real, operative, and valid, and so deserve to be taken seriously, even when they tend to produce different outcomes than other mechanisms operating in the same context. We can then incorporate their insights about particular causal influences into a larger, more complicated model of a multiplicity of influences that can operate simultaneously in concert with, on different tracks from, or at odds with each other.

Begin with a simple example. Some secularization theorists have claimed that modernity's religious pluralism corrodes and weakens religions.[36] Theorists of religious economies, however, have argued the opposite, that religious pluralism strengthens religions.[37] These would appear to be mutually

---

in the background. To do better, we need to banish the ghosts of positivism and welcome critical realism.

36. Berger. *Sacred Canopy.*
37. Stark and Finke. *Acts of Faith.*

exclusive positions. Pluralism cannot simultaneously weaken and strengthen religions, right? Wrong. Religious pluralism *can* do both, in different ways for different reasons. To see how and why, we need to pay less attention to general regularities represented by correlations between variables, and instead concentrate on the operation of causal mechanisms. To do so for the example in question: Religious pluralism can undermine religions by fostering doubts among practitioners about the probability of the truth of their own religion when so many other religions exist. That is one possible causal mechanism triggered by pluralism: cognitive doubt. That mechanism does not always operate, but it sometimes does, particularly under certain social conditions. On the other hand, religious pluralism sometimes strengthens religions by prompting some religious actors to mobilize resources to promote their religions in the face of competition. That is another possible causal mechanism triggered by pluralism: resource mobilization and deployment.

When research is framed by positivist assumptions, which focus on regular associations of observed events, either one or the other of these claims is expected to be true, and the other will therefore necessarily be false. That is exactly what scholarship in the last decades has assumed about pluralism and religious strength—which led to a dead end.[38] But positivism is wrong, and thus so too is the mutually exclusive perspective it sets up. The *very same* social facts can activate multiple distinct causal mechanisms that tend to produce *different* results. With this possibility in mind, we realize that what is really valuable in traditional secularization theory and more recent work on religious economies is not their competing claims about the effects of pluralism on religion. What is valuable in them is their *descriptions of particular causal mechanisms* by which the very same factor—pluralism—can shape religion in *different* ways. Thus, when we focus on mechanisms of causation instead of regularities of association, we can embrace and capitalize upon the contributions of *both* theories. Then, what is valuable in these and all other theories can be built into a more inclusive, realistic framework of analysis of religion.

The main task in this effort is not testing hypotheses repeatedly until the accumulated findings eventually declare one theory to be the winner and the other falsified, or merely compiling a list of all causal mechanisms that may be relevant to the topic in question. The mission is instead to identify

---

38. Chaves and Gorski. "Religious Pluralism and Religious Participation."

in all plausible theories their accounts of causal mechanisms potentially at work, and then pull them together to develop a more comprehensive framework for understanding the many complicated social forces that shape religion. The goal is to formulate a clearer and more complex theoretical understanding of *what particular social contexts tend to trigger and accentuate which of the many possible relevant causal mechanisms, how those causal mechanisms generally operate as influences when set in motion together, and what characteristic outcomes they tend to produce.* In the end, we will have a general theory—indeed, one not limited to the allegedly unique influences of modernity—but a more complicated and realistic theory than the sort that positivism produces.

When we keep the complexity of religion and the many factors that influence it in mind, it becomes easy to see that the following additional claims about religion and modernity might all, in fact, be valid in different contexts and under different conditions:

- Religious pluralism tends to encourage more liberal, open, inclusive, and accommodating forms of religious community and practice.[39]
- Religious pluralism tends to encourage more conservative, traditionalist, sectarian forms of religious community and practice.[40]
- Religious pluralism provides a social setting in which religious groups that possess theological tools to sustain distinction-with-engagement will be more likely to thrive.[41]
- Religious pluralism tends to exert homogenizing influences that reduce the distinctions between different religious groups, producing organizational isomorphism.[42]
- Religious pluralism creates conditions in which religious organizations are predisposed to differentiate themselves from others in their identity and practice in order to target particular niche populations of the religious market.[43]

39. Wade Clark Roof. 2001. *Spiritual Marketplace.* Princeton: Princeton University Press.

40. Davidman. *Tradition in a Rootless World*; Almond and Appleby. *Strong Religion.*

41. Smith et al. *American Evangelicalism.* Also see Roland Robertson. 1992. *Globalization.* London: Sage.

42. Berger. *Sacred Canopy.* Pp. 148–149.

43. Stark and Finke. *Acts of Faith.* Pp. 195–198; Stephen Warner. 1993. "Work in Progress toward a New Paradigm in the Sociological Study of Religion in the United States." *American Journal of Sociology.* 89: 1044–1093.

- Socioeconomic development normally reduces human insecurity, which reduces the human demand for religion.[44]
- Socioeconomic development tends to reduce human insecurity, which frees people to focus on higher levels in the hierarchy of human needs, including spiritual self-development.[45]
- Modern science can undermine religious beliefs by replacing religious accounts of the world with naturalistic explanations.[46]
- Modern science can reinforce religious beliefs by revealing a cosmos of amazing complexity and beauty, discovering how extremely improbable ("fine tuning") are the conditions necessary for our reality to exist, and failing to answer pressing moral and ethical questions as well as metaphysical questions about the origin of all being.[47]
- The Protestant Reformation forced new forms of religious freedom and launched a series of religious innovations that sustain some of the most vibrant and robust religious communities in modernity.[48]
- The Protestant Reformation triggered a series of religious innovations that unintentionally set in motion powerful secularizing forces like epistemological conflict, individualistic religious authority, schism and fragmentation, and demystification.[49]
- Structural institutional differentiation tends to privatize religion and undermine religious authority by delegitimizing religious institutions' authority over many sectors of social life.[50]

44. Norris and Inglehart. *Sacred and Secular.*

45. Abraham Maslow. 2013. *A Theory of Human Motivations.* Eastford, CT: Martino Fine Books.

46. Bruce. *God Is Dead.* Pp. 26–28; Owen Chadwick. 1975. *The Secularization of the European Mind.* Cambridge: Cambridge University Press. Pp. 161–188.

47. Francis Collins. 2007. *The Language of God.* New York: Free Press; Gerald Schroede. 2002. *The Hidden Face of God.* New York: Free Press.

48. Perez Zagorin. 2005. *How the Idea of Religious Toleration Came to the West.* Princeton: Princeton University Press; Benjamin Kaplan. 2010. *Divided by Faith.* Cambridge: Belknap Press; Finke and Stark. *Acts of Faith.*

49. Brad Gregory. 2015. *The Unintended Reformation.* Cambridge, MA: Harvard University Press; Bruce. *God Is Dead.* Pp. 10–11; Jose Casanova. 1994. *Public Religions in the Modern World.* Chicago: University of Chicago Press. Pp. 20–25.

50. Thomas Luckmann. 1996. "The Privatization of Religion and Morality." In Paul Heelas, Scott Lash, and Paul Morris (eds.). *Detraditionalization.* Malden, MA: Blackwell. Pp. 72–86; Luckmann. 1967. *The Invisible Religion.* London: Macmillan; Bryan Wilson. 1976. *Contemporary Transformations of Religion.* Oxford: Clarendon. Pp. 1–37. Niklas Luhmann. 1990. "The Paradox of System Differentiation and the Evolution of Society." In Jeffrey Alexander and Paul Colomy

- Structural institutional differentiation, along with the expansion of religious freedom, tends to strengthen religion by providing religious institutions clarity of focus, identity, purpose, and function, and preventing religion from becoming entangled in politics, economics, and military life—entanglements that typically harm religious institutions in the long run.[51]
- Rationalization in modern social life is apt to erode religious worldviews through cognitive processes of demystification and the legitimation of secular naturalism.[52]
- Because it produces a world widely perceived as formal and meaningless, rationalization in modern social life tends to intensify demands for religious beliefs, experiences, and practices as people try to retain some degree of significance, feeling, and humane purpose in life.[53]
- New technologies of communication and transportation that radically compress time and space tend to corrode religious plausibility by fostering a kind of rationalized consciousness of amoral control of causes and interest in prediction.[54]
- New technologies of communication and transportation tend to enhance the capacities of religious people and organizations to mobilize people and resources for greater religious participation.[55]
- Cultural and moral relativism are likely to undermine the plausibility of specific religious beliefs and moral principles by generating epistemological uncertainties that accompany the confrontation with competing truth claims.[56]
- Cultural and moral relativism tend to create new and stronger demands for secure religious identities, cognitive certainty, and

(eds.). *Differentiation Theory and Social Change*. New York: Columbia University Press. Pp. 427, 432–433.

51. Finke and Stark. *Churching of America*.

52. Weber. *The Protestant Ethic*; Kenneth Allan. 2013. *The Social Lens*. Thousand Oaks, CA: Sage. Pp. 91–96.

53. Alexandra Walsham. 2008. "Historiographical Reviews: The Reformation and the 'Disenchantment of the World.'" *Historical Journal*. 51: 497–528; Harvey Cox. 2001. *Fire From Heaven*. Cambridge, MA: De Capo Press; Smith et al. *American Evangelicalism*. p. 116–117; Miller and Yamamori. *Global Pentecostalism*.

54. Bruce. *God Is Dead*. Pp. 28–29.

55. Richard Flory with Donald Miller. 2008. *Finding Faith*. New Brunswick, NJ: Rutgers University Press. Pp. 19–51.

56. Bruce. *God Is Dead*. P. 29; Berger. *Sacred Canopy*.

traditional practices, driving people to higher levels of religious commitment.[57]

- The more liberal and egalitarian certain societies and cultures become, the more traditional religious authorities and norms will be met with resistance, dissent, transgression, and demands for change by internal and alienated critics who give "voice" to disagreement and perhaps eventually "exit."[58]

- The more liberal and egalitarian certain societies and cultures become, the more traditional religious authorities and practices will appeal to a certain audience who rally to defend them.[59]

- The more liberal and egalitarian certain societies and cultures become, the more traditional religions will play the symbiotic role of indirectly and unintentionally supporting liberal, secular culture by providing temporary refuges of community and moral meaning and values.[60]

- Secular states that seek to control religions typically suppress religious vitality.[61]

- Secular states that seek to control religions tend to intensify religious identities and heighten the salience of religious differences and commitments.[62]

Rather than providing general laws of modernity and religion, all of these claims are true and operative in different contexts; they are specific causal capacities that tend under certain conditions to be activated. Some

57. James Hunter. 1981. "The New Religions." In Bryan Wilson (ed.). *The Social Impact of New Religious Movements*. New York: Rose of Sharon Press. Pp. 1–20; Davidman. *Tradition in a Rootless World*; Roland Robertson. 1992. *Globalization*. London: Sage; Roland Robertson. 2007. "Global Millennialism: A Postmortem on Secularization." In Peter Beyer and Lori Gail (eds.). *Religion, Globalization and Culture*. Leiden: Brill. Pp. 9–34.

58. See, for example, Timothy Shah, Thomas Farr, and Jack Friedman (eds.). 2016. *Religious Freedom and Gay Rights*. New York: Oxford University Press; Christel Manning. 1999. *God Gave Us The Right*. New Brunswick, NJ: Rutgers University Press; Philip Hammond. 1992. *Religion and Personal Autonomy*. Columbia: University of South Carolina Press; Mark Chaves. 1999. *Ordaining Women: Culture and Conflict in Religious Organizations*. Cambridge, MA: Harvard University Press; per Hirschman. 1970. *Exit, Voice, Loyalty*. Cambridge, MA: Harvard University Press.

59. Bell. *Winding Passage*; Anthony Giddens. 1991. *Modernity and Self-Identity*. Palo Alto: Stanford University Press. Pp. 194–196.

60. Robert Fowler. 1989. *Unconventional Partners*. Grand Rapids, MI: Eerdmans.

61. Stark and Finke. *Churching of America*. Pp. 218–258.

62. Saba Mahmood. 2016. *Religious Difference in a Secular Age*. Princeton: Princeton University Press; also see Jonathan Fox. 2015. *Political Secularism, Religion, and the State*. Cambridge: Cambridge University Press.

FIGURE 5.3. Ultra-Orthodox Jews living in New York City—among the most modern and pluralistic urban centers on earth—illustrate how traditional religious communities of practice can, under the right conditions, readily coexist with and even capitalize on aspects of modern technology, rationality, and pluralism. (Copyright: Mendy Hechtman/Flash 90)

of these may reinforce each other. Some may counteract each other. Some may "ricochet" off each other. Some may neutralize others, although those others may not neutralize them. And some may simply be "indifferent" to each other. The job in the critical realist study of religion, therefore, is first to think long and hard about causal mechanisms and second to conduct conceptually informed empirical research to investigate which combinations of causal mechanisms tend to be operative under which conditions and with what effect. If we succeed in this difficult task, we will be able to explain religion with much greater nuance and success than any positivist-informed framework ever could (figure 5.3).

This outlook means that studies of religion need to take very seriously causal multiplicity, complexity, interactions, and contingency. We need to pay much greater attention to the ways that different types of social contexts create distinct situations that tend to activate particular combinations of causal mechanisms that in turn may produce different (or similar) results. To do this well, we need, before designing our research programs and gathering data, to spend plenty of time and effort reflecting on our questions, cases, and the causal influences most likely to be relevant for them. We then need to focus our empirical research not on correlating readily measured variables, but finding ways directly and indirectly to observe causal mechanisms at work and the variety of outcomes that they are prone to producing. Combinations of reinforcing, neutral, and opposing causal influences will likely prove at least as important as any one mechanism. Ultimately, rather than ending up with one theory that supposedly explains the fate of religion in modernity, we will have a more complex account emphasizing history, culture, contingency, and complexity.[63]

Conclusion

What, then, is religion's future? The most reliable answer is that religion will likely always play a significant role in many if not most human societies. Exactly what kind of role it plays, however, will vary by place and over time. At least some humans will continue to practice their religions, as people have done for all of known human history. Religious life in various parts of the world will ebb and flow in various ways, and religious institutions and traditions will strengthen and weaken over time, depending on other multifaceted influences. Among them will be how various religious traditions can navigate the often conflicting demands—conservative and liberal, obedient and dissenting, consolidating and transgressing, traditional and innovative—of religious practitioners in today's globalizing world. But, given the human condition and the nature of religion's appeal to humanity, religious practices are not apt to disappear, or even come close to disappearing, anytime in the foreseeable future. A variety of powerful causal forces do indeed work against religious belief and practice, perhaps especially in the modern world—secularization surely happens under certain conditions. But numerous other powerful causal influences simultaneously encourage the practice of religion. Exactly which of those causal mechanisms operates under what social conditions to produce differing religious outcomes we cannot predict according to some general law of social life. That can only be discovered through careful, theoretically informed, empirical research— which is what this book intends to encourage.

63. For example, see the developing theory of multiple modernities. S. Eisenstadt. 2000. "Multiple Modernities." *Daedalus.* 129: 1–29; Ibrahim Kaya. 2004. "Modernity, Openness, Interpretation." *Social Science Information.* 43: 35–57; Peter Katzenstein. 2006. "Multiple Modernities as Limits to Secular Europeanization?" In Timothy Byrnes and Peter Katzenstein (eds.). *Religion in an Expanding Europe.* Cambridge: Cambridge University Press; Masoud Kamali. 2006. *Multiple Modernities, Civil Society, and Islam.* Liverpool: Liverpool University Press; S. N. Eisenstadt. 2003. *Comparative Civilizations and Multiple Modernities.* Leiden, The Netherlands: Brill Academic.

Conclusion

No citizen of the world today can afford to be ill-informed about religion. Modernity has not done away with religion and does not look like it will anytime soon. Religion remains vitally important around the globe, not only despite modernity but in part because of it. Religion has arguably even enjoyed a resurgence since the end of the Cold War in the last decade of the twentieth century and the acceleration of globalization in the twenty-first. Anyone trying to comprehend our contemporary world while neglecting religion is attempting the impossible. Their comprehension will be incomplete and slanted, at best. Among the powerful, such an approach could lead to terrible and costly policy and military miscalculations. Those who understand religion well, by comparison, will be positioned not only to comprehend the world more accurately, but also to exert more intelligent and humane influences in it.

The academic scholarship on religion today is rich and diverse. Many scholars in various disciplines in social science and the humanities study religion the world over and produce works of insight and importance. But these works often provide more breadth and diversity than coherence and integration. One can find all manner of books and articles on myriad aspects of religion all around the globe and across history—which is fantastic. Harder to find are tight, accessible works that pull together some of these rich studies' most important insights into basic summary statements that can orient our thinking and bring conceptual organization to the vast scholarly works.

But that is what is needed to promote a better scholarly and public understanding of religion. It is what I hope this book accomplishes.

I have only addressed certain absolutely central theoretical questions about religion. Other important issues—such as religious conversion, religion and immigration, and religious radicalization—I have not been able to speak to here. In fact, when this book's theory is taken into the real world, a vast range of empirical research questions opens up for inquiry. Some require field studies in sites all around the globe, others greatly improved methods of survey research, still others historical approaches, and yet others careful laboratory and natural-field experiments. I have, for decades, learned from the scholarship of many colleagues working from a variety of meta-theoretical backgrounds. My wager with this book, however, is that future social science scholarship can be improved by working more intentionally and consistently within the frameworks of critical realism and personalism.

To what ends? Better causal explanations? Yes. More intelligent policy decisions? Certainly. The critique of dehumanizing abusive powers? Absolutely. All of these are essential. But for me, the greatest success would be if, as a result of academic scholarship, ordinary people from all walks of life come to understand religion better than they do today, become more equipped to explain with reasonable empathy why other religious people and institutions live and act as they do, and so approach our religiously pluralistic world with less suspicion and hostility, carry on more invigorating and fertile conversations, and together enjoy greater mutual respect and peace.

Research Questions

For readers with empirical research interests in religion, this appendix suggests a set of research questions that follow the argument of this book, chapter by chapter, in hopes of prompting ongoing empirical inquiry that will be focused, coherent, and cumulative. In this, scholars of religion should resist the general notion in social science that religion only matters insofar as it helps explain things of (supposedly) "real" importance, such as politics, inequality, or social movements. That prejudice, which is internalized and honored even by many religion scholars, reflects unacknowledged materialist and utilitarian biases that are common in the social sciences, but not so defensible when spelled out. Religion is just as important, interesting, and enlightening a subject of study in its own right as are the economy, politics, race, gender, or any other human social institution. I agree with Riesebrodt that "the sociology of religion has shown mainly an instrumental interest in religion; it has given little attention to religion itself," and I endorse his "plea for taking an interest in religious phenomena themselves, qua religious phenomena, but doing so empirically, as an investigation into their institutionalized and appropriate meaning."[1] The study of religion is not academically justified only when religious independent variables prove statistically significant in multivariate analyses of non-religious dependent variables. If the goal of social science is to comprehend the full range of activities, conditions, and occurrences in human social life in order to understand the world and our own experience in it—as I think it should be—then religion *in and of itself* has "real" importance and merits serious scholarly attention. I hope this book's theory helps promote that end.

1. Riesebrodt. *Promise of Salvation.* P. 79.

Chapter 1

1.3

From figure 1.1 we can derive a series of elementary research questions that we might ask to better understand any given religion. Each major question is associated with a labeled arrow (a, b, c., etc.) in figure 1.1, as follows:

1. What are the complexes of culturally prescribed practices that practitioners are expected to perform in a religion?
   a. What practices are essential or mandatory? Which are only recommended or routine? Which are optional or exceptional?
   b. Exactly who must or ought to perform these practices and why is that so? What kind of designated person? Individuals or groups?
   c. Under what conditions of place, time, or circumstance are the practices to be performed?
   d. What conditions define the correct and invalid performance of the practices?
   e. How are the practices believed to be efficacious? What are their believed causal powers? How certain or tentative are the desired outcomes of the practices?
2. What premises about superhuman powers do the religious practices presuppose?
   a. What kind of being, reality, or existence are the superhuman powers believed to have?
   b. What kind of nature and character, and related capacities and powers, are the superhuman powers believed to have?
3. What rationales link the premises about superhuman powers to the complex of religious practices?
   a. What specific substantive beliefs concerning the existence and nature of the superhuman powers give rise to or legitimate the particular prescribed practices?
   b. How exactly are those linkages explained and justified as authoritative? Tradition? Law? Divine command? Or something else?
4. How do performances of the prescribed complex of religious practices influence the premises about superhuman powers that the practices themselves presuppose?
   a. How, if at all, do the performances of practices over time influence the objective content of the premises? Reinforced stasis? Unintended slippage? Intentional revision?
   b. How does carrying out the practices over time influence

individual practitioners' subjective beliefs in the premises?
Reinforced stasis? Strengthening and deepening? Weakening and
retreating?

5. What are the actual results of the performed complexes of
practices, and how are they interpreted by human participants and
observers?

   a. What change (or lack of change) happens that was the intended
   result of executing the prescribed practices?

   b. How are those changes or lack of changes given meaning through
   interpretation by the religious practitioners or other observers?

6. How, if at all, do the actual and interpreted outcomes of the
performed religious practices influence (i) the premises about
superhuman powers that the practices presuppose, and (ii) the
performance of the actual practices themselves?

   a. How are "successful" outcomes understood and communicated in
   ways that influence the premises or practices?

   b. How are unsuccessful or ambiguous outcomes interpreted—in
   particular, in ways that avoid threats to the legitimacy of the
   premises or practices?

   c. Under what conditions are either the premises about superhuman
   powers or the complexes of prescribed practices doubted,
   questioned, revised, or abandoned because of particular
   outcomes?

7. How did the religious tradition prescribing the complex of practices
come into being, and how did those origins and subsequent
experience shape exactly who gained authority to control the belief
content of the religious tradition, its prescribed practices, and who
else would be deemed an acceptable practitioner?

   a. How are power, authority, influence, continuity, and boundaries
   governed and with what consequences within and beyond the
   religious tradition?

   b. Who "owns" the religious tradition, and how exactly do they
   manage to maintain their ownership over time? What kinds of
   challenges to the authority of ownership arise, and how are they
   handled?

   c. How do religions interact with the subjective beliefs,
   interpretations, and feelings of their practitioners who transgress
   or dissent or distance themselves from the official or dominant
   culture and practices of the tradition? How do those interactions

affect who continues to practice the religion over time and who exits?

8. What does the apparently increasingly popular self-description of "spiritual but not religious" mean for those who claim it and for how religion itself may be evolving in its relation to larger culture? What significance does "spiritual but not religious" have for more conventional religious traditions and practices?

Chapter 2

9. What new religious causal powers in the form of institutional and social-structural facts and capacities have emerged and are sustained through the exercise of religious practices by adherents of particular traditions?

   a. What *other* causal powers besides the 18 described in chapter 2 can religions generate?

   b. Which of religion's emergent causal powers provide religious adherents capacities to act as *agents in the world*?

   c. Which of religion's emergent causal powers give religions' leaders and members capacities to *shape and control religious adherents*?

10. What kinds of secondary causal powers appear to be *universal* for all religions, and which are *particular* to some types of religions? Are there characteristic patterns to be observed?

    a. Does the nature of the postulated *superhuman powers* affect the character of the emergent causal powers that can emerge from practices seeking access to them?

    b. Does the character of the culturally prescribed *practices* affect the character of the emergent causal powers resulting from their performance?

11. In what ways are the emergent causal powers generated by the practices of particular religious traditions related to each other? Are there any basic patterns of *internal* structure or "grammar" of religion's emergent powers to be observed?

12. What causal mechanisms account for the *strengthening* and *weakening* of religion's emergent causal powers over time?

13. What specific conditions tend to give rise to the kind of *extra depth, intensity, and tenacity* to human commitments and actions found at times in religious contexts, as suggested in this chapter? What

combinations of circumstances and factors are apt to bring out distinctive causal tendencies in religious people and communities?

14. What is the full range of types of causal social mechanisms by which religions exercise and express their causal powers? Can we develop a nearly comprehensive typology of the means of religious influence that capture the many levels, proximities, temporal horizons, and processes of the mechanisms of operation?

15. Under what conditions do the multivocality and polysemy of the contents of religious traditions allow for religious causal influences to be expressed in typical ways versus in creative and unexpected ways? Can we identify any general patterns of influence that might explain the varying directions that the social, political, economic, and military implications of religious teachings take in particular instances?

16. Under what conditions are emergent religious causal powers used to bolster the established religious culture and practices versus challenge, transgress, or dissent from the status quo? When do the causal capacities play a conserving and reinforcing role, and when do they play a self-critiquing, reforming, or revolutionary role?

17. In what ways does religion function as a social control mechanism? Whose interests do various forms of religious social control serve? Under what conditions do religions break out of the strictures of social control and operate in fundamentally different modes?

    a. How and why are minority or historically subservient groups (regarding gender, race, ethnicity, social class, sexual proclivities, etc.) officially and in practice defined and treated in the religious tradition, and what consequences does that have for community solidarity and conflict in ways that influence group commitment, affiliation, and disaffiliation?

18. What specific conditions tend to guide religious beliefs, goals, and behaviors in *positive* and *negative* directions? Under what conditions is religion inclined to promote the human good and when does it turn dark?

    a. In what ways and under what conditions are negative or destructive expressions of religious causal powers logically inherent to or native within the religious tradition (multivocality and polysemy notwithstanding) as opposed to an unusual divergence from or mutation of the mainstream tradition?

Chapter 3

19. What *kinds of attributions* concerning the potential causal influences of superhuman powers do specific religious traditions tend to foster as a result of their premises about the nature, capacities, and tendencies of those powers?

    a. What causal influences do religious practitioners have *reason to expect* from their superhuman powers in response to the practices they perform?

    b. How and why do different religious traditions, groups, and perhaps persons vary in *how closely they monitor* and evaluate the responses of superhuman powers to their religious practices? To whom does that matter a lot versus not matter much, and why?

    c. What patterns of differences in religious attributions are discernable between religions engaging *personal versus non-personal* superhuman powers? What explains that?

20. When and why do religious practitioners attribute causal influences not (only) to naturalistic causes but (also) to superhuman powers?

21. What *social processes* form expectations among religious practitioners about the ways they anticipate superhuman powers to respond to their practices?

    a. How do *group and institutional dynamics of interaction and culture* form the particular patterns of religious attribution-making in different religious traditions? What explains that?

    b. What kinds of *cognitive biases and "lubricants"* generally shape the religious attribution-making and evaluation of superhuman powers' (non-)responses of causal influence in the lives of religious practitioners?

22. How do placebo effects work social-psychologically to enhance the plausibility of religious attributions among religious practitioners? What kinds of religious placebos work most consistently, and how might that vary by religious tradition or other difference?

23. How do different religious traditions and groups *respond* to the possible outcomes they may attribute to superhuman powers—ranging from complete success to rejection—when they confront them?

    a. Which outcomes tend to *strengthen* and which *undermine* individual and collective religiousness? Which normally have no effect?

b. What resources and strategies do religions offer their practitioners to *manage attributed outcomes that are less optimal* than outright success? How successful are those resources and strategies?

c. Under what outcome conditions do religious practitioners tend to *neglect or abandon* engaging in religious practices because of their apparent lack of efficacy?

24. What kinds of *identity and boundary work* may religious practitioners engage in vis-à-vis people outside of their religious group or tradition to protect the plausibility of their religious attributions in the face of potential non-belief and skepticism?

25. How might processes of making religious attributions interact with the operations of *power, authority, and control* in religious communities? Does the making of religious attributions shape religion's powers of social control, managing dissent, or legitimating exclusion?

Chapter 4

26. What do religious people pray for and more generally seek from their superhuman powers; and how might that vary, if at all, cross-nationally?

27. Does empirical evidence tend to confirm the Default Religious Laxity tendency described in chapter 4?

a. What casual mechanisms, under what social conditions, are apt to reduce the frequency or intensity of religious practice?

b. Are some religious traditions more or less immune to the Default Religious Laxity tendency? What about them makes that so?

c. What causal mechanisms in particular social contexts or religious traditions work against the Default Religious Laxity tendency?

28. Does empirical evidence tend to support the Vulnerable Religious Demand tendency described in chapter 4?

a. What kinds of vulnerabilities are inclined to increase the frequency or intensity of religious practice? Do particular thresholds of vulnerability especially encourage religious practice?

b. Are different religious traditions more responsive to the

Vulnerable Religious Demand tendency? What about them makes that so?

29. What biological, genetic, neurochemical, and other bodily factors dispose some people toward or against engaging in religious practices?

30. What demographic or other measurable factors tend to be associated with greater belief and participation in religious practices, and what causal mechanisms underlie those associations?

    a. How might those factors and associated mechanisms vary by distinct religious traditions?

    b. How might those factors and associated mechanisms vary by time period and geographical location for the same religious tradition?

31. Under what types of social conditions and situations do various kinds of people practicing different religious traditions shift from relying only on non-religious (human) causal capacities to seek good outcomes and address problems to turning, through religious practices, to superhuman powers for blessings and deliverance?

    a. How much are those turning points determined by the prescriptions of religious traditions and how much are they chosen by religious practitioners in light of personal preferences?

32. What distinctive human causal capacities, in addition to those described in chapter 4, enable humans to be uniquely religious?

    a. Does any form of brain damage or other debilitation diminish human capacities to be religious? Which, why, and how?

33. In what ways do human neurology, cognition, perception, memory, language, symbolization, understanding of causation, awareness of death, or any other factor tend to make religion "natural" for human beings to practice and believe?

34. Under what conditions, if any, can traditions that have lost much of the ontological core of religious life sustain communities of religious practice by supplying only secondary reinforcements for practicing religion? Which, if any, types or combinations of secondary reinforcements of religion can sustain people's religious practices even in the absence of strong belief in the existence of superhuman powers or the efficacy of religious practices aimed at them?

35. Which kinds of (actual or ex-)religious practitioners tend to feel discounted, stigmatized, or excluded, and under what conditions? What do religious traditions and communities do to help create

classes of people who withdraw from religious practice or question or discount their religious identity?

    a. Why and how do different religious traditions alienate new members (children and youth), prospective practitioners, and former practitioners? How do religions themselves contribute to the production of less- and non-religious people?

36. How and with what cognitive, emotional, and volitional materials do religious practitioners piece together "multiple, overlapping patchworks" of reasons for starting or continuing to practice religion?

    a. How many and what combinations of reasons typically sustain strong religious practice?

    b. What critical thresholds or junctures may exist in the disintegration of "multiple, overlapping patchworks" of reasons for practicing religion, leading to its reduction or cessation?

    c. How might the configuration of effective and ineffective patchworks of reasons vary by religious tradition?

37. What resources do religions possess for generating emotional energy, both positive and negative?

    a. Which of those are common to any organization or community and which are perhaps unique to religion?

    b. Under what conditions do religions tend to create high emotional energy versus low emotional energy?

    c. How do organizational dynamics of power, status, voice, inclusion, and exclusion shape the experiences of prospective, actual, and former religious practitioners on the matter of emotional energy?

    d. How do different kinds of religious organizations and communities manage or cope with developing trends toward high and low emotional energy?

38. What patterns of associations might we discover between systems of material and financial support for religious specialists at the micro-, meso-, and macro-social levels, and the types and levels of religious engagement among lay religious practitioners? How do political economies of religious communities and organizations influence the kinds and amounts of religious practices in them?

39. Given the apparent naturalness of religion for humans, what social conditions tend to give rise to significant populations of secular

people and institutions, for whom religion is uninteresting, irrelevant, or worthless?

40. Under what conditions and why do some people engage in the kind of denial of real religious commitments and motivations involved in "religious muting" mentioned in this chapter?

Chapter 5

41. What social conditions tend to give rise to the emergence of new religious movements and schisms from established religions? What causal mechanisms account for that?

    a. What factors have the greatest impact on which new religious movements and schisms succeed and which fail?

42. Under what specific social conditions do established religions tend to decline and disappear over time? What are the primary causal mechanisms at work?

    a. Under what conditions are religions replaced by rival religions? Under what conditions do they instead fade and become extinct or near extinct on their own?

43. How much and in what ways—given the content of religious histories, traditions, teachings, and texts—are religions able internally to adapt to changed cultural and institutional environments? How much internal diversity is sustainable under what conditions?

    a. What causal mechanisms tend to spur significant internal changes to religious traditions?

    b. What kind of processes of innovation and conflict take place inside of religious traditions amid such religious change?

    c. How do particular kinds of religious traditions negotiate processes of identity and difference as they change internally?

    d. How might religious organizational structures influence processes of internal religious transformation?

    e. How might internal religious transformations relate to larger processes of religious change in societies?

44. Why and how do religious traditions migrate geographically? When and why are geographic migrations attempted and under what conditions do they tend to succeed or fail?

    a. What causal influences does geographical migration have on religious cultures and traditions? How does the experience of migration itself provoke or obstruct religious change?

45. What are the significant recurring causal mechanisms that tend to promote, sustain, and strengthen religious practices?

    a. Under what social conditions are those causal influences activated?

    b. Which causal influences may work synergistically or in conjunction to support religion?

    c. How might different causal mechanisms be more or less important for particular religious traditions?

46. What are the significant recurring causal mechanisms that tend to weaken religious plausibility, practice, and influence?

    a. Under what social conditions are those causal influences triggered?

    b. Which causal influences tend to work together to undermine religion?

    c. How might different causal mechanisms be more or less important in eroding the strength of particular religious traditions?

47. Under what conditions do internal religious challenges, conflict, and dissent lead to exclusions (shunning, excommunications, de facto marginalization), schisms, withdrawal, or new religious movements as opposed to internal reform or revolutionary change? In these processes of conflict, who ends up able and unable to remain within the religious tradition or community and why?

INDEX

A NOTE ON THE TYPE

This book has been composed in Adobe Text and Gotham. Adobe Text, designed by Robert Slimbach for Adobe, bridges the gap between fifteenth- and sixteenth-century calligraphic and eighteenth-century Modern styles. Gotham, inspired by New York street signs, was designed by Tobias Frere-Jones for Hoefler & Co.